Mrs BEETON'S
Book of
BAKING

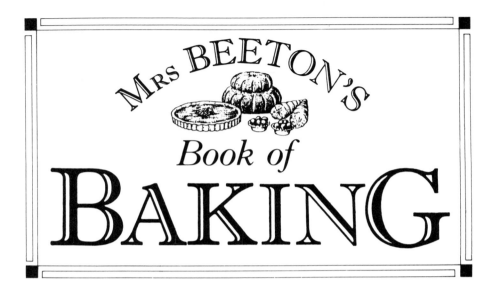

Mrs BEETON'S
Book of
BAKING

Consultant Editor **Bridget Jones**

WARD LOCK

First published 1991 by Ward Lock
Villiers House, 41/47 Strand, London WC2N 5JE

First paperback edition 1993

A Cassell imprint

Editor: Barbara Croxford
Designer: Cherry Randell
Photography by Sue Atkinson
Home Economist: Sarah Maxwell
Illustration: Tony Randell
Text: Typeset by Best-set Typesetter Ltd

Printed and bound in Great Britain by
The Bath Press
British Library Cataloguing in Publication Data
Beeton, Mrs. *1836-1865*
  Mrs. Beeton's book of baking.
  1. Baking – Recipes
  I. Title   II. Jones, Bridget
  641.71

ISBN 0-7063-7176-3

CONTENTS

Useful Weights and Measures   6

Following the Recipes   8

Essential and Useful Utensils for Baking   10

A Guide to Ingredients   15

Basic Techniques and Methods   24

Savoury Bakes   30

Pastries   50

Soufflés   88

Puddings   94

Cakes and Biscuits   102

Gâteaux   125

Yeasted Breads   131

Sweet Yeast Doughs   146

Breads Without Yeast   164

Teabreads and Muffins   167

Scones   179

Pizza and Dough Bakes   182

Index   189

USEFUL WEIGHTS AND MEASURES

USING METRIC OR IMPERIAL MEASURES

Throughout the book, all weights and measures are given first in metric, then in Imperial. For example 100 g/4 oz, 150 ml/¼ pint or 15 ml/1 tbsp.

When following any of the recipes use either metric or Imperial – do not combine the two sets of measures as they are not interchangeable.

EQUIVALENT METRIC/IMPERIAL MEASURES

Weights The following chart lists some of the metric/Imperial weights that are used in the recipes.

METRIC	IMPERIAL
15 g	½ oz
25 g	1 oz
50 g	2 oz
75 g	3 oz
100 g	4 oz
150 g	5 oz
175 g	6 oz
200 g	7 oz
225 g	8 oz
250 g	9 oz
275 g	10 oz
300 g	11 oz
350 g	12 oz
375 g	13 oz
400 g	14 oz
425 g	15 oz
450 g	16 oz
575 g	1¼ lb
675 g	1½ lb
800 g	1¾ lb
900 g	2 lb
1 kg	2¼ lb
1.4 kg	3 lb
1.6 kg	3½ lb
1.8 kg	4 lb
2.25 kg	5 lb

Liquid Measures The following chart lists some metric/Imperial equivalents for liquids. Millilitres (ml), litres and fluid ounces (fl oz) or pints are used throughout.

METRIC	IMPERIAL
50 ml	2 fl oz
125 ml	4 fl oz
150 ml	¼ pint
300 ml	½ pint
450 ml	¾ pint
600 ml	1 pint

Spoon Measures Both metric and Imperial equivalents are given for all spoon measures, expressed as millilitres and teaspoons (tsp) or tablespoons (tbsp).

All spoon measures refer to British standard measuring spoons and the quantities given are always for level spoons.

Do not use ordinary kitchen cutlery instead of proper measuring spoons as they will hold quite different quantities.

METRIC	IMPERIAL
1.25 ml	¼ tsp
2.5 ml	½ tsp
5 ml	1 tsp
15 ml	1 tbsp

Length All linear measures are expressed in millimetres (mm), centimetres (cm) or metres (m) and inches or feet. The following list gives examples of typical conversions.

METRIC	IMPERIAL
5 mm	¼ inch
1 cm	½ inch
2.5 cm	1 inch
5 cm	2 inches
15 cm	6 inches
30 cm	12 inches (1 foot)

OVEN TEMPERATURES

Whenever the oven is used, the required setting is given as three alternatives: degrees Celsius (°C), degrees Fahrenheit (°F) and gas.

The temperature settings given are for conventional ovens. If you have a fan oven, adjust the temperature according to the manufacturer's instructions.

°C	°F	GAS
110	225	¼
120	250	½
140	275	1
150	300	2
160	325	3
180	350	4
190	375	5
200	400	6
220	425	7
230	450	8
240	475	9

MICROWAVE INFORMATION

Occasional microwave hints and instructions are included for certain recipes, as appropriate. The information given is for microwave ovens rated at 650-700 watts.

The following terms have been used for the microwave settings: High, Medium, Defrost and Low. For each setting, the power input is as follows: High = 100% power, Medium = 50% power, Defrost = 30% power and Low = 20% power.

All microwave notes and timings are for guidance only: always read and follow the manufacturer's instructions for your particular appliance. Remember to avoid putting any metal in the microwave and never operate the microwave empty. See also page 63.

NOTES FOR AMERICAN READERS

In America dry goods and liquids are conventionally measured by the standard 8-oz cup. When translating pints, and fractions of pints, Americans should bear in mind that the U.S. pint is equal to 16 fl oz or 2 cups, whereas the Imperial pint is equal to 20 fl oz.

EQUIVALENT METRIC/AMERICAN MEASURES

Liquid Measures

METRIC/IMPERIAL	AMERICAN
150 ml/¼ pint	⅔ cup
300 ml/½ pint	1¼ cups
450 ml/¾ pint	2 cups
600 ml/1 pint	2½ cups
900 ml/1½ pints	3¾ cups
1 litre/1¾ pints	4 cups (2 U.S. pints)

Weights

450 g/1 lb butter or margarine	2 cups (4 sticks)
100 g/4 oz grated cheese	1 cup
450 g/1 lb flour	4 cups
450 g/1 lb granulated sugar	2 cups
450 g/1 lb icing sugar	3½ cups confectioners' sugar
200 g/7 oz raw long-grain rice	1 cup
100 g/4 oz cooked long-grain rice	1 cup
100 g/4 oz fresh white breadcrumbs	2 cups

Terminology Some useful American equivalents or substitutes for British ingredients are listed below:

BRITISH	AMERICAN
aubergine	eggplant
bicarbonate of soda	baking soda
biscuits	cookies, crackers
broad beans	fava or lima beans
chicory	endive
cling film	plastic wrap
cornflour	cornstarch
courgettes	zucchini
cream, single	cream, light
cream, double	cream, heavy
flour, plain	flour, all-purpose
frying pan	skillet
grill	broil
minced meat	ground meat
shortcrust pastry	basic pie dough
shrimp	prawn
spring onion	scallion
sultana	golden raisin
swede	rutabaga

FOLLOWING THE RECIPES

There are a few basic culinary rules that can be applied when following all recipes or preparing any food. Good kitchen practice, accuracy when following recipes and care when cooking food are the general principles which should be applied to all cooking processes. Certain pastries, cakes and biscuits are particularly delicate and special attention should be paid to their preparation. Follow these guidelines to ensure both kitchen safety and success.

BEFORE YOU START

The starting point for making any recipe is to read it through, checking that you have all the ingredients that are listed, in the right quantities, and all the cooking utensils that are needed. As well as checking these obvious points, make sure that you will have enough time to prepare and cook the recipe; this is particularly important if you are making a dish that may require lengthy cooking.

It may seem very obvious, but do clear the work surface before you start – it is all too easy to begin a baking session in enthusiasm when the kitchen is already crowded with dishes waiting to be washed after a meal, or from a previous cooking task. The lack of space and the mess suddenly become all too apparent when a soufflé is removed from the oven and there is not a space anywhere to put it down.

Assemble all the ingredients, utensils and baking tins. If you want to make any adjustments to the quantities – for example preparing a large batch of scones – then work through the ingredients list, jotting down the quantities you intend to prepare, or noting any other changes so that you will be consistent as you weigh and prepare the recipe. It is very easy to forget to double up just one item when preparing a double quantity of mixture and it can be disastrous!

Lastly, make sure the oven is empty, ready for use and that the shelves are in position.

CHOICE OF INGREDIENTS

Information on basic ingredients is given on pages 15-23, but in general all ingredients should be fresh and of good quality. The rule for baking is to have foods such as butter, margarine, eggs and milk at room temperature unless otherwise stated in the recipe. Always wash eggs under cool water before cracking them open.

KITCHEN HYGIENE

Always make sure that areas where food is prepared are thoroughly clean, that all utensils are clean and dry and that dish cloths and tea-towels are scrupulously clean. And the same applies to your hands – do not handle raw food, then cooked food without washing your hands in between. Keep all utensils for raw and cooked food separate or washed between use.

WEIGHING AND MEASURING

It is important to follow the recipes closely for success. Use only one set of measures, either metric or Imperial. Use an accurate set of scales for weighing, a measuring jug for measuring quantities of fluid and British standard spoon measures.

Weigh all the ingredients before you begin to prepare the mixture so that they are all ready to be added as they are needed. It is a good idea to weigh dry ingredients, such as flour and sugar, before softer foods, like butter or margarine, as this saves having to wash the scoop or container on the scales in between weighing the items. Keep the prepared ingredients separate until they are ready to be mixed in the right order.

PREPARING TINS AND HEATING THE OVEN

Always make sure you have the correct size and shape of tin and prepare it in advance according to the instructions given in the recipe, or by following specific advice given by the bakeware manufacturer as appropriate. If you are unsure as to exactly how to line tins, then check with the chapter that explains and illustrates all the basics.

Prepare the oven, taking care to select the right temperature, at the stage suggested in the recipe.

MIXING THE INGREDIENTS

Follow the recipe method closely, taking note of any advice on the texture or colour of the mixture so that you know what you should be aiming for. If you are unsure of any term or process, then check it in the chapter on basics or in the glossary as appropriate.

The majority of baking mixtures should be baked as soon as they are prepared unless the recipe states otherwise. When preparing biscuits always observe suggested chilling times before baking.

COOKING TIMES

Check the cooking time before you put the dishes, breads, cakes or biscuits into the oven, setting a timer as a reminder. Many recipes give a range of times within which the item should be cooked, so check on the cooking progress at the first suggested time. Before opening the oven door make sure that you know what you are looking for in the finished item, then you will be able to decide quickly whether it is cooked or not.

REMOVING FOOD FROM THE OVEN

Make sure that you have a clear space on which to put the baked goods as soon as they are removed from the oven. Have a heat-proof mat or stand on the work surface and always remember to use a thick oven glove to protect your hands.

Have a wire rack ready to receive the cooked food if the recipe suggests that it ought to be transferred to one. You may need a palette knife to slide biscuits off a baking sheet, or a small knife to loosen a cake around the sides of a tin. If you are removing a cake from a loose-bottomed tin, then have a suitable vessel ready to support the middle of the tin allowing the side to slide down. A storage jar with a heat-resistant top is ideal for this.

FINISHING THE RECIPE

Follow the advice given in the recipe for cooling and finishing the baked items. Some recipes offer guidance on storing the baked goods, otherwise follow the general instructions at the beginning of the sections.

ESSENTIAL AND USEFUL UTENSILS FOR BAKING

This section provides a guide to the essential and useful utensils for baking. For preparing a simple cake, or a batch of small cakes, very little is needed in the way of equipment but if you bake regularly, or enjoy experimenting with more complicated baking recipes, then it is worth discovering the wide variety of utensils and baking tins which are available. One of the most important pieces of equipment for baking is the oven. For good results you should have an oven which has a reliable thermostat, keeping the temperature constant and accurate, and which cooks evenly throughout the cavity. It is a good idea to have the oven professionally checked if you have doubts about its technical performance.

SMALL UTENSILS FOR PREPARING MIXTURES

Bowls and Basins   One of the first items of equipment to consider has to be a container in which to mix all the ingredients. There are all sorts of mixing bowls and basins available, from glazed earthenware through to flimsy plastic. The size of bowl will depend on the amount of mixture which you are preparing and the method used to mix the ingredients; for example, if fat has to be rubbed into flour, then the bowl should be big enough to allow you to do this even if the quantities used are small. As well as the main mixing bowl you may have to use another container for beating eggs or for combining other ingredients.

Fairly heavy bowls are best for creaming ingredients together since they tend to be more stable. As well as glass and earthenware, the choice includes heavy plastic bowls which have a rubber strip on the base to prevent them from slipping on the surface. Some bowls have rims or handles to make them easy to hold with one hand while you are working.

If you bake frequently, then it is a good idea to invest in a set of basins and bowls of different sizes. Remember that those which are made of ovenproof glass can also be very useful for many other kitchen tasks, and make sure that you have some basins that will withstand the heat when placed over a saucepan of hot water.

After use wash bowls and basins in hot soapy water and rinse them under clean hot water. Drain and dry them thoroughly before storing, preferably in a closed cupboard, away from dust. Take care when stacking basins to avoid jamming them together.

Kitchen Scales   More so than in any other area of cooking, when baking it is vital to weigh ingredients accurately and for this you will need a reliable set of kitchen scales. There are many types and a wide range of prices from which to select. Scales graduated in either metric or Imperial are available and many types provide the facility for measuring both.

Good quality balance scales are usually very accurate and they can be used with either metric or Imperial weights. They should always be used on a level work surface, with the correct scoop as supplied by the manufacturer.

A good beam scale also provides an accurate means of weighing ingredients. A sliding device is used to select the required weight before the ingredients are added to the scoop which should balance perfectly when the amount is correct. These tend to be more fiddly to use and they are not the most popular type of scales.

Digital scales vary in accuracy according to their type, and often according to cost. They are neat and clean, and they can be free standing or wall mounted. Always follow the manufacturer's instructions closely when using them and do make sure that batteries are replaced when necessary to ensure continued accuracy.

Spring scales indicate the weight on a dial. This is probably the least accurate type of scale but this is usually only a problem when weighing small quantities, or preparing very precise mixtures. Before buying this type of scale make sure that the dial registers small quantities as well as large ones. Instead of the traditional scoop, some scales of this type have mixing bowls, measuring jugs or neat streamlined containers to hold the ingredients. They can be free standing or wall mounted.

Whichever type you choose, always follow the manufacturer's instructions. If necessary check that the dial or digital indicator registers zero before adding ingredients. Keep the container for food scrupulously clean, washing and drying it after each use. All scales should be kept in a dry place and for convenience they are often positioned on the work surface, with the scoop (or its equivalent) inverted for cleanliness when not in use.

Measuring Spoons and Jugs It is vital to have a set of measuring spoons which comply with British Standard measures. All spoon measures given throughout the book refer to these, and serving spoons must not be used instead. Most kitchen shops, hardware stores and department stores stock spoon measures, often with metric equivalents, and these are usually quite inexpensive.

Measuring jugs are available in many shapes and sizes, and they should always be used for accuracy when using liquids.

Spoons and Spatulas A wooden spoon is used for beating fat with sugar (known as creaming) or for similar tasks. The spoon should have a handle which is long enough for the mixture to be beaten efficiently but it should not be too long for comfort. Firm, rigid plastic spoons which are as strong as wooden spoons are an alternative and these are preferable in terms of hygiene.

A large metal spoon is necessary for folding in dry ingredients, for example when making a sponge cake. Any suitable serving spoon can be used for this purpose.

A plastic spatula is useful for scraping all the mixture from the inside of a bowl; select one with a large, flexible end.

Knives A kitchen knife is used for cutting up and chopping ingredients. A round-bladed knife or small palette knife is used for smoothing mixture and easing cakes away from the edge of a tin. A large palette knife or metal spatula is used for lifting baked items off hot baking sheets.

Sieve and Sifter A fine metal or plastic sieve is used for sifting flour or a similar dry ingredient before adding it to a mixture.

A sifter is useful for sprinkling caster or icing sugar over finished baked goods but it is not an essential piece of equipment.

Fine Grater A fine grater is usually used for grating lemon or orange rind which is added to mixtures. Most large graters have the facility for grating coarsely and finely. A very fine, small nutmeg grater is useful for grating whole nutmegs but the ground spice can be used for baking.

Citrus Squeezer Lemon or orange juice is sometimes added to mixtures for baking and a citrus squeezer is used to extract the juice from the fruit. A wide variety of types are available, some quite inexpensive, and it is a good idea to look for one which includes a strainer to prevent the pips from dropping in when the juice is measured.

Whisk A whisk is used for whisking egg whites or similar tasks. Either a balloon or coiled whisk is ideal for light tasks; a rotary whisk can be useful for heavier work.

Cutters Pastry cutters or biscuit cutters are available in metal or plastic, in fluted or plain rounds, squares or a variety of other shapes.

Pastry Brush Useful for greasing tins with a little oil. After use the brush should be washed in very hot soapy water, rinsed and thoroughly dried.

Oil Well A handy gadget for those who often need to grease tins: a small plastic container complete with brush and cover to hold oil ready for greasing tins.

Wire Racks Most cakes, teabreads and biscuits are turned out of the tin and placed on a wire rack to cool. For making sandwich cakes it is wise to have two cooling racks.

ELECTRICAL APPLIANCES

Food Mixers These take the hard work out of beating and creaming cake mixtures. The smaller, hand-held mixers or beaters or those with an optional stand are ideal for making light cakes, for whisking eggs for a Swiss roll or sponge, or for whisking egg whites. The large, free-standing mixers are useful for preparing large quantities of heavy mixtures, for example fruit cakes. Although these appliances are used for creaming and beating they cannot be used for folding in.

Food Processors Most food processors have an optional attachment for mixing or beating, usually a plastic blade. They are ideal for preparing one-stage cake mixtures but it is important to avoid processing the ingredients for too long. Some food processors have the facility for whisking egg whites.

BAKING TINS

Baking Sheets These come in a variety of sizes, some with edges, others without. They can also have a non-stick coating. Many new ovens come complete with a baking sheet provided by the manufacturer. The sheets should always be cooled after cooking, then washed in hot, soapy water and dried thoroughly before storing in a dry cupboard. Do check that a large sheet will fit inside your oven before you buy one.

Plain Deep Cake Tins For baking large cakes, these can be square or round, in one piece or with a loose bottom. They are available with a variety of non-stick coatings. The loose-bottomed tins are useful for making semi-rich cakes or deep sponges which can be difficult to remove from one-piece tins. Very rich, heavy cakes are easy to remove from tins, and are often allowed to cool completely or partly cool in the tin before being transferred to a wire rack. All tins should be thoroughly washed and dried after use and before being stored in a dry cupboard. Follow the manufacturers' instructions for the treatment of specific non-stick coatings.

Springform Tins These are deep, round tins which have a spring clip to hold the side together and a loose base which is removed when the clip is loosened. They are ideal for light cakes which can be difficult to remove from tins. These tins usually have a choice of bases, including a ring-tin base.

Cake Forms Cake forms are useful for baking large, rich fruit cakes. The form consists of the sides for the tin and this is placed on a baking sheet. The 'tin' is then lined with greaseproof paper and greased before the mixture is added.

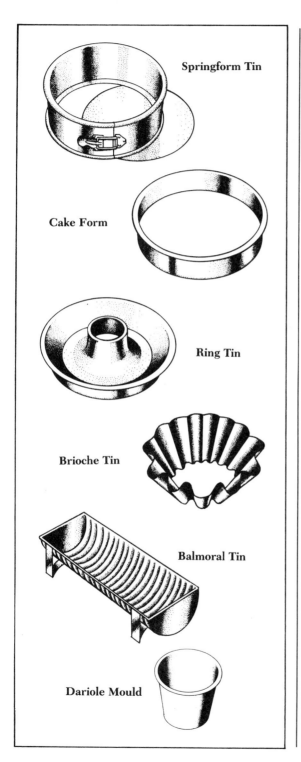

Springform Tin

Cake Form

Ring Tin

Brioche Tin

Balmoral Tin

Dariole Mould

Sandwich Tins Shallow, straight-sided tins, usually round, often with a non-stick coating, which are used to make cakes in pairs; for example Victoria sandwich. The tins can be base lined before use if the mixture is likely to stick during cooking.

Shallow Tins Available in various shapes, round, oblong or square with straight or slightly sloping sides. They can be plain or fluted, with or without a non-stick coating.

Swiss Roll Tins Large, very shallow tins, oblong in shape and usually in two sizes. They may have a non-stick coating but these tins are usually lined with grease-proof paper before use.

Loaf Tins Narrow, deep and long, these are used for making bread, teabreads and and semi-rich fruit cakes. They are available with non-stick coatings but are often lined before use. Tins which can have adjustable sides to make them larger or smaller are also available.

Ring Tins With rounded or square bottoms, good for making light cakes. Kugelhopf moulds are deep and highly decorated.

Brioche Tin A large, round fluted tin with sloping sides. Useful for baking light cakes as well as for the traditional rich bread.

Balmoral Tin A long, narrow tin, with a base which is semi-circular in shape and sometimes supported by metal stands at both ends. This type of tin has decorative ridges from side to side all along its length and is not as deep as a loaf tin.

Patty Tins Usually in the form of a tray of six or twelve individual hollows, these are used for baking individual cakes and tartlets. They can be deep or shallow, patterned or plain, with or without a non-stick coating.

Dariole Moulds Also known as castle tins, these are small, deep tins which are usually about 150 ml/¼ pint in capacity or slightly less. Used to make English-style Madeleines, plain cakes coated in jam and coconut.

Shaped Tins Cake tins are available in a wide variety of different shapes, from large and small heart-shaped tins to numeral shapes, hexagonal tins, oval shapes and so on. Many of these can be hired from cook shops and hardware stores to make special, one-off cakes.

OVENPROOF CAKE DISHES

With the development of microwave cooking, and particularly combination microwave cooking, more glassware cooking dishes are available in shapes suitable for baking cakes which can withstand the temperatures in the conventional oven. As well as ordinary ovenproof glassware, some dishes are available with a non-stick coating. They are available as deep round dishes, shallow round dishes, loaf dishes and fluted dishes similar to brioche tins. If you do want certain dishes for dual purpose use then these are suitable.

DISPOSABLE ITEMS

Greaseproof Paper This is widely used in baking. It is used for lining cake tins, for rolling up in cakes which are to be cooled before filling and for making icing bags to be used for intricate icing.

Non-stick Baking Parchment This is a non-stick paper which does not need greasing and which is particularly useful for items which tend to stick during cooking, for example very delicate biscuits or meringues. It can be used in place of greaseproof paper for base lining sandwich tins.

Paper Cake Cases These may be plain or patterned, and are used instead of patty tins for baking small cakes. The paper cases are stood on baking sheets or they can be placed in the patty tins for support. Large cake cases are available for putting inside tins when making semi-rich cakes or deep sponges. Small paper cake cases, of the type generally used for confectionery, may be used to make petits fours.

Wax Paper This is not as widely used as greaseproof paper but it can be used for lining tins when making certain delicate cakes. It is similar to greaseproof paper but has a wax coating on one side.

Rice Paper A fine, opaque paper which is edible. It is used as a base for macaroons and similar mixtures which tend to stick during cooking. The edges are trimmed but the rice paper base bakes into the mixture and is eaten with it.

Cooking Foil Not widely used in baking but it is useful for loosely covering the top of cakes which are cooked for a long period of time, and which may begin to darken too much on top before the middle is cooked.

Brown Paper Although this is not used in direct contact with the food, it is wrapped neatly around the outside of tins when baking heavy, rich mixtures in a cool oven for long periods of time. By wrapping several thicknesses of paper around the outside of the tin the cake is prevented from forming a dry crust during cooking.

DECORATING EQUIPMENT

Specialist equipment for decorating cakes is listed in the chapter on cake decorating. A few items are useful for the preparation of certain mixtures; for example when piping biscuits.

Piping or Icing Bags Large piping bags are usually made of nylon or heavy cotton which is treated with a moisture-proof coating. They can be lightweight or firmer. They are useful for piping biscuits or sponge fingers. Bags should always be thoroughly washed, rinsed and dried after use and they should be boiled occasionally.

Large Piping Nozzles Large plain and fluted nozzles are used for piping uncooked, soft biscuit mixtures; also meringue-type mixtures as well as for piping choux pastry, cream and other fillings for cakes.

A GUIDE TO INGREDIENTS

The following information outlines the main ingredients which form the basis for many of the recipes, with notes on the different types which are available and how they should be stored. Do read the information supplied on packaging and take advantage of leaflets and advice which are offered by manufacturers. Remember, most manufacturers want to help you to achieve the best results when using their products and they can also be helpful in solving any particular problems which you may encounter.

FLOUR

There is a wide range of flours available and the choice depends on the purpose for which it is required. Flour is obtained by milling wheat. The wheat grain is made up of various parts: the *endosperm* which is the starchy part and which is intended to provide food for the growing plant; the *outer bran layers* which are the main source of fibre; the *aleurone* which is a layer between the bran and the endosperm, providing protein, vitamins and minerals; and the *germ*, or *wheatgerm*, which is rich in protein, oil and vitamins. (The germ is the part of the grain that will grow if it is planted.)

The grain is broken down by milling. During this process either all or part of the grain can be used to make the flour. Each type of flour has a different composition and they can be broadly grouped according to the percentage of the whole cleaned wheat grain which they contain; this is known as the extraction rate. The extraction rate is given on the packet and this is useful for checking the difference between the types of brown flour that are available.

Wholemeal or Wholewheat Flour This flour contains all the wheat grain with nothing added or taken away during processing and milling. This is known as 100% extraction flour and the preferred term is wholemeal, although both names are used. When 'whole' is included in the name of the flour it means it contains all the grain.

Brown Flour This type of flour usually contains about 85% of the wheat grain (85% extraction rate) and it is most often sold under particular brand names. The term 'wheatmeal' was at one time used for this type of flour but this was confusing and its use is now illegal.

White Flour This type of flour usually contains about 75% of the wheat grain although some white flours have a lower extraction rate. Most of the bran and wheatgerm are removed during the milling process in order to produce white flour.

81% Extraction Flour   This is a flour which bridges the gap between brown and white flour and it is sold under various brand names. The extraction rate is given on the packets.

Stoneground Flour   This term is used for wheat which is ground between two stones instead of by modern roller methods and it does not reflect the composition of the flour.

As well as the composition of the flour which depends on the amount of the grain which it contains, other processes go to make up the different types of flour.

Plain Flour   This is flour which does not have any raising agent added. It is the common term used for plain white flour. It is used for certain types of cake mixture, pastry and for making biscuits.

Self-raising Flour   This is flour which has a raising agent added to it. When used in recipes the term usually relates to white flour but self-raising wholemeal or brown flours are also available. The amount of raising agent to flour is carefully balanced during the production process so that it gives perfect results in the majority of baking recipes. When self-raising brown flour is required this is stated in the ingredients list.

Soft Flour   This is usually white. This flour has a low protein content and it is very light. It is manufactured for use in light cake or biscuit mixtures, for example Victoria sandwich cakes, Genoese sponge cakes or piped biscuits, or for making pastry. It is one of the most 'modern' types of flour and many manufacturers offer guidance on its use and sample recipes.

Strong Flour   This is usually white. It has a high protein content and it is used in yeast mixtures, particularly in bread making.

Malted Wheat Flour   This is brown flour to which malted wheat is added to give a distinctive texture and flavour. Again the main use for this type of flour is in bread but it can be used in savoury biscuits.

STORING FLOUR

Flour should be kept in a cool, dry, airy place. The bag of flour can be placed in an airtight tin or the flour can be turned into a storage jar with a tight-fitting lid. The jar should always be thoroughly washed and dried before it is filled with a new batch of flour. Do not add new flour to the remains of an older batch.

Plain white flour can be stored for four to six months but self-raising flour does not keep as well and it should be stored for up to two or three months. Wholemeal and brown flours have a higher fat content than white flour so they may go rancid if they are not properly stored or if they are kept for too long. These should be kept for up to two months, so it is best to buy small quantities frequently. Store wholemeal and brown flours in a cool, dry place and keep them separate from white flour as they should be used sooner.

CORNFLOUR

Cornflour is produced from maize and it is quite different from wheat flour. It is very fine, almost pure starch, and it is sometimes combined with wheat flour in certain cake and biscuit recipes.

RAISING AGENTS

For the majority of cake mixtures a raising agent is added to make the cake rise during cooking. In the case of a whisked mixture, such as a whisked sponge, air is incorporated into the mixture during whisking and it acts as the raising agent since it expands as the mixture is heated in the oven. Self-raising flour is used in the majority of cake recipes and it is not usually necessary to add any additional raising agent, although there are exceptions to this rule.

A combination of acid and alkaline substances are used to make most cake mixtures rise. When they are moistened and heated in combination they produce a gas (carbon dioxide) and it is the gas bubbles which make the mixture rise. The heat of the oven sets the cake and this traps the bubbles in place. Alternatively, yeast can be used as a raising agent, mainly for breads and buns. Yeast ferments with sugar and moisture in the presence of warmth and it produces carbon dioxide, the bubbles of which are trapped during proving (or the rising process) and baking.

Baking Powder Baking powder is the most common leavening agent used in baking when self-raising flour is not used for a recipe. Baking powder is made up of bicarbonate of soda (alkaline), selected acids and a certain amount of starch. These ingredients are combined in the exact proportions required to produce a rise when the powder is both moistened and heated. It is important to use the correct amount of baking powder as suggested in the recipe because too much can cause failure just as too little will result in inadequate rising.

Bicarbonate of Soda Bicarbonate of soda is used in certain recipes, for example gingerbread. Once it is moistened the bicarbonate of soda quickly starts to produce the bubbles which result in a rise, so recipes which contain bicarbonate of soda must be cooked as soon as they are mixed.

Cream of Tartar This is an acid which can be combined with bicarbonate of soda and used instead of baking powder. To be used in this way, two parts of cream of tartar should be mixed with one part of bicarbonate of soda. This is a common raising agent for scones.

Yeast In warm conditions, when combined with moisture and sugar, yeast produces carbon dioxide to make doughs and selected cake mixtures rise. Either fresh or dried yeast can be used successfully in making bread and heavy doughs.

Fresh yeast is sometimes available from bakers. It should be creamy in colour, have a slightly beery smell, be cool to the touch and easy to break. It should be blended with warm liquid for use.

Dried yeast is available in packets and tins and it keeps very well if unopened (for up to one year). Once opened it keeps for about two to three months. Before use the dried yeast is reconstituted by sprinkling it over lukewarm liquid and leaving it, loosely covered, in a warm place until it has dissolved and the liquid is frothy. The yeast liquid should be stirred to make sure that all the grains of dried yeast have dissolved before it is mixed with other ingredients.

Easy-blend yeast is a dried yeast which must be added straight to the dry ingredients. When this is used the manufacturer's instructions should be followed closely for good results.

Storing Raising Agents All dry raising agents should be stored in an airtight container in a cool, dry place. Old, stale raising agents will not give the required results, so they should be stored for no more than two or three months, then discarded. Dried yeast should be stored in a cool, dry place in an airtight container. Fresh yeast wrapped in polythene can be kept for up to a week in the refrigerator or it can be frozen, well wrapped, for up to a month.

FAT

The majority of baked goods include a certain amount of fat and the richer types have a high proportion of fat added. There are various fats which can be used but the majority are made from butter or margarine.

Butter This gives an excellent flavour in cooking. If it is allowed to soften at room temperature, butter creams extremely well. When taken straight from the refrigerator and rubbed into dry ingredients, it is ideal for making cakes and biscuits. It can also be melted with other ingredients before being added to the dry ingredients.

There are two types of butter to choose from: the first is sweet cream butter which is salted or slightly salted. The second is lactic butter which is slightly salted or unsalted and may be referred to as 'continental'.

Traditionally, the sweet cream varieties are the most popular and they form the largest proportion of butter produced in the United Kingdom, the Republic of Ireland and New Zealand. This type of butter is produced by churning cream which has been allowed to stand for approximately twelve hours. The addition of salt produces the characteristic flavour and improves the keeping quality of the butter.

A certain amount of lactic butter is produced in the United Kingdom but the majority is imported. A culture of lactic acid is added to the cream before it is churned; this results in a slightly acidic flavour.

In addition a number of regional butters are produced in the United Kingdom. These have subtle individual flavour qualities that are appreciated on bread. These are not usually specified for use in recipes.

When buying butter always check the sell-by date which is given on the packet. (Remember that sell-by dates are for guidance only and they are not a compulsory feature.) Store butter in the refrigerator, neatly packed in its original wrapping. The keeping quality of butter does vary according to its type and packaging. Butter in foil packaging keeps slightly better than butter in parchment packing, and salted butter keeps nominally better than the unsalted type. The foil-wrapped butter can be kept for up to eleven weeks in the refrigerator; butter in parchment for seven weeks.

Butter can be frozen, when the unopened pack should be enclosed in a sealed polythene bag. The unsalted type will keep best in the freezer and it can be stored for up to six months. Salted butter can be frozen for up to three months.

All butter should be well wrapped during storage as it absorbs flavours and odours.

To clarify butter, heat gently until melted, then stand for 2-3 minutes. Pour off clear yellow liquid on top and allow to solidify. This is the clarified butter.

Margarine Margarine is probably the most popular fat used in baking as it is less expensive than butter and yet gives comparable results, although the flavour is not as good. Generally, it is made of 80% fat and a maximum of 16% water, with added flavouring, colouring and emulsifiers.

Margarine is produced from blended edible oils and soft fats and the type used is specified on the packet or tub. Fish oil and soft animal fats can be used in combination with vegetable oils; some margarines use vegetable oils only. There are two types, either hard, block margarine or soft, tub margarine. The texture of the margarine depends on type of oils or fats used and on the manufacturing process. For creaming, the block margarine should be allowed to soften at room temperature in the same way as butter. Soft margarine can be used straight from the refrigerator. The nature of the processing method results in soft margarine being whipped before packing so that it is particularly light and will cream easily with sugar. Soft margarine is particularly useful for making one-stage mixtures.

Lard Lard is white, melted and clarified pork fat which was once very popular for cooking. It is used mainly in pastry.

Dripping This is melted down meat fat – usually beef – and it has a distinctive flavour. It is not an ingredient which is commonly used in baking but it is used in traditional, and very economical, recipes.

When it is used in baking recipes, dripping obtained from meat should be clarified. To do this the fat is heated gently in a large saucepan with the same volume of cold water until the water just begins to boil. All scum must be removed as it rises to the surface and the dripping is allowed to simmer in the water for 5 minutes. The liquid is then strained through a muslin-lined sieve into a clean bowl. The bowl is covered and the fat allowed to solidify in a cool place. The dripping is lifted off the water in one piece and any sediment on its underside is scraped off. Lastly, the dripping is heated very gently until all spitting and bubbling ceases, to evaporate all the water.

Oil Some recipes are developed specifically to use oil in certain doughs but otherwise this fat is not used for baking. However, it is the most convenient form of fat for greasing baking tins.

Low-fat Spreads These spreads should not be confused with margarine. They are manufactured specifically for spreading and they are not recommended instead of margarine or butter for baking since they have a high water content and they contain little fat, as the term suggests. The fat content of the spread should be given on the container and this varies according to the product.

SUGAR

Sugar, in its many forms, is widely used in cooking and it is a vital ingredient in ensuring the success of many baking recipes. Its prime function is to sweeten, but certain types of sugar also add flavour to cake and biscuit mixtures. It is important that the correct proportion of sugar is used, as stated in the recipe, and that it is incorporated into the mixture correctly.

As well as sugar, syrup and treacle are used for certain recipes; these ingredients are derived from sugar.

Granulated Sugar This is probably the most common type of sugar and it should be used in recipes where the term 'sugar' is used in the ingredients list. It is used in recipes that contain enough liquid for it to dissolve completely or where the cooking temperature and time are adequate to ensure that it dissolves. For example, it is used in rubbed-in mixtures and for melted mixtures. It can be used for creamed mixtures but caster sugar gives better results.

Caster Sugar This is finer than granulated sugar, it dissolves more quickly and it is the most suitable sugar for creaming with fat or for use in whisked mixtures. It gives more volume and a lighter result than granulated sugar in these recipes. In addition, caster sugar can be sprinkled over cooked sponge cakes and plain biscuits to enhance their appearance.

Soft Light Brown Sugar The term used to describe this type of sugar varies according to the manufacturer; for example it may be sold as 'light golden soft sugar'. It is a fine-grained sugar which has cane molasses added, to provide flavour as well as darkening the colour. It is used in light fruit cakes or in other baking recipes and adds flavour as well as sweetening the mixture.

Soft Dark Brown Sugar Again the term used varies according to the manufacturer and this type of sugar may be sold as 'rich dark soft sugar'. It is similar to the soft light brown sugar but it contains more cane molasses, giving it a richer flavour and darker colour. It is used in rich fruit cakes or gingerbreads and it can be used to make certain biscuits.

Muscovado Sugar Muscovado sugar is very dark, moist and fairly fine-grained. It is unrefined cane sugar and it has a very dark, almost black, colour and strong flavour. It is not widely used in baking but it can be used in making rich fruit cakes to give a very dark colour and rich flavour to the mixture.

Raw Cane Sugar This is sugar which contains a certain amount of the impurities from sugar cane which are otherwise removed during the processing of white sugars. Some brown sugars are first refined, then molasses is added to contribute the characteristic flavour and colour. Raw cane sugars are not refined first – the darker varieties naturally contain the most impurities and molasses; the lighter types contain fewer impurities. The composition of the product is indicated on the packet and if the sugar has first been refined, then had molasses added (or caramel), then this will be indicated by an ingredients list.

Demerara Sugar Demerara sugar is light brown in colour, with a fairly rich flavour and large crystals. It is not widely used in baking but it can be sprinkled over the top of certain types of cakes (for example, loaf cakes) before cooking as a topping.

Icing Sugar This is very fine, powdered sugar which is not commonly used in cake mixtures but which forms the basis for many different types of icing. It is ideal for sweetening whipped cream as it dissolves very rapidly. It is also useful for sprinkling over cooked cakes, sweet buns and biscuits once they are cooled.

Lump Sugar This is made from granulated sugar which is moistened with syrup and moulded. The lumps or cubes of sugar are dried and packed into boxes. It does not have a role to play in baking recipes other than for crushing and sprinkling over cakes, buns and biscuits as decoration.

Preserving Sugar As its name implies this sugar is manufactured specifically for use in preserves. It has very large crystals and it can be sprinkled over loaf cakes before cooking.

Golden Syrup This is a blend of sugar syrup, caramel and flavourings. It is used in certain baking recipes instead of sugar. It can be used to glaze the top of light fruit cakes just before they are served.

Black Treacle This is made from molasses and sugar syrup. It has a very dark colour and strong flavour and it is used in certain baking recipes, for example gingerbread, or it is added to rich fruit cakes.

Molasses Molasses is the very dark, thick syrup which is drained from raw sugar cane. It is interchangeable with black treacle.

Storing Sugar All types of sugar, syrup and treacle should be stored in airtight containers and kept in a cool, dry place. Soft brown sugar may harden slightly during storage but it usually softens again if it is warmed briefly in a cool oven (or for a few seconds in the microwave). Icing sugar does not have a long shelf life as it does harden and it is vital that there are no lumps in it if it is used to prepare icings. Syrup and treacle tins should be wiped clean with absorbent kitchen paper after use and they must be stored in a dry place. Do not use the contents of old tins which may have rusted or been damaged.

EGGS

Eggs play a vital role in cake making. They are used to lighten cakes and to ensure that they rise and set during cooking. In some mixtures, where a high proportion of eggs is used, they are the only raising agent.

The eggs can be used whole or they may be separated before they are added to the mixture. Whisked with sugar, they may form the basis for the mixture and the other ingredients will be folded into them. For some recipes the egg yolks are incorporated first, then the whisked whites are folded into the mixture. In this case a little of the whites should be stirred in first to soften the bulk of the mixture before the rest of the whites are folded in.

In some recipes just the whites or yolks are used; for example, meringues require the whites only and biscuits often use just yolks. Other recipes may call for more whites than yolks in order to produce a very light mixture. Eggs are an important ingredient in soufflés (page 88).

Buying eggs   Eggs come in different sizes and they are also categorized by quality. Two quality grades of whole eggs are sold, either A or B quality and this is clearly stated on the box. There are regulations that have to be observed for the sale of pre-packed eggs, and certain information has to be included on the outside of the box.

Firstly, the class of eggs must be clearly marked and the number of eggs in the box indicated. The size of the eggs must also be shown along with the registered number of the packing station, the name and address of those responsible for packing and the date on which the eggs were packed. In addition there may be a sell-by date, although this is optional – always look out for this and make sure that it has not expired if it is included.

Egg Sizes   Class A eggs are graded in sizes from 1-7 and the sizes most commonly available are 2-4.

Size 1 – 70 g and over
Size 2 – 65 g and under 70 g
Size 3 – 60 g and under 65 g
Size 4 – 55 g and under 60 g
Size 5 – 50 g and under 55 g
Size 6 – 45 g and under 50 g
Size 7 – under 45 g

Size 3 are the most suitable for baking unless otherwise stated; for example if large eggs are called for then use size 2.

Storing Eggs   Eggs should be stored in the refrigerator, preferably in their box, and the pointed end of each egg should be kept downwards to help prevent breakage, reduce evaporation and help to prevent any odours being absorbed.

Using Eggs   For many recipes it is best if eggs are used at room temperature so they should be removed from the refrigerator about 30 minutes before they are to be used. However this is not essential. It is very important that eggs are clean and they should be washed under cool water and dried before they are cracked, taking care not to break them, of course. It is best to crack eggs individually into a mug, cup or small basin before adding them to mixtures and any broken shell should be removed.

Eggs are a protein food and they should be treated with the same standards of hygiene that are adopted for all raw meat, fish and poultry. All utensils must be thoroughly clean before use and hands should be washed before and after breaking eggs, particularly if cooked food is handled after raw eggs. Ang unused beaten egg should be kept in a tightly covered container and placed in the refrigerator. It should be used within twenty-four hours. Egg whites can be frozen in a clean, airtight, rigid container. Remember to label the container with the number of whites which it contains. Once thawed, egg whites should always be used immediately.

DRIED FRUIT

Dried fruit includes raisins, sultanas, currants, dates, glacé cherries, candied peel and other fruits such as apricots, pears, peaches and apples. The smaller dried fruits, candied peel and cherries are those which are most commonly used when making cakes, teabreads and sweet breads. Most dried fruit is cleaned and seeded before it is packed and sold, but any stalks that may be left should be removed.

Raisins   Raisins are dried grapes and the best are those obtained by drying the varieties of muscatel grape. These have to be mechanically seeded during processing. Alternatively, seedless grapes are dried. This avoids the necessity for seeding, but the quality of the raisins is not as good.

Sultanas These are dried, seedless green grapes and they are lighter in colour than raisins. They re slightly softer than raisins, and should be plump and sweet.

Currants These are smaller, darker and more shrivelled than raisins. They are dried, small black grapes which are produced mainly in Greece. Currants are used in large quantities for rich fruit cakes.

Dates Dried stoneless dates are sold ready for cooking, either in the form of a block which should be chopped before use or ready chopped and lightly coated in sugar. Both types are more suitable for cooking than the dessert dates which are boxed whole.

Figs Whole figs are dried. They should be chopped before use, although they are not as widely used as the smaller dried fruits.

Prunes There are two main types of dried prune available, either the whole dried fruit that must be washed and soaked overnight or for several hours before use or the stoned, ready-to-eat variety that is more convenient. Prunes are obtained by drying plums and they should be dark and shiny in appearance.

Chopped Mixed Peel This is the mixed peel of citrus fruits, preserved by impregnating it with sugar. Lemon, orange and citron peel is usually included. Alternatively whole pieces of candied citrus peel can be purchased and individually chopped.

Glacé Cherries These are used in a wide variety of mixtures and they may be used as decoration. If they are very sticky, then they should be washed and thoroughly dried before use. The best way to do this is by placing the cherries in a sieve to wash them, then draining them well before drying them on absorbent kitchen paper. Before they are incorporated into many cake mixtures the cherries are dusted with a little of the measured flour.

Storing Dried Fruit Always keep dried fruit in clean, dry, airtight containers. They should be kept in a cool, dark cupboard that is quite dry.

NUTS

Nuts are used to flavour cakes, breads and biscuits and to give texture to certain mixtures. They are also used for decorating.

Almonds These can be purchased shelled with their skins on, blanched with skins removed, split, flaked or chopped. It is often a good idea to compare supermarket prices with those in wholefood shops.

To blanch almonds, place them in a saucepan with plenty of cold water and bring them just to the boil. Drain the nuts in a sieve and rinse them under a cold running tap, then pinch off their skins. Dry the blanched nuts on absorbent kitchen paper.

To split almonds, use a small, sharp, pointed kitchen knife and slide it into the side of the warm nuts.

To brown or roast almonds place them on a piece of foil on a baking sheet or in the grill pan and cook them under the grill, turning them frequently and taking care to prevent them from burning. Alternatively, they can be roasted by placing them on a baking sheet in a warm oven.

Ground almonds are used in cake and biscuit mixtures or to make marzipan and almond paste for covering and decorating cakes.

Walnuts These are not usually blanched before use in baking mixtures. They are also used for decorating. Walnuts are sold in halves or pieces, with pieces the most economical buy if the nuts are to be chopped.

Hazelnuts These can be bought with their skins on, skinned or chopped, and toasted. They are used to flavour cakes and biscuits or to coat the sides of gâteaux.

To remove the skins from hazelnuts, place them under the grill or in the oven, and roast them, turning frequently, until the skins can be rubbed off. To rub the skins off, place the nuts in a paper bag or in a cloth to avoid burning your fingers.

Hazelnuts can be ground in a food processor, coffee grinder (for small amounts), blender or in a rotary grater.

Peanuts Readily available shelled, either salted or unsalted, peanuts are most often used to make biscuits.

Pistachios Delicately flavoured nuts, tinged with green. They are often sold in their shells which are split open but not removed. They are expensive, so their use is limited.

Brazils, Pecans and Other Nuts A variety of other nuts are also used in cakes and biscuits. These are usually available ready shelled, particularly from wholefood shops.

Chopped Mixed Nuts These are an inexpensive alternative to chopped walnuts or hazelnuts but they can be dominated by the flavour of peanuts.

Desiccated Coconut This is finely shredded, dried coconut which is used in cakes and biscuits. It is also used to coat the outside of some baked items.

Long-thread Coconut Desiccated coconut which is very coarsely shredded to give long threads. Useful for decorating purposes but not usually incorporated into mixtures.

FLAVOURING INGREDIENTS

As well as the basic ingredients which go to make up baking mixtures, a wide variety of flavourings can be added. Here are notes on just a few of the most popular ingredients used for flavouring baked goods.

Vanilla A strong flavouring which comes from the seed pods of an orchid. The flavour develops during a period of maturation after the pods have been picked, by the action of enzymes naturally present. True vanilla essence is extracted from the black pods. Vanilla is expensive and the pods are usually sold individually or in pairs. As an alternative to real vanilla, a synthetically produced essence is readily available.

Vanilla is very strong and should be used sparingly. A vanilla pod can be placed in a jar of caster sugar to make vanilla sugar. The pod and sugar should be left to stand for at least three or four weeks. Shake the jar frequently to impart the flavour to the sugar.

Almond Essence Another strong flavouring which must be used with care. It is added to certain mixtures instead of the nuts. It can have a very synthetic flavour and must be used sparingly.

Ground Mixed Spice This mixture of spices is used to flavour cakes, teabreads and biscuits. It usually consists of cinnamon, cloves, ginger and nutmeg.

Ground Ginger Another spice which is used to flavour both cakes and biscuits. It has a strong flavour and should be used according to recipe directions.

Ground Cinnamon A sweet spice which is used to flavour sweet mixtures. A little ground cinnamon can be mixed with caster sugar to make cinnamon sugar and this is used to dust sweet baked goods.

Nutmeg This can be purchased ready ground or the whole nuts can be freshly grated on a small, tough grater as the spice is required. Freshly grated nutmeg has the best flavour.

Grated Fruit Rind The grated rind of oranges and lemons is often used to flavour cakes, doughs and biscuits. The fruit should be washed and dried before the rind is grated on a fine grater. When grating the rind avoid including any of the bitter pith which lies underneath.

BASIC TECHNIQUES AND METHODS

PREPARING TINS FOR BAKING

There is nothing quite as distressing as battling unsuccessfully to release a beautifully cooked cake in one piece from an ill-prepared tin. Difficulties with turning cakes out of tins can often be avoided if the tin is properly prepared in the first instance. Each recipe offers guidance on the size and shape of tin required and the method by which it should be prepared before the mixture is turned into it. Good cake tins are those to which the cooked mixture is not supposed to stick but this is little consolation when there is a fair chance that the tin you intend to use is quite likely to end up with the cake firmly stuck to it. So, if you have doubts about whether a particular tin is going to release the cake easily, do plan ahead and at least line the bottom of the tin. There are four main ways to prepare tins:

1 Bun tins, patty tins and baking sheets should be greased. In some instances the sheets should be dusted with flour after greasing.

2 For rubbed-in cakes each tin should be greased and the base should be lined. The lining paper should be greased before the mixture is placed in the tin.

3 For creamed mixtures it is best to line the base of each tin and in some cases, where the cake requires lengthy cooking, the sides of the tin should also be lined. The lining paper should be greased. The same preparation applies to cakes made by the melted method, for example gingerbread.

4 For whisked sponge cakes each tin should be greased and dusted with a little flour. If the tin is one to which the cake may stick on the base, then a circle of paper should be used to line the base of the tin. The floured sides of the tin provide a surface to which very light sponge mixtures may adhere as they rise during cooking.

Non-stick Tins Many non-stick tins do not have to be lined before they are used. The manufacturer's instructions should be followed carefully when preparing this type of tin.

FAT FOR GREASING

The most convenient fat for greasing is oil. A special 'oil well' gadget is designed to hold a small amount of oil with a suitable brush ready for greasing tins. Alternatively a few drops of oil can be tipped into the tin and brushed evenly over its surface. Lard or other white cooking fat is suitable for greasing tins but butter and margarine are not recommended. If butter or margarine is used it should be clarified first to remove all excess moisture and salt which it contains.

The purpose of greasing is obvious – to prevent the cake from sticking to the tin or to the lining paper. The process of lining tins is made easy if the tin itself is lightly greased first. The lining paper clings to the greased surface, allowing it to be pushed neatly up against the sides. Where the lining paper overlaps slightly, the under-piece should be lightly greased so that the top piece clings to it and stays in place.

CHOICE OF LINING PAPER

Greaseproof paper is the most common form of lining which is used when preparing tins. However non-stick baking parchment is available and this can be used instead. Follow the manufacturer's instructions when using this product as, in many cases, it does not require greasing before the cake mixture is placed on it. Heavy, re-usable non-stick baking paper is also available and this is particularly useful if you want to make a semi-permanent lining for a frequently used tin. The tin should of course be washed and the paper wiped clean between uses. Again the manufacturer's instructions should be followed for using this type of paper.

For making small cakes, paper cake cases can be used, either by standing them on a baking sheet or placing them in patty tins. If the cases are fairly flimsy, it is best to place them in tins for support. It is also possible to purchase large fluted paper cases that can be used to line full-sized cake tins. This is particularly useful if the cake is to be frozen once it is cooked.

For making rich fruit cakes, the tins are best lined with a double thickness of grease-proof paper. To protect the outside of the cake, near the sides and base of the tin, a thick piece of brown paper or newspaper can be tied securely around the outside of the tin, or a piece can be placed on a baking sheet underneath the tin. This is really only necessary when large cakes are baked for several hours and there may be a danger of the outside crust becoming dry.

LINING A SQUARE TIN

1 Place the tin flat on a single or double thickness of lining paper and draw all around the outside of the bottom. Cut out the shape as above, cutting slightly inside the pencil mark to allow for the thickness of the tin.

2 Measure a strip of paper for the sides of the tin as for lining a round tin. Make sure that there is enough to go all the way around the inside of the tin and that the strip is wide enough for a 2.5 cm/1 inch fold all around the bottom as well as to stand at least 2.5 cm/1 inch above the rim of the tin.

3 Lightly grease the tin and place one square of paper in the base if a double thickness is used; grease this lightly. Make a 2.5 cm/1 inch fold all along one side of the strip of paper.

4 Carefully lift the strip of paper into the sides of the tin. Have a pair of scissors ready to snip and fit the corners of the paper into the tin. The overlap in the strip of paper should be positioned on one side of the tin, not at a corner.

5 Press the paper against the sides of the tin and into the first corner. Snip into the corner of the strip of paper sitting in the base of the tin.

6 Overlap the paper in the base of the tin in the first corner, to make a neat squared lining. Continue to press the paper smoothly against the side of the tin up to the next corner, then cut and fi the paper as before. Fit the paper into all four corners in this way.

7 Place the square of lining paper in the base of the tin and brush all the inside evenly with a little oil.

LINING A ROUND TIN

1 Place the tin on a single or double piece of lining paper and draw around the outside edge of the bottom in pencil. Remove the tin and cut out the circle of paper, cutting slightly inside the drawn circle to allow for the thickness of the tin and to ensure that the paper will fit neatly inside the base of the tin.

2 Cut out a strip of paper which is long enough to go around the outside of the tin and overlap by 5 cm/2 inches. The paper should be at least 5 cm/2 inches wider than the depth of the tin, to allow for 2.5 cm/1 inch to sit neatly in the bottom of the tin and at least 2.5 cm/1 inch standing above the rim of the tin.

3 Make a 2.5 cm/1 inch fold all along one side of the strip of paper. Open out the fold and snip diagonally from the edge in as far as the foldline at 1-2.5 cm/½-1 inch intervals all along the length of the paper.

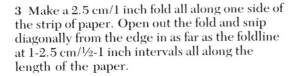

4 Very lightly grease the inside of the tin. If you are using a double thickness of paper, then place one circle in the base of the tin and grease it very lightly. If you are using a single thickness, then put the lining paper around the sides first. Carefully lower the strip of paper into the tin, placing the snipped folded edge downwards. The fold in the base of the strip should tuck neatly all around the inside of the bottom of the tin and the pieces of snipped paper should be overlapped. Place the circle of lining paper in the base of the tin.

5 Lightly grease the lining paper all over, making sure that it is pressed well into the shape of the tin.

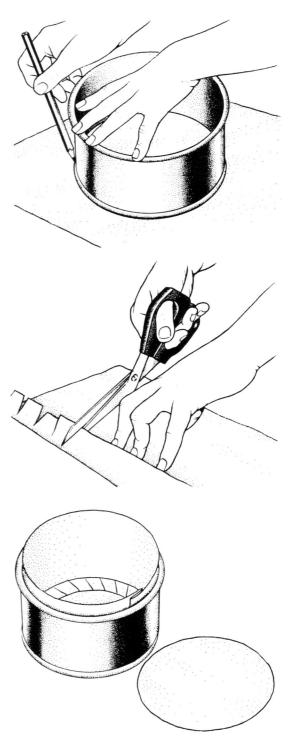

LINING A SWISS ROLL TIN

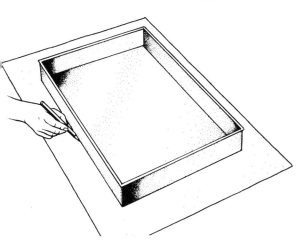

1 Stand the tin on a sheet of greaseproof paper and draw all around the outside of the bottom. Remove the tin.

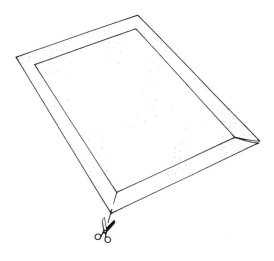

3 Cut from each outer corner of the paper into the corner of the drawn shape of the tin.

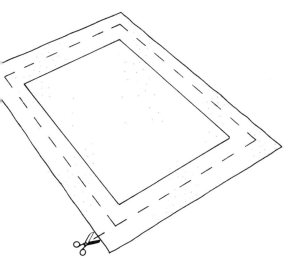

2 Cut out the shape, about 5 cm/2 inches outside the drawn shape. This is to allow enough paper to line the sides of the tin and to stand about 2.5 cm/1 inch above the rim of the tin. The paper should not stand more than 2.5 cm/1 inch above the rim as this may impair the process of browning.

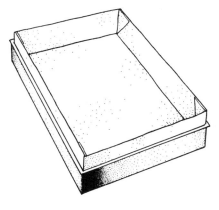

4 Lightly grease the inside of the tin. Turn the paper over so that the pencil mark is facing downwards, into the tin. Press the paper into the tin, overlapping it at the corners to make a neatly squared lining.

5 The paper will stay in place at the corners if it is greased between the overlap. Grease the lining paper evenly.

LINING A LOAF TIN

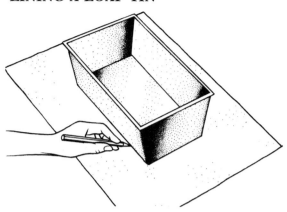

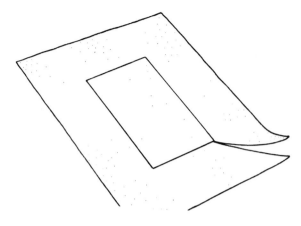

1 Cut a piece of paper large enough to cover the bottom of the tin, to come up both sides and the ends and to stand at least 2.5 cm/1 inch above the tin.

2 Stand the tin in the middle of the paper and draw all around the outside of the bottom.

3 Cut in from each outer corner of the piece of paper to the corner of the drawn shape.

4 Lightly grease the tin, then turn the paper over so that the pencil marks are downwards and lift the paper into the tin.

BASE LINING TINS

If the recipe suggests that the base of the tin should be lined, then simply place the tin on a piece of paper, draw around the outside edge and cut out the shape. Lightly grease the base of the tin so that the paper will stay firmly in place. Place the piece of paper in the base of the tin, then grease the paper and the sides of the tin.

GREASING AND FLOURING TINS

Lightly grease the inside of the tin. Place a spoonful of flour in the tin. Hold the tin at an angle and turn it around and around, tapping the sides as you turn the tin, so that the flour evenly coats the inside. Tip out any excess flour.

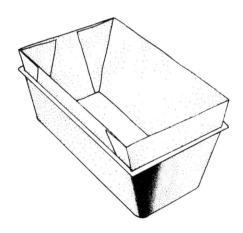

5 Press the paper neatly into the tin, overlapping the cut corners to make neat squares. Grease lightly between the overlap so that the paper clings together.

6 Grease the lining paper well.

PREPARING TINS FOR PASTRY

Pastries with a high fat content are often cooked on ungreased tins. For example, generally there is no need to grease tins for short crust, puff, flaky and rough puff pastry items. However, fillings or toppings which spill on baking tins may stick.

CHOUX PASTRY Plain items may be cooked on ungreased tins, although many cooks prefer to lightly grease the surface. Instead of greasing, the tins should be rinsed with cold water before the paste is spooned or piped on them. Steam from the water helps to give the pastry a good rise.

HOT WATER CRUST PASTRY This is often used to line intricate moulds or tins with sharp corners, therefore the surface is usually well greased for easy removal of the cooked pastry.

PHYLLO PASTRY This contains little fat and tins should always be greased before the pastry is placed on them.

PREPARING BAKING DISHES

When cooking pasta, vegetables and other foods to be served from the baking dish, the fat used for greasing will affect the flavour of the finished dish. Butter, margarine or an oil with distinct flavour, such as olive oil, may be used fairly generously to contribute to the food. Alternatively, a light oil, such as safflower or sunflower oil, may be used very sparingly to prevent food sticking but without making the result greasy. For example, when baking gougère, the dish may be buttered or very lightly greased according to taste.

SAVOURY BAKES

This chapter offers a sample of the many types of savoury dishes that can be cooked by baking, from tempting first courses to traditional ways with potatoes and piping hot pasta specialities.

The aim in this section is to pass on ideas about the types of savoury foods that can be baked and the way in which they are prepared before cooking.

CHOICE OF DISHES

There is an excellent choice of ovenproof dishes available and many attractive designs that are ideal for presenting as well as cooking the food. Always check that a dish is ovenproof before putting it in the oven.

Oven to Table Ware Patterned and plain dishes include chunky pottery as well as elegant white dishes. Soufflé dishes, ramekins, flan dishes and casseroles in a variety of shapes and sizes are all included.

Ovenproof Glassware There is a choice of manufacturers producing plain or smoked glass, fine ovenproof glass and opaque, patterned glass.

Freezer to Oven Ware Certain ovenproof glassware is designed to withstand the sudden change in temperature inflicted when a dish is taken straight from the freezer and put in a hot oven. Make certain that the manufacturer suggests this use of a product. Most ovenproof dishes do not stand up to such sudden changes in temperature – they may not crack immediately but they craze or break with repeated use.

Fireproof Cookware As well as traditional-style casseroles, look for glassware and pottery that is manufactured to withstand hob use, grilling and baking.

CARE OF OVENPROOF DISHES

Always have a heatproof mat ready on the work surface before removing a dish from the oven. Never put a hot baking dish in water (unless the manufacturer recommends this). Leave the dish to cool before filling it with soapy water. Soaking for a few hours usually softens baked on food.

FREEZING SAVOURY BAKES

Many savoury bakes freeze successfully. Remember that the storage life of the cooked dish is only as long as the shortest recommended freezer life of the ingredients.

■ Cool cooked food quickly, keeping it covered all the time.

■ Make sure the pack is airtight and waterproof.

■ Label the pack with the date, name of the dish and any notes about the storage time or the way in which the food should be reheated.

■ Thaw the dish in the refrigerator.

■ Always reheat thawed cooked food thoroughly to the original cooking temperature before serving.

■ Food may be heated from frozen – the oven should be set at a low setting and the food should be covered until it has thawed. The temperature may be increased and the food uncovered so that it browns and forms a crust.

CHEESE AND ASPARAGUS CUSTARD

It is important to cook asparagus upright, so that the stalks are poached while the delicate tips are gently steamed. If the asparagus is too tall for the saucepan, cover it with a dome of foil, crumpled around the pan's rim, instead of using the lid. You can buy special asparagus pans from specialist kitchen shops.

butter for greasing
1 bundle small or sprue asparagus, trimmed, or 225 g/8 oz canned or frozen asparagus
100 g/4 oz cheese, grated
4 eggs
salt and pepper
500 ml/17 floz milk

Butter a 750 ml/1¼ pint ovenproof dish. Tie fresh asparagus in small bundles. Add enough salted water to a deep saucepan to cane three-quarters of the way up the stalks. Bring to the boil. Wedge the bundles of asparagus upright in the pan, or stand them in a heatproof container in the pan. Cover and cook gently for about 10 minutes, depending on the thickness of the stalks. Drain carefully. Drain canned asparagus or cook frozen asparagus according to the directions on the packet.

Set the oven at 150°C/300°F/gas 2. Cut the asparagus into short lengths and put into the prepared dish, with the tips arranged on the top. Sprinkle the grated cheese over the asparagus. Beat the eggs, salt and pepper together lightly and stir in the milk. Strain the custard into the dish.

Stand the dish in a shallow tin containing enough warm water to come half-way up the sides of the dish. Bake for 1½ hours, until the custard is set in the centre.

SERVES 4

HOT STUFFED AVOCADOS

Illustrated on page 33

2 large avocados
100 g/4 oz cooked smoked haddock or cod
50 g/2 oz ricotta cheese
lemon juice
salt and pepper
chopped parsley
about 25 g/1 oz fresh white breadcrumbs
butter
lemon rind to garnish

Set the oven at 200°C/400°F/gas 6. Cut the avocados in half lengthways and remove the stones.

Flake the fish and mix with the ricotta. Fill the hollows of the avocados with the fish mixture. Sprinkle the surface of the avocado and fish with lemon juice, and season the avocado only with a sprinkling of salt and pepper. Stir some parsley into the breadcrumbs, then spoon over the avocados. Dot with a very little butter.

Place the avocados in a baking dish. Bake for 15-20 minutes. Garnish with lemon. Serve at once with toast.

SERVES 4

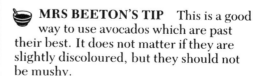 **MRS BEETON'S TIP** This is a good way to use avocados which are past their best. It does not matter if they are slightly discoloured, but they should not be mushy.

EGGS IN COCOTTES

25 g/1 oz butter
4 eggs
salt and pepper
60 ml/4 tbsp milk or cream

Butter 4 ramekins or cocottes at least 3.5 cm/1¼ inches deep, and stand them in a baking tin containing enough warm water to come half-way up their sides. Set the oven at 180°C/350°F/gas 4.

Break an egg into each warm dish and add salt and pepper to taste. Top with any remaining butter, cut into flakes. Spoon 15 ml/1 tbsp milk or cream over each egg.

Bake for 6-10 minutes, depending on the thickness of the dishes. The whites of the eggs should be just set. Wipe the outsides of the dishes and serve at once.

SERVES 4

VARIATIONS

☐ Shake ground nutmeg or cayenne pepper over the eggs before cooking.
☐ Sprinkle the eggs with very finely grated cheese before cooking.
☐ Put sliced, fried mushrooms, chopped ham, cooked diced chicken or lightly sautéed, diced Italian sausage in the bottom of each dish before adding the eggs.
☐ Put 15-30 ml/1-2 tbsp spinach purée in the dishes before adding the eggs.

MOULDED EGGS

50 g/2 oz butter
30 ml/2 tbsp finely chopped parsley
4 eggs
4 slices of white bread

Butter 4 dariole moulds generously, reserving the remaining butter. Set the oven at 180°C/350°F/gas 4.

Coat the insides of the moulds lightly with the parsley. Break an egg into each, then put them in a baking tin. Pour on enough warm water to come half-way up the sides of the moulds. Bake for 10-12 minutes, until the whites are just firm.

Meanwhile, cut a circle 7.5 cm/3 inches in diameter from each slice of bread and fry in the remaining butter, until golden brown on each side. Loosen the cooked eggs in the moulds, turn out on to the fried bread, and serve immediately.

SERVES 4

VARIATIONS

☐ About 15 ml/1 tbsp finely chopped chives can be used instead of the parsley.
☐ Use 25 g/1 oz mushrooms, finely chopped, cooked in butter and drained instead of the parsley.
☐ Use 25 g/1 oz minced ham mixed with 10 ml/2 tsp chopped parsley instead of the parsley alone.
☐ The bread can be toasted and buttered instead of fried.
☐ The eggs can be turned out on to rounds of pastry or into shallow pastry cases.
☐ Large flat mushrooms, lightly cooked in butter, can be used instead of the bread.
☐ Tomatoes, peeled, cut in half and seeded, can be used instead of the bread.

Hot Stuffed Avocados (page 31) and Stuffed Mushrooms (page 41)

Gratin Dauphinoise (page 43) and Stuffed Cabbage Leaves (pages 42)

Pasticcio di Lasagne Verdi (page 46) and Cannelloni with Mushroom Stuffing (page 47)

Polenta with Smoked Sausage (page 48) and Corn Pudding (page 49)

Leek Tart (page 58) and Quiche Lorraine (page 59)

Cornish Pasties (page 62)

Orange Boats and Parisien Tartlets (both on page 66)

Mince Pies (page 65)

CHICKEN AND HAM SCALLOPS

25 g/1 oz butter
250 g/9 oz cooked chicken
100 g/4 oz cooked ham
salt and pepper
good pinch of grated nutmeg
60 ml/4 tbsp fine dried white breadcrumbs

SAUCE
25 g/1 oz butter
25 g/1 oz plain flour
300 ml/½ pint milk, chicken stock or a
    mixture

Butter 6 deep scallop shells, reserving the remaining butter. Set the oven at 190-200°C/375-400°F/gas 5-6.

To make the sauce, melt the butter in a saucepan. Stir in the flour and cook over a low heat for 2-3 minutes, without colouring. Over a very low heat, gradually add the liquid, stirring constantly. Bring to the boil, stirring, and simmer for 1-2 minutes until smooth and thickened. Add salt and pepper to taste. Leave to cool.

Remove any skin and bone from the chicken. Chop the meat coarsely and place in a bowl. Chop the ham finely and add it to the chicken. Moisten the mixture well with some of the sauce. Add salt and pepper to taste and a good pinch of grated nutmeg.

Fill the prepared scallop shells with the mixture, sprinkle evenly with breadcrumbs and flake the rest of the butter on top. Bake for about 20 minutes, until golden brown.

SERVES 4 TO 6

VARIATIONS

CHICKEN AND CHEESE SCALLOPS
Omit the ham, substitute 5 ml/1 tsp lemon juice for the grated nutmeg and add 5 ml/1 tsp chopped parsley to the mixture. Mix 20 ml/4 tsp grated cheese with the breadcrumbs. Bake as above or place under moderate grill for 4-6 minutes to brown.

BROWNED CHICKEN SCALLOPS Heat the chicken and ham mixture gently in a saucepan before putting it into scallop shells. Cover with breadcrumbs and butter as before, then put under moderate grill for 4-6 minutes to brown the top.

STUFFED MUSHROOMS

Illustrated on page 33

fat for greasing
12 large flat mushrooms
1 onion, finely chopped
25 g/1 oz butter or margarine
50 g/2 oz cooked ham, finely chopped
15 ml/1 tbsp fresh white breadcrumbs
10 ml/2 tsp grated Parmesan cheese
10 ml/2 tsp chopped parsley
white wine
salt and pepper

Generously grease an ovenproof dish. Set the oven at 190°C/375°F/gas 5.

Clean the mushrooms and remove the stalks. Place the caps in the prepared dish, gills uppermost. Chop the stalks finely. Melt the butter or margarine in a pan and gently fry the mushroom stalks and onion for 5 minutes. Add the ham to the onion mixture together with the breadcrumbs, cheese and parsley. Add just enough white wine to bind the mixture together. Add salt and pepper to taste. Divide the stuffing mixture between the mushroom caps.

Cover and bake for 25 minutes.

SERVES 6

STUFFED CABBAGE LEAVES

Illustrated on page 34

fat for greasing
8 large cabbage leaves

STUFFING
  1 onion, finely chopped
  15 ml/1 tbsp oil
  400 g/14 oz minced beef
  1(400 g/14 oz) can tomatoes
  10 ml/2 tsp cornflour
  15 ml/1 tbsp Worcestershire sauce
  2.5 ml/½ tsp dried mixed herbs
  15 ml/1 tbsp chopped parsley
  salt and pepper

SAUCE
  juice from the canned tomatoes
  15 ml/1 tbsp tomato purée
  20 ml/4 tsp cornflour

Remove the thick centre stems from the cabbage leaves then blanch them in boiling water for 2 minutes. Drain well.

To make the stuffing, heat the oil in a pan and gently fry the onion for 5 minutes. Add the mince and cook, stirring until the beef has browned. Drain the tomatoes and reserve the juice. Add the tomatoes to the meat mixture. Blend the cornflour with the Worcestershire sauce and stir into the meat mixture with the herbs and salt and pepper. Cover and cook for 20 minutes, stirring occasionally.

Grease a shallow ovenproof dish. Set the oven at 190°C/375°F/gas 5.

Divide the stuffing between the cabbage leaves and roll up, folding over the edges of the leaves to enclose the meat completely.

Place in the prepared dish and cover with foil. Bake in the oven for 20 minutes.

Meanwhile to make the sauce, blend the reserved juice from the tomatoes with the tomato purée and make up to 250 ml/8 fl oz with water. Blend the cornflour with 15 ml/1 tbsp of the sauce. Pour the rest of the sauce into a pan and bring to the boil. Pour in the blended cornflour and bring to the boil, stirring all the time, until the sauce has thickened. Add salt and pepper to taste. Pour the sauce over the cabbage leaves just before serving.

SERVES 4

BAKED STUFFED PEPPERS

  butter or margarine for greasing
  4 green peppers
  1 small onion, finely chopped
  400 g/14 oz lean minced beef
  100 g/4 oz cooked rice
  salt and pepper
  good pinch of dried marjoram
  250 ml/8 fl oz tomato juice
  strips of pepper, to garnish

Grease an ovenproof dish. Set the oven at 180°C/350°F/gas 4. Cut a slice off the top of the peppers, then remove the membranes and seeds. Blanch in a saucepan of boiling water for 2 minutes.

Mix the onion, beef, rice, salt, pepper and marjoram together in a bowl. Stand the peppers upright in the prepared dish; if they do not stand upright easily, cut a thin slice off the base. Divide the stuffing mixture between the peppers. Pour the tomato juice around the base of the peppers.

Cover and bake for 1 hour. Garnish with strips of pepper.

SERVES 4

BAKED STUFFED MARROW

For a different presentation, the marrow can be peeled, cut into rings, seeded, then stuffed.

fat for greasing
1 marrow
1 small onion, finely chopped or grated
200 g/7 oz minced beef
100 g/4 oz pork sausagemeat or 100 g/4 oz extra minced beef
25 g/1 oz fresh white breadcrumbs
15 ml/1 tbsp chopped parsley
15 ml/1 tbsp chopped chives
5 ml/1 tsp Worcestershire sauce
salt and pepper
1 egg, beaten

SAUCE
25 g/1 oz butter
25 g/1 oz plain flour
300 ml/½ pint milk, stock or a mixture (see method)
75-100 g/3-4 oz Cheddar cheese, grated
pinch of dry mustard

Generously grease a large, shallow casserole. Set the oven at 180°C/350°F/gas 4. Halve the marrow lengthways and scoop out the seeds. Lay each half, side by side, in the prepared casserole.

Put the onion into a bowl with the beef, sausagemeat, if used, breadcrumbs, parsley, chives, Worcestershire sauce and salt and pepper. Mix well. Bind the mixture with the beaten egg.

Divide the stuffing between each marrow half. Cover the dish and bake for 1 hour.

Strain off most of the liquid in the casserole. Meanwhile to make the sauce, melt the butter in a saucepan. Stir in the flour and cook over a low heat for 2-3 minutes, without colouring. Over a very low heat, gradually add the liquid (the casserole juices may be used), stirring constantly. Bring to the boil, stirring, and simmer for 1-2 minutes until smooth and thickened. Add the cheese, mustard and salt and pepper to taste.

Pour the cheese sauce over the marrow and bake, uncovered, for a further 20 minutes, until the sauce is golden brown.

SERVES 4 TO 6

GRATIN DAUPHINOIS

Illustrated on page 34

25 g/1 oz butter
1 kg/2¼ lb potatoes, thinly sliced
1 large onion, about 200 g/7 oz, thinly sliced
200 g/7 oz Gruyère cheese, grated
salt and pepper
grated nutmeg
125 ml/4 fl oz single cream

Butter a 1.5 litre/2¾ pint casserole, reserving the remaining butter. Set the oven at 190°C/375°F/gas 5. Bring a saucepan of water to the boil, put in the potatoes and onion, then blanch for 30 seconds. Drain.
Put a layer of potatoes in the bottom of the prepared casserole. Dot with a little of the butter, then sprinkle with some of the onion and cheese, a little salt, pepper and grated nutmeg. Pour over some of the cream. Repeat the layers until all the ingredients have been used, finishing with a layer of cheese. Pour the remaining cream on top.

Cover and bake for 1 hour. Remove from the oven and place under a hot grill for 5 minutes, until the top of the cheese is golden brown and bubbling.

SERVES 6

DUCHESSE POTATOES

These attractive potatoes make a popular garnish to dinner party fish and meat dishes.

butter or margarine for greasing
450 g/1 lb old potatoes
25 g/1 oz butter or margarine
1 egg or 2 egg yolks
salt and pepper
grated nutmeg (optional)
beaten egg for brushing

Butter a baking sheet. Cut the potatoes into pieces and cook in a saucepan of salted water for 15-20 minutes. Drain thoroughly, then sieve.

Set the oven at 200°C/400°F/gas 6. Beat in the butter or margarine and egg or egg yolks. Add salt and pepper to taste and the nutmeg, if used. Spoon the mixture into a piping bag fitted with a large rose nozzle. Pipe rounds of potato on to the prepared baking sheet. Brush with a little beaten egg. Bake for about 15 minutes, until the potatoes are golden brown.

SERVES 6

> **🥣 MRS BEETON'S TIP** The potatoes can be piped on to the baking sheet, then baked when required. If a piping bag is not available, shape the potato into diamonds, rounds or triangles. Criss-cross the tops with a knife, brush with egg, and bake as above.

ANNA POTATOES

These sliced potato layers, baked until golden, make an unusual dinner party vegetable.

fat for greasing
1 kg/2¼ lb even-sized potatoes
salt and pepper
melted clarified butter (see Mrs Beeton's tip)

Well grease a 20 cm/8 inch round cake tin and line the base with greased greaseproof paper. Set the oven at 190°C/375°F/gas 5.

Trim the potatoes so that they will give equal-sized slices. Slice them very thinly using either a sharp knife or a mandoline. Arrange a layer of potatoes, slightly overlapping, in the base of the tin. Add salt and pepper to taste, then spoon a little clarified butter over them. Make a second layer of potatoes and spoon some more butter over them. Complete these layers until all the potatoes have been used. Cover the tin with greased greaseproof paper and foil.

Bake for 1 hour. Check the potatoes several times during cooking and add a little more clarified butter if they become too dry. Invert the tin on to a warm serving dish to remove the potatoes, and serve as soon as possible.

SERVES 6

🍴 **MRS BEETON'S TIP** To clarify butter, put the butter in a saucepan and heat gently until it melts. Continue to heat slowly without browning, until all bubbling ceases (this shows that the water content has evaporated). Remove from the heat and skim off any scum that has risen to the top. Let it stand for a few minutes for any sediment to settle, then gently pour off the clear butter into a bowl or jar, leaving the sediment behind. If there is a lot of sediment, it may be necessary to strain the fat through a fine sieve or scalded muslin.

MOUSSAKA

Moussaka can be made a day ahead, then reheated, covered, in the oven.

fat for greasing
1 aubergine
salt and pepper
1 large onion, chopped
1 garlic clove, grated
30 ml/2 tbsp olive oil
500 g/18 oz minced lamb or beef
10 ml/2 tsp chopped parsley
2 tomatoes peeled, seeded and chopped
150 ml/¼ pint dry white wine
300 ml/½ pint milk
1 egg
2 egg yolks
pinch of grated nutmeg
75 g/3 oz Kefalotiri or Parmesan cheese, grated

Grease a 20 × 10 × 10 cm (8 × 4 × 4 inch) oven-to-table baking dish. Set the oven at 180°C/350°F/gas 4. Cut the aubergine into 1 cm/½ inch slices, sprinkle them with salt and put to one side on a large platter.

Heat the olive oil, and gently fry the onion and garlic for about 10 minutes until the onion is soft. Add the mince and continue cooking, stirring with a fork to break up any lumps in the meat. When the meat is thoroughly browned, add salt, pepper, parsley and tomatoes. Mix well, then add the white wine. Simmer the mixture for a few minutes to blend the flavours, then remove from the heat.

In a bowl, beat the milk, egg, egg yolks, salt and a good pinch of grated nutmeg together. Add about half the cheese to the egg mixture, then beat again briefly.

Rinse and drain the aubergine slices and pat dry with absorbent kitchen paper. Place half in the bottom of the prepared dish and cover with the meat mixture. Lay the remaining aubergine slices on the meat and pour the milk and egg mixture over them. Sprinkle the remaining cheese on top.

Bake for 30-40 minutes, until the custard is set and the top is light golden brown. Serve from the dish.

SERVES 4

🍴 **MRS BEETON'S TIP** To peel tomatoes, hold each tomato on a fork over a gas flame or under a grill until the skin blackens and splits, then skin. Alternatively, place the tomatoes in a heatproof bowl. Cover with boiling water and leave for 1 minute. Drain and skin.

PASTICCIO DI LASAGNE VERDE

Illustrated on page 35

Green lasagne or lasagne verdi is pasta into which spinach has been worked at the dough-making stage. A crisp salad is the ideal accompaniment for this dish.

fat for greasing
250 g/9 oz green lasagne
salt and pepper
50 g/2 oz lard or 60 ml/4 tbsp oil
50 g/2 oz onion, chopped
1 garlic clove, chopped
50 g/2 oz celery, chopped
50 g/2 oz carrot, chopped
50 g/2 oz lean minced lamb
500 g/18 oz lean minced beef
300 ml/½ pint beef stock
50 g/2 oz tomato purée
75 g/3 oz walnut pieces, finely chopped
50 g/2 oz sultanas
250 g/9 oz tomatoes, peeled, seeded and chopped
50 g/2 oz red pepper, seeded and chopped
150 ml/¼ pint cold sauce
(see Stuffed Baked Cannelloni, right)

Grease a shallow ovenproof dish. Cook the lasagne in a saucepan of boiling salted water for 15 minutes. Drain, rinse under hot water, then place on a slightly dampened, clean tea-towel, side by side but not touching. Leave to dry.

Heat the lard or oil in a frying pan and cook the onion, garlic, celery and carrot for 5 minutes. Add the mince and brown it lightly all over. Add the stock, tomato purée and salt and pepper to taste. Bring "o the boil, reduce the heat and simmer for 30 minutes. Set the oven at 180°C/350°F/gas 4.

Line the bottom of the dish with half the pasta and cover with the meat mixture, then sprinkle with the nuts, sultanas, tomatoes and red pepper. Cover with the remaining pasta. Coat with the cold sauce and bake for 20 minutes.

SERVES 4

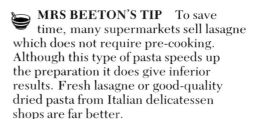

MRS BEETON'S TIP To save time, many supermarkets sell lasagne which does not require pre-cooking. Although this type of pasta speeds up the preparation it does give inferior results. Fresh lasagne or good-quality dried pasta from Italian delicatessen shops are far better.

STUFFED BAKED CANNELLONI

butter for greasing
16-20 cannelloni
15 ml/1 tbsp olive oil
300 g/11 oz frozen chopped spinach
salt and pepper
1.25 ml/¼ tsp grated nutmeg
150 g/5 oz ricotta or cottage cheese
50 g/2 oz cooked ham, finely chopped
25 g/1 oz dried white breadcrumbs
25 g/1 oz Parmesan cheese, grated

SAUCE
50 g/2 oz butter
50 g/2 oz plain flour
600 ml/1 pint milk
75 g/3 oz any strong hard cheese

Butter an ovenproof dish. To make the sauce, melt the butter in a saucepan. Stir in the flour and cook over a low heat for 2-3 minutes, without colouring. Over a very low heat, gradually add the milk, stirring constantly. Bring to the boil, stirring, and simmer for 1-2 minutes until smooth and thickened. Add the cheese and salt and pepper to taste.

Cook the cannelloni in a saucepan of boiling salted water with the oil for 10-15 minutes until al dente. Drain well.

Place the spinach in a pan and cook for a few minutes. Drain thoroughly. Mix together the spinach, salt, pepper, nutmeg, soft cheese and ham. Spoon the mixture into the cannelloni. Place in the prepared ovenproof dish. Pour the sauce over the cannelloni.

Bake for 15-20 minutes. Mix together the crumbs and Parmesan, then sprinkle over the dish. Place under a hot grill for 2-3 minutes to brown the top.

SERVES 4

> 🥄 **MRS BEETON'S TIP**   The oil added to the pasta cooking water helps to prevent the tubes sticking together and it assists in preventing the water from frothing up during cooking.

◆

CANNELLONI WITH MUSHROOM STUFFING

Illustrated on page 35

butter for greasing
16-20 cannelloni
15 ml/1 tbsp olive oil
750 ml/1¼ pints sauce made without
    cheese (see Stuffed Baked Cannelloni,
    left)
50 g/2 oz butter
200 g/7 oz button mushrooms, thinly sliced
50 g/2 oz Parmesan cheese, grated
50 g/2 oz Gruyère cheese, grated
50 g/2 oz Parma ham, finely shredded
15 ml/1 tbsp fine dried breadcrumbs
15 ml/1 tbsp single cream or top of the
    milk

Butter a shallow ovenproof dish. Cook the cannelloni in a saucepan of boiling salted water with the oil for 10-15 minutes until al dente. Drain well. Simmer 500 ml/18 fl oz of the Béchamel sauce until well reduced and very thick. Put to one side.

Melt 25 g/1 oz of the butter in a pan and gently cook the mushrooms for 2 minutes. Add to the sauce with 25 g/1 oz of the Parmesan. Leave to cool for 10 minutes.

Spoon the cooled mixture into the cannelloni. Place in the prepared ovenproof dish. Sprinkle the Gruyère and ham over the cannelloni, then sprinkle with the breadcrumbs. Add the cream or top of the milk to the remaining sauce and pour over the pasta. Top with the remaining Parmesan and butter.

Bake for 15-20 minutes, until lightly browned. Cover with greased foil if browning too much before the end of cooking.

SERVES 4

SEMOLINA GNOCCHI

Serve this Italian-style dish with a tomato sauce or spicy savoury sauce.

fat for greasing
500 ml/17 fl oz milk
100 g/4 oz semolina
salt and pepper
1.25 ml/¼ tsp grated nutmeg
1 egg
100 g/4 oz Parmesan cheese, grated
25 g/1 oz butter

Grease a shallow ovenproof dish. Bring the milk to the boil in a saucepan. Sprinkle in the semolina and stir over low heat until the mixture is thick. Mix in the salt, pepper, nutmeg, egg and 75 g/3 oz of the Parmesan. Beat the mixture well until smooth. Spread on a shallow dish and leave to cool.

Set the oven at 200°C/400°F/gas 6, if using. Cut the cooled semolina mixture into 2 cm/¾ inch squares or shape into rounds. Place in the prepared ovenproof dish and sprinkle with the remaining cheese; dot with butter. Brown under the grill or in the oven for 8-10 minutes.

SERVES 4

MRS BEETON'S TIP Canned chopped tomatoes make a quick sauce. Add them to a chopped onion cooked in butter or oil until soft. Simmer for 5 minutes, then season to taste and add plenty of chopped parsley. Herbs, such as bay and marjoram, and garlic may be added; with a little red wine and larger simmering the sauce is rich and excellent.

POLENTA WITH SMOKED SAUSAGE

Illustrated on page 36

The sausages used in this satisfying dish are dried continental ones. They have a high meat content and require a little cooking before eating.

400 g/14 oz polenta
salt and pepper
400 g/14 oz chorizo, cabanos or other
    small smoked sausages
200 g/7 oz tomato purée
50 g/2 oz Parmesan cheese, grated
25 g/1 oz dried white breadcrumbs
25 g/1 oz butter

Bring 500 ml/17 fl oz water to the boil in a large saucepan. Stir in the polenta and salt and pepper to taste. Cook for 10-15 minutes, stirring all the time. Leave to cool.

Cook the sausages in boiling water for 10 minutes. Remove from the pan and leave to cool. Remove the skins and cut into 2 cm/¾ inch slices.

Set the oven at 180°C/350°F/gas 4. Put a layer of polenta in the bottom of an ovenproof dish, cover with a layer of sausages, some tomato purée, Parmesan, salt and pepper. Repeat the layers until all the ingredients have been used. Sprinkle the breadcrumbs over the mixture. Dot with the butter. Bake for 25-30 minutes.

SERVES 3 TO 4

POLENTA WITH CHEESE

*Polenta is also known as maize flour and
cornmeal.*

5 ml/1 tsp salt
200 g/7 oz polenta
50 g/2 oz butter
50 g/2 oz Parmesan cheese, grated

Bring 500 ml/17 fl oz water to the boil in
a saucepan with the salt. Add the polenta
and stir well with a wooden spoon. Cook
for 20-30 minutes, stirring all the time.
When the mixture leaves the sides of the
saucepan cleanly, stir in the butter and
Parmesan quickly and thoroughly.

Put the mixture on a dish which has been
sprinkled with cold water. Cut into slices
to serve.

SERVES 3 TO 4

VARIATION

Cut cold polenta into pieces, 1 cm/½
inch thick. Place in a pie dish and cover
with a thick layer of grated cheese. Continue layering the polenta and cheese until
all the polenta has been used up. Top with
a thick layer of cheese and dot with butter.
Bake in the oven at 190°C/375°F/gas 5 for
20-25 minutes.

CHEESE PUDDING

butter for greasing
100-150 g/4-5 oz Cheddar or Gruyère
    cheese, grated
2 eggs, beaten
250 ml/8 fl oz whole or skimmed milk
100 g/4 oz fresh white breadcrumbs
salt (optional)

Butter a 600 ml/1 pint ovenproof dish.

Set the oven at 180°C/350°F/gas 4.

Combine the cheese, eggs and milk in a
bowl. Add the breadcrumbs with a little
salt, if needed. Mix thoroughly, then pour
into the prepared dish.

Bake for 25-30 minutes, until set in the
centre and browned on top. Serve hot.

SERVES 4

CORN PUDDING

Illustrated on page 36

fat for greasing
100 g/4 oz plain flour
5 ml/1 tsp salt
2.5 ml/½ tsp black pepper
2 eggs, beaten
500 ml/17 fl oz milk
400 g/14 oz fresh or frozen sweetcorn
    kernels

Grease a 1.5 litre/2¾ pint pie or ovenproof dish. Set the oven at 180°C/350°F/
gas 4.

Sift the flour, salt and pepper into a
bowl. Add the beaten eggs, stirring well.
Beat together with the milk and then the
corn to form a batter. Turn into the
prepared dish. Bake for 1 hour. Serve hot.

SERVES 6

PASTRIES

**Whether puffed and risen or layered and crisp, good pastry
is the trademark of a competent cook. The selection of
recipes in this section illustrates the versatility of pastry
cookery and provides a framework within which to perfect
skills and develop ideas.**

Good pastry should be light in texture. A few simple rules will help to ensure success with all types. Always weigh ingredients accurately as it is important that the correct proportions of fat, flour and liquid are used. Keep all ingredients, utensils and your hands as cool as possible.

RUBBING IN

The first stage in making several types of pastry is to rub the fat into the flour. This basic technique is used for other purposes in cookery so it is worth getting it right. Cut the fat into small pieces and mix it with the flour. Using just the tips of your fingers, lift a little of the mixture and rub the fat with the flour once or twice. Let the mixture fall back into the bowl before lifting another small portion and rubbing again. Continue in this way until the mixture has the texture of fine breadcrumbs.

It is important that you lift the mixture and rub it lightly to incorporate air into it. If you pick up too much mixture and push it back into the palms of your hands, air will not mix with it and the pastry will be heavy. Once you have mastered the technique you will find it quick and easy to perform; in fact, the quicker the process is completed, the lighter the pastry.

ADDING LIQUID TO SHORT PASTRIES

The term 'short' is used to describe pastry that is not made heavy by the addition of too much liquid. The 'melt-in-your-mouth' texture that is characteristic of good 'short' pastry is the result of using the right proportion of fat to flour and just enough liquid to hold the pastry together as it is rolled.

When making sweet pastry dishes, various types of short pastry may be used and the difference may be in the liquid added to bind the ingredients. Plain short crust pastry is bound with a little water. The water should be very cold (preferably iced) and just enough should be added to bind the rubbed in mixture into lumps. The lumps are gently pressed together so that the pastry just holds its shape. It should not be sticky.

Sweet short crust or a richer pastry for making flans may be bound with egg yolk instead of, or as well as, a little water. Egg yolk contains a high proportion of fat so the resulting pastry will be very short. Adding sugar to pastry also tends to give a short and crumbly texture. Some rich pastry is made very short by adding extra fat, usually butter, to give a good flavour as well as a short texture.

ADDING LIQUID TO PUFF PASTRY OR FLAKY PASTRY

The dough for this type of pastry has only a small proportion of the fat rubbed in, with the majority of the fat incorporated by rolling it with the pastry. A little extra liquid is added to make a dough that is just slightly sticky. This type of dough holds the fat which is added in lumps or a block during rolling. The resulting pastry is not short; it is crisp and it forms distinct layers. Puff pastry is lighter and has more layers than flaky pastry.

The layers in puff and flaky pastry trap air to make the pastry rise during cooking. A strengthening substance called *gluten* is naturally present in flour; this is developed by rolling the pastry. The process of rolling and folding actually serves to toughen the basic dough. Adding the fat each time the pastry is rolled means that the dough does not form into a solid mass but retains very fine layers. The air trapped between these layers expands as the dough is heated and so the pastry rises. Because the dough itself is toughened by the gluten, the layers set and give the finished pastry its characteristic crisp texture.

ROLLING OUT

Whatever type of pastry you are handling, you should always roll it out very lightly. Use a very light dusting of flour on the work surface. There should be just enough to prevent the pastry from sticking; short pastries usually require less than puff or flaky pastries. Too much flour at this stage may spoil the balance of ingredients.

Never turn pastry over during rolling. The pastry should be lifted occasionally and turned around to prevent it sticking to the surface. Push the rolling pin away from you in short, quick strokes. Keep the rolling pin lightly dusted with flour.

When rolling out pastry, try to establish the shape as soon as you begin. For example, if you are lining a round flan dish start with a ball of pastry which is flattened into a roughly circular shape. If you want to end up with an oblong sheet of pastry, form the pastry into an oblong lump and flatten it slightly before rolling it.

LIFTING ROLLED-OUT PASTRY

To lift a sheet of pastry, dust the rolling pin lightly with flour and place it in the middle of the pastry. Fold half the pastry over it, then use the rolling pin to lift the pastry into position.

LINING A FLAN TIN OR DISH

Roll the pastry out to a size that will cover the base and come up the sides of the dish with a little extra to spare. Lift the pastry on the rolling pin, then lower it loosely over the tin or dish.

Quickly work around the dish, lifting the edge of the pastry with one hand and pressing it down into the corner of the dish with the forefinger and knuckle of the other hand. When the pastry is pressed neatly all around the base of the dish, press the excess around the edge of the dish so that it falls backwards slightly.

Roll the rolling pin across the top of the dish to trim off excess pastry. If you are lining a tin its edge will cut off the pastry; if using a dish you will have to gently pull away the excess pastry edges.

BAKING BLIND

Pastry cases that are cooked and cooled before they are filled have a sheet of greaseproof paper and baking beans placed in them to prevent the base of the pastry from puffing up. This is known as baking blind (see illustration overleaf). The paper and baking beans are usually removed once the pastry has cooked enough to set, and the pastry case returned to the oven to allow it to brown slightly.

In some recipes, the pastry case is partially baked before it is filled, and the cooking is completed with the filling. The technique of baking blind would be used to partially bake the pastry.

Clear instructions are given in individual recipes. Ceramic baking beans may be purchased for baking blind, or ordinary dried peas or beans may be used. These are sprinkled over the greaseproof paper to weight the pastry slightly. Dried peas or beans used for this purpose may be cooled and stored in an airtight container and used over and over again. However, they may not be cooked to be eaten in another recipe.

MAKING TURNOVERS

Turnovers may be cut in circles or squares. The size to which the pastry should be rolled depends on the recipe.

Use a saucer or plate to mark out circles; small turnovers are made by using large round biscuit cutters. When using a saucer or plate, place it on the pastry and cut around it with a small pointed knife.

Put the filling on one half of the pastry. Dampen all around the pastry edge, then fold the pastry over the filling. Press the pastry edges together well to seal in the filling in a neat semi-circular turnover.

To make triangular turnovers, roll out the pastry into a large square. Use a large,

clean ruler and a small, pointed knife to trim off the pastry edges.

Cut the pastry into four squares of equal size. Place some filling on one half of each

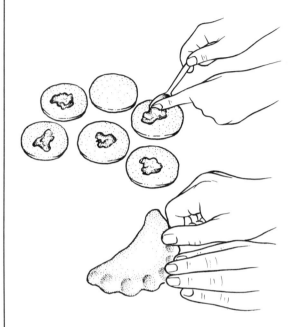

pastry square, in a corner, and dampen the edges.

Fold the corner of pastry opposite the filling over to enclose it completely and to make a neat triangle. Press the edges together to seal in the filling.

PASTRY PIES

Roll out the pastry about 5 cm/2 inches larger than the top of the dish. Cut off a strip from the edge of the pastry. Dampen the edge of the dish and press the strip of pastry on to it.

Fill the dish, dampen the pastry edge and lift the pastry lid over the top.

Press the edges of the pastry to seal in the filling. Holding the pie dish slightly raised in one hand, use a sharp knife to trim all around the edge of the dish. Keep the knife pointing outwards so that only the excess pastry is trimmed off.

KNOCKING UP

Knocking up is the term used for neatly sealing the pastry edges together. Press down and outwards on the pastry edge with the knuckle and forefinger of one hand, at the same time knocking the pastry edge inwards with the blunt edge of a round-bladed knife.

SCALLOPED EDGES

The traditional edge for a sweet pie is small scallops (large ones are used for savoury pies). Use the blunt edge of a knife to pull the pastry inwards as you push the edge out towards the rim of the dish with the finger of your other hand.

FORKED EDGE

A simple edging technique is to press all around the pastry with a fork. However, the edge does sometimes tend to become slightly too brown if the pastry is pressed very thin.

PLAITED EDGE

Re-roll leftover pastry and cut out three long, thin strips. Plait these together all around the edge of the pie.

DECORATIONS USING CUTTERS

Use small cocktail cutters to cut out pastry shapes. Dampen these and overlap them around the edge of the pie.

PASTRY LEAVES

Roll out a strip of pastry – the wider the strip, the longer the leaves – and cut it into diamond shapes. Mark veins on the leaves and pinch one end of each into a stalk.

IMAGINATIVE DESIGNS

Roll out pastry trimmings and cut out apples, pears, cherries or strawberry shapes to

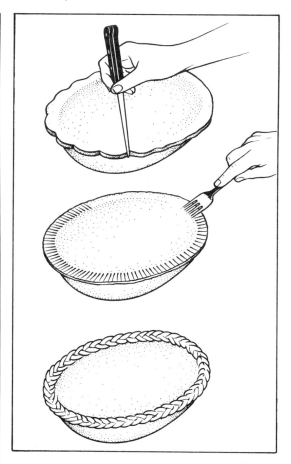

decorate the top of the pie. Dampen the pastry to keep the decorations in place. Alternatively, cut out letters to spell 'apple', 'pear' or whichever fruit is appropriate for the filling and press them on the pie.

SUET CRUST PASTRY

Suet crust pastry is quick and easy to make. Shredded suet is combined with self-raising flour and the ingredients mixed to a soft dough with cold water. The quantity of water should give a soft but not sticky dough which may be kneaded very lightly into a smooth shape. The pastry rises to give a light, slightly spongy texture. Suet pastry is cooked by steaming, boiling or baking.

CHOUX PASTRY

Although many people shy away from making choux pastry, it is not difficult. However, it is important that all the ingredients are accurately measured and that a few rules are observed:

The water and fat must be heated together gently until the fat melts, and the mixture brought to the boil as quickly as possible. Do not bring the water to the boil before the fat melts.

The flour must be tipped into the liquid all at once, the pan removed from the heat and the mixture stirred to make a smooth paste that comes away from the sides of the pan in a clean ball. Do not beat the mixture at this stage or it will become greasy. If the mixture is too wet put the pan back on the heat and stir gently until the paste comes away from the sides of the pan. This paste must be cooled slightly before the eggs are added.

Lastly, eggs are beaten into the paste. At this stage the mixture should be thoroughly beaten until it is smooth and glossy. The paste should be soft enough to pipe but it should not be runny. Use at once.

PHYLLO PASTRY

This Greek pastry contains little fat. It is made with a strong flour. It is available both chilled and frozen, ready rolled in very thin sheets.

Two or three sheets are layered together before they are wrapped around a filling. Each sheet is brushed with melted butter. The pastry is very delicate to handle as it rapidly becomes brittle once unpacked. Always keep the pastry covered with cling film or under dampened tea-towels when you are not working with it as it dries rapidly if exposed to the air. Make sure the work surface is perfectly dry before unrolling the pastry. Any dampness will cause the pastry to stick, soften and break up.

PASTRY TECHNIQUES

■ Work in a cool place; keep hands, utensils and all ingredients cool.

■ Weigh and measure all ingredients accurately.

■ Handle pastry as lightly as possible, and work as quickly as you can, at all stages.

■ Use the minimum amount of flour for rolling out.

■ Chill short crust, flaky and puff pastry for 20-30 minutes before rolling it out.

■ Chill finished short crust, puff or flaky pastry goods for 15 minutes before baking.

SOME COMMON FAULTS WITH PASTRY AND HOW TO AVOID THEM

Short Crust Pastry   (or similar pastries)

Hard, tough pastry

■ Too little fat used

■ Too much liquid added

■ Pastry handled too much or too heavily

■ Too much flour used for rolling out

Grainy, flaky or blistered pastry

■ Fat not rubbed in sufficiently

■ Water not mixed in well

■ Pastry rolled out twice

■ Too much flour used for rolling

Pastry too short, very crumbly (collapses)

■ Too much fat used

■ Fat overworked into flour

■ Too little liquid used

HOT WATER CRUST PASTRY

By comparison to the other pastries, hot water crust is a heavy dough. Plain flour is bound to a dough with a mixture of water and lard, heated together until boiling.

Hot water crust pastry should be mixed, then lightly kneaded until smooth. If it is overworked it becomes greasy. Once mixed, the pastry should be kept warm in a bowl placed over hot (not simmering) water. To prevent the surface from drying, the dough should be closely covered with a polythene bag.

Hot water crust pastry is usually used for moulding pies both large and small. When hot it is malleable and the surface of the dough is easily smoothed. Also, while hot the edges of the dough seal together easily and they may be pinched into a neat border.

As the pastry cools it becomes more difficult to manage and tends to crack on the surface. When moulding pie cases around the outside of a container, the pastry has to be cooled before it may be filled and covered; during this time the pastry for the lid should be kept just warm over hot water. The method which gives a better finish is to line a mould with pastry, then fill and cover it at once.

If the sides of a mould are removed so that the pastry may brown, it is important to work quickly once the mould is not supporting the pie, otherwise the soft pastry may collapse. Before removing the sides of the mould, have beaten egg ready to brush the pastry. Brush the pastry quickly and put the pie back into the oven. The egg helps to strengthen and seal the pastry quickly.

If the sides of a moulded pie begin to bulge, quickly wrap a double-thick band of foil around the pie, placing it halfway up the depth. Put the pie back in the oven until the pastry sets.

PUFF PASTRY

225 g/8 oz plain flour
1.25 ml/¼ tsp salt
225 g/8 oz butter, chilled
5 ml/1 tsp lemon juice
flour for rolling out

Sift the flour and salt into a bowl. Rub in 50 g/2 oz of the butter. Add the lemon juice and enough cold water to mix the ingredients to a smooth, fairly soft dough. The mixture should take about 100 ml/4 fl oz water but this must be added by the spoonful to avoid making the dough too wet. Wrap the dough in cling film and chill briefly.

Shape the remaining butter into a rectangle measuring about 10 × 7.5 cm/4 × 3 inches, then chill again. On a lightly floured surface, roll out the dough into an oblong measuring about 25 × 15 cm/10 × 6 inches, or slightly smaller. Place the butter in the middle of the dough, then fold the bottom third over it and fold the top third down to enclose the butter completely.

Press the edges of the dough together with the rolling pin. Give the dough a quarter turn in a clockwise direction. Roll out the dough into an oblong as before, fold it again, then wrap in cling film. Chill for 30 minutes. Roll and fold the pastry 6 times in all, chilling well each time. To remember the number of rollings, mark dents in the dough with your fingertips – 1 dent after the first rolling, 2 after the second and so on.

After the process of rolling and folding is complete, chill the pastry again before using it as required.

MAKES ABOUT 450 G/1 LB

FLAKY PASTRY

Flaky pastry does not have as many layers as puff pastry. It contains less fat to flour and the dough is rolled and folded fewer times.

225 g/8 oz plain flour
1.25 ml/¼ tsp salt
175 g/6 oz butter or 75 g/3 oz each butter
   and lard, chilled
5 ml/1 tsp lemon juice
flour for rolling out

Sift the flour and salt into a bowl. If using butter and lard, mix them together roughly. Rub in a quarter of the fat, keeping the remaining fat chilled. Stir in the lemon juice and enough cold water to mix the ingredients to a soft dough. The mixture should take about 100 ml/4 fl oz water but this should be added by the spoonful to avoid making the dough too wet.

On a lightly floured surface, roll out the dough into an oblong measuring about 25 × 15 cm/10 × 6 inches. Mark the dough into thirds. Cut the fat into 3 equal portions. Dot one portion of fat over the top two-thirds of the dough, in neat lumps.

Fold the bottom third of the dough up over the middle portion, then fold the top third down so that the lumps of fat are enclosed completely. Press the edges of the dough together with the rolling pin. Give the dough a quarter turn in a clockwise direction, then roll out as before.

Repeat the process of dotting the dough with fat, folding and rolling it, twice more. Chill the dough briefly between each rolling. Finally, fold and roll the pastry once more, without any fat, then chill again before using it as required.

MAKES ABOUT 450 G/1 LB

ROUGH PUFF

A slightly easier version of puff, all the fat must be well chilled for success. For best results, chill the bowl of flour too; always make sure your hands are very cold by holding them under cold running water before handling the dough.

225 g/8 oz plain flour
1.25 ml/¼ tsp salt
175 g/6 oz butter, cut in chunks and
   chilled
5 ml/1 tsp lemon juice
flour for rolling out

Sift the flour and salt into a bowl. Add the butter and mix in lightly using a round-bladed knife. Mix in the lemon juice and enough ice-cold water to make a soft dough. The mixture should take about 100 ml/4 fl oz (or very slightly more) but add the water a spoonful at a time to avoid making the dough too wet. The dough should be soft and very lumpy.

On a lightly floured surface, roll out the dough into an oblong, keeping the corners square. Mark the oblong of dough into thirds, then fold and roll it as for flaky pastry. Repeat the process 4 times in all, chilling the dough between each rolling or as necessary.

The rolled dough should be smooth. Wrap it in cling film and chill well before rolling it out to use as required.

MAKES ABOUT 450 G/1 LB

PASTRY VARIATIONS

SHORT CRUST

The half fat to flour proportions may be varied and additional ingredients can be added to enrich and flavour the dough.

Wholemeal Pastry All wholemeal flour may be used but the result tends to be slightly gritty. Additional fat must be used with all wholemeal flour to avoid producing a very heavy dough. Best results are obtained by using either half or three-quarters wholemeal flour to white flour.

Rich Pastry Plain rich pastry may be made by increasing the proportion of fat to three-quarters the weight of flour. Butter may be used for a good flavour. The dough may be further enriched by binding the dry ingredients with egg yolk. Use for sweet pies, savoury and sweet flans, pasties or savoury pies served cold.

Sweet Pastry A small quantity of sugar may be added to the rubbed-in mixture (about one eighth of the weight of flour). This is usually used with rich pastry (above). Ideal for sweet flan cases or mince pies.

Cheese Pastry Finely grated matured cheese may be added to pastry, in the proportions of a quarter cheese to flour. This may be increased slightly but if too much cheese is added the result will be heavy and greasy. The flavour of the cheese may be made more pronounced by adding mustard (either powder or mixed). Cheese pastry is ideal for vegetable pasties and pies or cheese straws.

Herbs Chopped fresh or dried herbs may be added to all savoury pastry.

Other Flavourings Chopped plain or roasted nuts and grated citrus rind may be added to savoury or sweet pastries.

Ground almonds combine well with grated orange rind in a sweet, rich pastry.

PUFF, ROUGH PUFF AND FLAKY

These pastries are not usually varied.

Uses They are ideal for sweet and savoury cooking, for small and large items. Being rich, they are ideal for making special items and for desserts. The puffed pastries may be substituted for short crust as a covering for pies, for making turnovers and other pastry cases. However, the puffed pastries do not make good bases (for example in flans and tarts) as the filling placed on top tends to inhibit the rising and the result can be a heavy, rather fatty layer of pastry underneath. The exceptions are small tartlets with light fillings.

Puff pastry is used for making vols-au-vent; all three may be used for pastry horns and other shallow puffed items.

CHOUX

Choux pastry is another versatile basic.

Cheese Choux Grated mature cheese may be added in the proportions of 50 g/2 oz to each 2-egg batch. Too much cheese will make the paste greasy and heavy. Useful for small buns or gougère.

Herbs Chopped parsley, snipped chives and other fresh herbs may be added.

Cooked Meat and Other Flavourings Chopped cooked ham or bacon, diced cooked chicken, chopped spring onion, chopped capers, diced stoned olives and flaked almonds are all good candidates for flavouring choux pastry. The almonds may be used with sweet or savoury recipes.

HOT WATER CRUST

This is a savoury pastry which is used mainly for raised pies. It is also used for small pies, such as pork pies and Scottish pies filled with lamb.

PRAWN QUICHE

150 g/5 oz Cheddar cheese, grated
200 g/7 oz peeled cooked prawns
juice of ½ lemon

SHORT CRUST PASTRY
100 g/4 oz plain flour
2.5 ml/½ tsp salt
50 g/2 oz margarine (or half butter, half lard)
flour for rolling out

BECHAMEL SAUCE
½ small onion, thickly sliced
½ small carrot, sliced
½ small celery stick, sliced
300 ml/½ pint milk
1 bay leaf
few parsley stalks
1 thyme sprig
1 clove
3 white peppercorns
1 blade of mace
25 g/1 oz butter
25 g/1 oz plain flour
30 ml/2 tbsp single cream (optional)

Set the oven at 200°C/400°F/gas 6. To make the pastry, sift the flour and salt into a bowl, then rub in the margarine until the mixture resembles fine breadcrumbs. Add enough cold water to make a stiff dough. Press the dough together.

Roll out the pastry on a lightly floured surface and use to line an 18 cm/7 inch flan tin or ring placed on a baking sheet. Line the pastry with greaseproof paper and fill with baking beans. Bake 'blind' for 20 minutes, then remove the paper and beans. Return to the oven for 5-7 minutes, then remove.

Meanwhile to make the sauce, combine the onion, carrot, celery, milk, herbs, spices and salt to taste in a saucepan. Heat to simmering point, cover, turn off the heat and allow to stand for 30 minutes to infuse. Strain the milk.

Melt the butter in a saucepan. Stir in the flour and cook over low heat for 2-3 minutes, without colouring. Over a very low heat, gradually add the flavoured milk, stirring constantly. Bring to the boil, stirring, and simmer for 1-2 minutes until smooth and thickened. Add half the cheese and all the prawns to the sauce. Mix well and add the lemon juice.

Pour the mixture into the baked pastry case and sprinkle with the remaining cheese. Brown under the grill.

SERVES 4

LEEK TART

Illustrated on page 37

8 small leeks, trinmed and washed
2 eggs
salt and pepper
grated nutmeg
25 g/1 oz Gruyère cheese, grated

SHORT CRUST PASTRY
100 g/4 oz plain flour
1.25 ml/¼ tsp salt
50 g/2 oz margarine (or half butter, half lard)
flour for rolling out

SAUCE
15 g/½ oz butter
15 g/½ oz plain flour
150 ml/¼ pint milk or milk and leek cooking liquid

Set the oven at 200°C/400°F/gas 6. To make the pastry, sift the flour and salt into a bowl, then rub in the margarine until the mixture resembles fine bread-crumbs. Add enough cold water to make a stiff dough. Press the dough together.

Roll out the pastry on a lightly floured surface and use to line an 18 cm/7 inch flan tin or ring placed on a baking sheet. Line the pastry with greaseproof paper and fill with baking beans. Bake 'blind' for 20 minutes, then remove the paper and beans. Return to the oven for 5 minutes, then leave to cool. Reduce the oven temperature to 190°C/375°F/gas 5.

Using the white parts of the leeks only, tie them into 2 bundles with string. Bring a pan of salted water to the boil, add the leeks and simmer gently for 10 minutes. Drain, then squeeze as dry as possible. Slice the leeks thickly.

To make the sauce, melt the butter in a saucepan. Stir in the flour and cook over a low heat for 2-3 minutes, without colour-ing over a very low heat, gradually add the liquid, stirring constantly. Bring to the boil, stirring, and simmer for 1-2 minutes.

Beat together the eggs and white sauce, then add salt, pepper and nutmeg to taste. Stir in half of the Gruyère. Put a layer of sauce in the cooled pastry case, cover with the leeks, then with the remaining sauce. Sprinkle with the rest of the Gruyère. Bake for 20 minutes or until golden on top.

SERVES 8

> ☆ **FREEZER TIP** The cooled, filled tart freezes well for up to 3 months. Thaw the tart in the refrigerator for several hours. Alternatively, it may be cooked slowly from frozen until thoroughly reheated, covering with foil.

QUICHE LORRAINE

Illustrated on page 37

6 rindless streaky bacon rashers
3 eggs
300 ml/½ pint single cream
2.5 ml/½ tsp salt
grinding of black pepper
pinch of grated nutmeg
25 g/1 oz butter

SHORT CRUST PASTRY
100 g/4 oz plain flour
2.5 ml/½ tsp salt
50 g/2 oz margarine (or half butter, half lard)
flour for rolling out

Set the oven at 200°C/400°F/gas 6. To make the pastry, sift the flour and salt into a bowl, then rub in the margarine until the mixture resembles fine bread-crumbs. Add enough cold water to make a stiff dough. Press the dough together.

Roll out the pastry on a lightly floured surface and use to line an 18 cm/7 inch flan tin or ring placed on a baking sheet. Line the pastry with greaseproof paper and fill with baking beans. Bake 'blind' for 20 minutes until the rim of the pastry is slightly browned but the base still soft. Remove the paper and beans. Reduce the oven temperature to 190°C/375°F/gas 5.

Cut the bacon in strips 2 cm × 5 mm/ ¾ × ¼ inch. Dry fry for 2 minutes. Drain and scatter the strips over the pastry base. Press in lightly. Beat the eggs, cream, salt, pepper and nutmeg. Pour the mixture into the pastry case and dot with butter. Bake for 30 minutes. Serve at once.

SERVES 4 TO 6

VEGETABLE FLAN

50 g/2 oz young carrots, sliced
about 100 g/4 oz frozen or canned
   sweetcorn kernels, drained
50 g/2 oz shelled peas

SAUCE
   25 g/1 oz butter
   25 g/1 oz plain flour
   250 ml/8 fl oz milk
   100 g/4 oz Cheddar cheese, grated
   salt and pepper

WHOLEMEAL SHORT CRUST PASTRY
   75 g/3 oz plain flour
   75 g/3 oz wholemeal flour
   2.5 ml/½ tsp salt
   75 g/3 oz margarine (or half butter, half
      lard)
   flour for rolling out

Set the oven at 200°C/400°F/gas 6. Mix the flours and salt in a bowl, then rub in the margarine. Add enough cold water to make a stiff dough.

Roll out the pastry on a lightly floured surface and use to line a 23 cm/9 inch flan tin. Line the pastry with greaseproof paper and fill with baking beans. Bake for about 20 minutes. Remove the paper and beans; cook for 5-7 minutes. Set aside.

Cook the carrots and peas separately. Drain and add salt and pepper. Set aside. To make the sauce, melt the butter in a saucepan. Stir in the flour and cook over a low heat for 2-3 minutes without colouring. Over a very low heat, gradually add the milk, stirring constantly. Bring to the boil, stirring, and simmer for 1-2 minutes until smooth and thickened. Remove from the heat. Stir in the cheese, and add salt and pepper to taste.

Spread the cheese sauce in the pastry case and top with the vegetables.

SERVES 6

DURHAM RABBIT PIE

200 g/7 oz cooked rabbit
50 g/2 oz boiled bacon, without rinds
4 eggs
salt and pepper
beaten egg or milk for glazing

SHORT CRUST PASTRY
   225 g/8 oz plain flour
   2.5 ml/½ tsp salt
   100 g/4 oz margarine (or half butter, half
      lard)
   flour for rolling out

Set the oven at 200°C/400°F/gas 6. To make the pastry, sift the flour and salt into a bowl, then rub in the margarine until the mixture resembles fine breadcrumbs. Add enough cold water to make a stiff dough. Press the dough together with your fingertips.

Roll out the pastry on a lightly floured surface and use half of it to line a 20 cm/8 inch pie plate. Use the remainder for the lid.

Chop the rabbit meat and bacon finely and mix together. Place the mixture on the pastry in the form of a cross, leaving the outside 1 cm/½ inch of pastry uncovered. Break an egg carefully into each uncovered pastry triangle, taking care not to break the yolks. Add salt and pepper to taste. Dampen the edges of the pastry and cover with the remaining pastry. Brush with egg or milk. Bake for 30-40 minutes. Serve hot as a supper dish.

SERVES 4

WILTSHIRE PIE

This unusual pie is served cold, turned upside down. A delicious potato pastry is used; for convenience freshly made-up instant potato can be used to make this pastry. Serve with salad.

dripping for greasing
4-6 slices of cooked breast of veal or
    chicken
4-6 slices of cooked lean lamb
4-6 slices of boiled bacon or pickled pork
salt
cayenne pepper
4 hard-boiled eggs
good pinch of ground mace
cooled and jellied stock (preferably made
    from veal bones)

POTATO PASTRY
    100 g/4 oz freshly cooked potatoes
    100 g/4 oz plain flour
    15 g/½ oz lard or dripping
    15 g/½ oz butter
    2.5 ml/½ tsp baking powder
    5 ml/1 tsp beaten egg
    15 ml/1 tbsp warm milk
    flour for rolling out

Grease a 1 litre/1¾ pint pie dish. Set the oven at 190°C/375°F/gas 5. To make the pastry, first mash the potatoes or rub them through a fine metal sieve. Leave until cold. Sift the flour into a bowl and rub in the fats. Add the cold potatoes, salt and baking powder. Add the beaten egg and enough milk to mix to a smooth dough; the amount of milk needed depends on the type of potato used.

Trim the meat slices, removing any skin and solid fat. Sprinkle with salt and cayenne. Lay half the slices in the prepared pie dish. Slice the eggs and arrange them on top of the meat. Sprinkle with salt, pepper and mace. Cover with the remaining meat slices, filling the dish. Melt the stock and pour in enough almost to fill the pie dish.

Roll out the pastry on a lightly floured surface and use it to cover the dish. Do not decorate. Make a small hole in the centre of the crust, then from the pastry trimmings make a button (or small round) of pastry of fit over it.

Bake for 45-60 minutes until the pastry is crisp and cooked through. Bake the button of pastry at the same time removing it when it is browned.

When the pie is cooked, pour in enough extra stock through the hole in the crust to fill the pie completely. Leave until cold and firm.

Insert the pastry button in the hole. With a sharp knife, loosen the side of the pie from the dish. Turn the pie carefully on to a serving plate so that the pastry is underneath. Serve cold.

SERVES 6

VARIATION

Any available cold cooked meat can be used.

CORNISH PASTIES

Illustrated on page 38

FILLING
1 large or 2 small potatoes
1 small turnip
1 onion
salt and pepper
300 g/11 oz lean chuck steak

PASTRY
500 g/18 oz plain flour
5 ml/1 tsp salt
150 g/5 oz lard
60 ml/4 tbsp shredded suet
flour for rolling out
beaten egg for glazing

Set the oven at 230°C/450°F/gas 8. To make the pastry, sift the flour and salt into a bowl. Rub in the lard, then mix in the suet. Moisten with enough cold water to make a stiff dough. Roll out on a lightly floured surface and cut into eight 16 cm/6½ inch rounds.

To make the filling, slice all the vegetables thinly, mix together and add salt and pepper to taste. Divide between the pastry rounds, placing a line of mixture across the centre of each round. Place equal amounts of meat on the vegetables.

Dampen the pastry edges of each round. Lift them to meet over the filling. Pinch together to seal, then flute the edges. Make small slits in both sides of each pasty near the top. Place the pasties on a baking sheet and brush with egg. Bake for 10 minutes, then reduce the oven temperature to 180°C/350°F/gas 4. Continue baking for a further 45 minutes, or until the meat is tender when pierced by a thin, heated skewer through the top of a pasty.

MAKES 8

LEEK TURNOVERS

These Welsh pasties make an ideal vegetarian snack.

10 large leeks, trinmed and washed
5 ml/1 tsp salt
5 ml/1 tsp lemon juice
5 ml/1 tsp sugar
125 ml/4 fl oz single cream
salt and pepper
beaten egg for glazing

SHORT CRUST PASTRY
450 g/1 lb plain flour
5 ml/1 tsp baking powder
100 g/4 oz lard
100 g/4 oz margarine
flour for rolling out

Set the oven at 200°C/400°F/gas 6. Remove the green part of the leeks and slice the white part only into 2 cm/¾ inch pieces. Put into a saucepan with just enough boiling water to cover. Add the salt, lemon juice and sugar. Cook for 5 minutes or until just tender. Drain and leave to cool.

To make the pastry, sift the flour, baking powder and a pinch of salt into a bowl. Rub in the lard and margarine. Mix to a stiff dough with cold water.

Roll out the pastry on a lightly floured surface to 1 cm/½ inch thick and cut into 10 oblong shapes, about 15 × 10 cm/6 × 4 inches. Lay the pieces of leek along the middle of each pastry piece. Moisten with a little cream and add salt and pepper to taste. Dampen the edges of the pastry and lift them to meet over the filling. Pinch and flute the edges to seal.

Place the pasties on a baking sheet and brush with egg. Bake for about 20 minutes.

MAKES 10

TRADITIONAL APPLE PIE

675 g/1½ lb cooking apples
100 g/4 oz sugar
6 cloves
caster sugar for dredging

SHORT CRUST PASTRY
350 g/12 oz plain flour
4 ml/¾ tsp salt
175 ml/6 oz margarine (or half butter,
    half lard)
flour for rolling out

Set the oven at 200°C/400°F/gas 6. To make the pastry, sift the flour and salt into a bowl, then rub in the margarine until the mixture resembles fine breadcrumbs. Add enough cold water to make a stiff dough. Press the dough together with your fingertips.

Roll out the pastry on a lightly floured surface and use just over half to line a 750 ml/1¼ pint pie dish. Peel, core and slice the apples. Place half in the pastry-lined dish, then add the sugar and cloves. Pile the remaining apples on top, cover with the remaining pastry and seal the edges. Brush the pastry with cold water and dredge with caster sugar.

Bake for 20 minutes, then lower the oven temperature to 180°C/350°F/gas 4 and bake for 20 minutes more. The pastry should be golden brown. Dredge with more caster sugar and serve hot or cold.

SERVES 6

MRS BEETON'S APPLE FLAN

6 eating apples
4 cloves
45 ml/3 tbsp medium-dry sherry
30 ml/2 tbsp soft light brown sugar
3 egg whites
45 ml/3 tbsp caster sugar

SHORT CRUST PASTRY
175 g/6 oz plain flour
2.5 ml/½ tsp salt
75 ml/3 oz margarine (or half butter,
    half lard)
flour for rolling out

Peel and core the apples, cutting each into 8 sections. Place in a heatproof bowl, add the cloves and sherry and cover closely. Place the bowl in a deep saucepan. Add boiling water to come halfway up the sides of the bowl and cook for 20 minutes until the apple sections are tender but whole.

Set the oven at 200°C/400°F/gas 6. Sift the flour and salt into a bowl, then rub in the margarine. Add enough cold water to make a stiff dough. Roll out the pastry on a lightly floured surface and use to line a 23 cm/9 inch flan tin. Line the pastry with greaseproof paper and fill with baking beans. Bake 'blind' for 20 minutes. Remove the paper and beans; cook for 5 minutes. Set aside.

Reduce the oven temperature to 140°C/275°F/gas 1. Arrange the apples in the flan. Sprinkle with 30 ml/2 tbsp of the cooking liquid and the brown sugar.

In a clean, grease-free bowl, whisk the egg whites until stiff. Whisk in 10 ml/2 tsp of the caster sugar and spread lightly over the apples. Sprinkle the remaining sugar over. Bake for 1 hour. Serve warm or cold.

SERVES 6

LEMON MERINGUE PIE

300 g/11 oz granulated sugar
45 ml/3 tbsp cornflour
45 ml/3 tbsp plain flour
grated rind of 2 lemons
30 ml/2 tbsp butter
75 ml/5 tbsp lemon juice
3 eggs, separated
75 g/3 oz caster sugar

SHORT CRUST PASTRY
175 g/6 oz plain flour
2.5 ml/½ tsp salt
75 g/3 oz margarine (or half butter, half lard)
flour for rolling out

Set the oven at 200°C/400°F/gas 6. To make the pastry, sift the flour and salt into a bowl, then rub in the margarine until the mixture resembles fine breadcrumbs. Add enough cold water to make a stiff dough. Press the dough together lightly.

Roll out the pastry on a lightly floured surface and use to line a 23 cm/9 inch pie plate. Line the pastry with greaseproof paper and fill with baking beans. Bake 'blind' for 15 minutes; remove paper and beans. Return to the oven for 5 minutes.

Meanwhile, mix the sugar, cornflour, plain flour and lemon rind and juice. Add 300 ml/½ pint boiling water and pour into a saucepan, then cook gently for 20 minutes.

Off the heat, add the butter and egg yolks. Beat well, then set aside to cool. Remove the pie from the oven and reduce the temperature to 180°C/350°F/gas 4.

In a clean, grease-free bowl, whisk the egg whites until stiff. Fold in the caster sugar. Pour the lemon custard into the baked pastry case and cover the top with the meringue, making sure that it covers the top completely. Bake for 12-15 minutes until the meringue is lightly browned. Cool before cutting.

SERVES 6

LEMON TARTLETS

50 g/2 oz butter
50 g/2 oz sugar
1 egg, beaten
grated rind and juice of ½ lemon
10 ml/2 tsp icing sugar

SHORT CRUST PASTRY
100 g/4 oz plain flour
1.25 ml/¼ tsp salt
50 g/2 oz margarine (or half butter, half lard)
flour for rolling out

Set the oven at 200°C/400°F/gas 6. To make the pastry, sift the flour and salt into a bowl, then rub in the margarine until the mixture resembles fine breadcrumbs. Add enough cold water to make a stiff dough. Press the dough together with your fingertips. Roll out and use to line twelve 7.5 cm/3 inch patty tins.

Cream the butter and sugar in a bowl until pale and fluffy. Beat in the egg. Add the lemon rind and juice. Fill the pastry cases with the mixture.

Bake for 15-20 minutes or until set. Leave to cool. Sift the icing sugar over the tartlets.

MAKES 12

MINCE PIES

Illustrated on page 40

Festive mince pies can also be made using flaky, rough puff or puff pastry with mouthwatering results. Use 200 g/7 oz flour quantity for these pastries.

350 g/12 oz mincemeat
25 g/1 oz icing or caster sugar for
    dredging

SHORT CRUST PASTRY
    300 g/10 oz plain flour
    5 ml/1 tsp salt
    150 g/5 oz margarine (or half butter, half
      lard)
    flour for rolling out

Set the oven at 200°C/400°F/gas 6. To make the pastry, sift the flour and salt into a bowl, then rub in the margarine until the mixture resembles fine breadcrumbs. Add enough cold water to make a stiff dough. Press the dough together with your fingertips.

Roll out the pastry on a lightly floured surface and use just over half of it to line twelve 7.5 cm/3 inch patty tins. Cut out 12 lids from the rest of the pastry. If liked, make holly leaf decorations from the pastry trimmings.

Place a spoonful of mincemeat in each pastry case. Dampen the edges of the cases and cover with the pastry lids. Seal the edges well. Brush the tops with water and add any pastry decorations. Dredge with the sugar. Make 2 small cuts in the top of each pie. Bake for 15-20 minutes or until golden brown.

MAKES 12

CHOCOLATE MERINGUE TARTLETS

fat for greasing
Short Crust Pastry as for Lemon Tartlets
    (left)
5 ml/1 tsp cornflour
5 ml/1 tsp cocoa, sifted
125 ml/4 fl oz milk
20 ml/4 tsp butter or margarine
20 ml/4 tsp sugar
2 large eggs, separated
few drops of vanilla essence
pinch of ground cinnamon
75 g/3 oz caster sugar

Grease twelve 7.5 cm/3 inch patty rins. Set the oven at 190°C/375°F/gas 5.

Roll out the pastry on a lightly floured surface and use to line the prepared patty tins.

Mix together the cornflour and cocoa in a saucepan and blend in the milk. Bring to the boil and cook for 2-3 minutes, stirring all the time. Cool slightly, then stir in the butter or margarine, sugar, egg yolks, vanilla essence and cinnamon. Half fill the pastry cases with the mixture. Bake for 10-15 minutes or until set. Reduce the oven temperature to 150°C/300°F/gas 2.

In a clean grease-free bowl, whisk the egg whites until stiff. Whisk in 10 ml/2 tsp of the caster sugar, then fold in almost all the rest, using a metal spoon. Pipe the mixture in a spiral or star on the tops of the tartlets. Dredge with the remaining caster sugar. Bake for 15-20 minutes or until the meringue is crisp and very lightly browned.

MAKES 12

ORANGE BOATS

Illustrated on page 39

ALMOND PASTRY
    100 g/4 oz plain flour
    30 ml/2 tbsp ground almonds
    50 g/2 oz butter
    1 egg yolk
    few drops of almond essence
    flour for rolling out

FILLING
    grated rind of 1 orange
    50 g/2 oz ground almonds
    75 g/3 oz caster sugar
    1 egg white

ICING
    50 g/2 oz icing sugar, sifted
    15 ml/1 tbsp orange juice

Set the oven at 190°C/375°F/gas 5. To make the pastry, sift the flour and salt into a bowl, then add the almonds. Rub in the butter until the mixture resembles fine breadcrumbs. Add the egg yolk, essence and cold water to make a stiff dough. Roll out the pastry and use to line 12 boat-shaped tartlet tins.

Mix the orange rind, ground almonds and caster sugar. In a clean, grease-free bowl, whisk the egg white until stiff, then fold it into the mixture. Fill the pastry cases two-thirds full with mixture. Bake for 20-30 minutes, until golden brown. Cool.

To make the icing, place the icing sugar in a bowl. Add the orange juice and about 15 ml/1 tbsp water to make a stiff icing. When the tartlets are cold, pipe a wavy thread of icing down the centre.

MAKES 12

PARISIAN TARTLETS

Illustrated on page 39

    50 g/2 oz butter
    50 g/2 oz caster sugar
    1 egg, beaten
    15 ml/1 tbsp cornflour
    15 ml/1 tbsp single cream or milk
    25 g/1 oz ground almonds
    25 g/1 oz plain cake crumbs
    2.5 ml/½ tsp ground cinnamon
    10 ml/2 tsp lemon juice
    caster sugar for dredging

SHORT CRUST PASTRY
    100 g/4 oz plain flour
    1.25 ml/¼ tsp salt
    50 g/2 oz margarine (or half butter, half lard)
    flour for rolling out

Set the oven at 200°C/400°F/gas 6. To make the pastry, sift the flour and salt into a bowl, then rub in the margarine until the mixture resembles fine breadcrumbs. Add enough cold water to make a stiff dough. Press the dough together with your finger-tips.

Roll out on a lightly floured surface and use to line twelve 7.5 cm/3 inch patty tins.

Cream the butter and sugar in a bowl until pale and fluffy. Add the egg and beat well. Blend the cornflour with the cream or milk, then stir this into the creamed mixture. Add the ground almonds, cake crumbs, cinnamon and lemon juice. Fill the pastry cases with the mixture.

Bake for 15-20 minutes until golden brown. Dredge with caster sugar when baked.

MAKES 12

MRS BEETON'S CHICKEN PIE

fat for greasing
1 chicken with giblets
1 onion, halved
salt and pepper
bouquet garni
1 blade of mace
2.5 ml/½ tsp grated nutmeg
2.5 ml/½ tsp ground mace
6 slices lean cooked ham
3 hard-boiled eggs
flour for dredging
Puff Pastry (page 55), using 150g/
    5 oz flour
beaten egg for glazing

HERB FORCEMEAT
50 g/2 oz shredded suet or margarine
100 g/4 oz fresh breadcrumbs
pinch of grated nutmeg
15 ml/1 tbsp chopped parsley
5 ml/1 tsp chopped fresh mixed herbs
grated rind of ½ lemon
1 egg, beaten

Lightly grease a 1.5 litre / 2¾ pint pie dish. For the herb forcemeat, melt the margarine, if using. Mix the breadcrumbs with the suet or margarine. Add the nutmeg, herbs and lemon rind. Add salt and pepper to taste, then bind with the beaten egg.

Skin the chicken and cut it into small serving joints. Put the leftover bones, neck and gizzard into a small pan with 250 ml/8 fl oz water. Add the onion to the pan with salt, pepper, bouquet garni and mace. Half cover and simmer gently for about 45 minutes until the liquid is well reduced and strongly flavoured. Put to one side.

Set the oven at 220°C/425°F/gas 7. Put a layer of chicken joints in the bottom of the prepared dish. Sprinkle with salt, pepper,

nutmeg and ground mace. Cover with a layer of ham, then with forcemeat; add salt and pepper to taste. Slice the eggs, place a layer over the forcemeat, and season again. Repeat the layers until the dish is full and all the ingredients are used, ending with a layer of chicken joints. Pour in 150-200 ml/ 5-7 fl oz water and dredge lightly with flour.

Roll out the pastry on a lightly floured surface to the same shape as the dish but 2.5 cm/1 inch larger all round. Cut off the outside 2 cm/¾ inch of the pastry. Lay the pastry strip on the rim of the dish. Dampen the strip and lay the lid on top. Knock up the edge, trim, then use any trimmings to decorate the crust with pastry leaves. Make a pastry rose and put to one side. Brush the pastry with the beaten egg. Make a small hole in the centre of the pie.

Bake for 15 minutes to set the pastry, then reduce the oven temperature to 180°C/ 350°F/gas 4, and cover the pastry loosely with greaseproof paper. Bake for 1-1¼ hours. Bake the pastry rose with the pie for the final 20 minutes but bake it separately. Test whether the joints are cooked through by running a small heated skewer into the pie through the central hole. It should come out clean with no trace of blood.

Just before the pie is cooked, reheat the stock and strain it. When the pie is cooked, pour the stock in through the central hole, then cover with the pastry rose.

SERVES 6 TO 8

 MRS BEETON'S TIP Boneless chicken and bought stock may be used instead of joints.

TURKEY BREASTS IN PASTRY

2 turkey breasts (about 500 g/18 oz each)
25 g/1 oz butter
175 g/6 oz mushrooms, finely chopped
50 g/2 oz onion, finely chopped
225 g/8 oz belly of pork, minced
50 g /2 oz sage and onion stuffing mix
salt and pepper
1 egg, beaten
Puff Pastry (page 55), using 225 g/
   8 oz flour
flour for rolling out

Set the oven at 220°C/425°F/gas 7. Remove the skin from the turkey breasts, then cut each across to make 2 thinner slices. Place each slice between sheets of greaseproof paper and flatten with a cutlet bat or rolling-pin.

Melt the butter in a pan and gently cook the mushrooms and onion until the onion is soft but not brown. Remove from the heat. Add the pork, stuffing mix, salt, pepper and half the beaten egg to the pan. Allow to stand for a few minutes for the crumbs to swell.

Roll out the pastry on a lightly floured surface into a 30 cm/12 inch square. Place 2 turkey pieces in the centre and spread the stuffing over them. Lay the remaining 2 turkey breasts on top to enclose the stuffing. Dampen the edges of the pastry lightly and fold it over the turkey. Place on a baking sheet with the seam underneath. Brush with the remaining egg and decorate with any pastry trimmings. Bake for 20 minutes, then reduce the oven temperature to 180°C/350°F/gas 4. Continue baking for a further 35 minutes. Serve hot, in slices.

SERVES 8

PASTRY HORNS

Illustrated on page 73

Puff Pastry (page 55), using 100 g/4 oz
   flour
flour for rolling out
beaten egg and milk for glazing

Roll out the pastry 5 mm/¼ inch thick on a lightly floured surface, then cut into strips 35 cm/14 inches long and 2 cm/¾ inch wide. Moisten the strips with cold water.

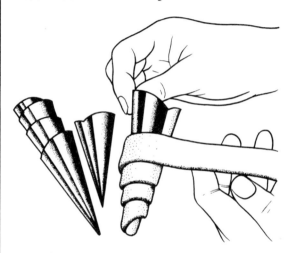

Wind each strip round a cornet mould, working from the point upward, keeping the moistened surface on the outside. Lay the horns on a dampened baking sheet, with the final overlap of the pastry strip underneath. Leave in a cool place for 1 hour.

Set the oven at 220°C/425°F/gas 7. Brush the horns with beaten egg and milk. Bake for 10-15 minutes or until golden brown. Remove the moulds and return the horns to the oven for 5 minutes. Cool completely on a wire rack. When cold, fill the horns with a sweet at savoury filling.

MAKES 8

FILLINGS FOR PASTRY HORNS AND
VOL-AU-VENT CASES

The basic pastry cases may be filled in a variety of ways, both savoury and sweet.

SEAFOOD FILLING For vols-au-vent. Melt 15 g/½ oz butter in a saucepan. Stir in 25 g/1 oz plain flour, then cook for 1 minute. Pour in 300 ml/½ pint milk, stirring all the time, and bring to the boil. Simmer for 3 minutes. Add a 200 g/7 oz can tuna (drained), 100 g/4 oz frozen peeled cooked prawns and seasoning to taste. Stir in 30 ml/2 tbsp chopped parsley and simmer for 3 minutes, stirring occasionally until the prawns are thawed. Spoon in the pastry cases and serve hot.

HAM AND TOMATO Mix 50 g/2 oz diced cooked ham with 2 peeled and diced tomatoes, 1 chopped spring onion and 100 g/4 oz soft cheese (full-fat soft cheese, ricotta, quark or low-fat soft cheese). Add salt and pepper to taste, then spoon into the pastry cases.

CHICKEN MAYONNAISE Dice 100 g/4 oz cooked chicken and bind with mayonnaise to a creamy mixture. Add 30 ml/2 tbsp snipped chives and salt and pepper to taste, then spoon the mixture into the pastry cases.

JAM AND CREAM Place 5 ml/1 tsp jam in each pastry case, then top with whipped cream. The cream may be flavoured with a little liqueur (such as Grand Marnier) or sherry and sweetened with a little caster or icing sugar before whipping. Sprinkle chopped nuts over the cream filling.

FRUIT HORNS Roughly chopped fresh fruit, such as strawberries or peach, may be mixed with lightly sweetened whipped cream to fill the pastry cases.

VOL-AU-VENT CASES

Illustrated on page 73

Puff Pastry (page 55), using 200 g/7 oz flour
flour for rolling out
beaten egg for glazing

Set the oven at 220°C/425°F/gas 7. Roll out the pastry on a lightly floured surface about 2 cm/¾ inch thick (1 cm/½ inch thick for bouchées). Cut into round or oval shapes as liked. Place on a baking sheet and brush the top of the pastry with beaten egg.

With a smaller, floured cutter, make a circular or oval cut in each case, to form an inner ring, cutting through about half the depth of the pastry. Bake until golden brown and crisp.

When baked, remove the inner circular or oval lid, then scoop out the soft inside while still warm to make room for the filling.

MAKES TWENTY-FOUR 5 CM/2 INCH OR TWELVE 7.5 CM/3 INCH BOUCHEES OR EIGHT 9 CM/3½ INCH OR TWO 15 CM/6 INCH VOL-AU-VENT CASES

 MRS BEETON'S TIP For a better appearance a separate piece of pastry can be baked for the lid instead of using the centre portion of the case.

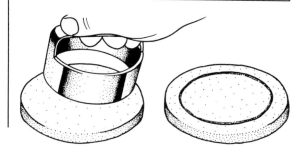

MILLE-FEUILLE GATEAU

PUFF PASTRY
200 g/7 oz plain flour
1.25 ml/¼ tsp salt
200 g/7 oz butter
2.5 ml/½ tsp lemon juice
flour for rolling out

FILLING AND TOPPING
300 ml/½ pint double cream
100 g/4 oz icing sugar, sifted
100 g/4 oz raspberry jam

Make the pastry. Sift the flour and salt into a mixing bowl and rub in 50 g/2 oz of the butter. Add the lemon juice and mix to a smooth dough with cold water.

Shape the remaining butter into a rectangle on greaseproof paper. Roll out the dough on a lightly floured surface to a strip a little wider than the butter and rather more than twice its length. Place the butter on one half of the pastry, fold the other half over it, and press the edges together with the rolling pin. Leave in a cool place for 15 minutes to allow the butter to harden.

Roll the pastry out into a long strip. Fold the bottom third up and the top third down, press the edges together with the rolling pin and turn the pastry so that the folded edges are on the right and left. Roll and fold again, cover and leave in a cool place for 15 minutes. Repeat this process until the pastry has been rolled out 6 times (see Mrs Beeton's Tip). Chill the pastry

well between each rolling, wrapping it in cling film to prevent it drying on the surface. The pastry is now ready for use.

Set the oven at 230°C/450°F/gas 8. Roll out the pastry on a lightly floured surface to a thickness of 3 mm/⅛ inch. Cut into six 15 cm/6 inch rounds. If work surface space is limited, it is best to cut the pastry into portions to do this. Either cut the pastry into six portions or cut it in half and cut out three circles from each half.
Place the pastry circles on baking sheets, prick well and bake for 8-10 minutes until crisp and golden brown. Lift the rounds off carefully and cool on wire racks.

In a bowl, whip the cream until thick. Make glacé icing by mixing the icing sugar with enough cold water to form an icing that will coat the back of the spoon. Coat one pastry layer with icing and set aside for the lid. Sandwich the remaining layers together lightly with the jam and cream. Put the iced layer on top. Serve as soon as possible.

SERVES 6 TO 8

MRS BEETON'S TIP Never rush the process of making puff pastry: always chill it if the fat begins to melt. It is a good idea to mark the pastry each time it is rolled, as it is easy to lose track of the number of times this process has been carried out.

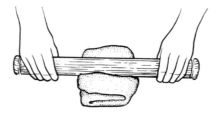
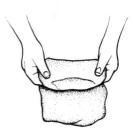

CREAM SLICES

Puff Pastry (page 55), using 100 g/4 oz
    flour
flour for rolling out
white Glacé Icing (page 103), using
    225 g/8 oz icing sugar
30 ml/2 tbsp smooth seedless jam
125 ml/4 fl oz sweetened whipped cream

Set the oven at 220°C/425°F/gas 7. Roll
out the pastry 1 cm/½ inch thick on a
lightly floured surface into a neat rectangle.
Cut into 8 oblong pieces 10 × 2 cm/4 ×
¾ inch. Place on a baking sheet and spread
the tops thinly with half of the icing.

Bake for 20 minutes or until the pastry is
well risen and the icing is slightly browned.
Leave to cool completely.

When cold, split in half crossways.
Spread the top of the bottom half with
jam, and the bottom of the top half with
cream; then sandwich the halves together
again. Spread a little icing on top of each
slice, over the browned icing.

MAKES 8

VARIATION

VANILLA SLICES Make as for Cream
Slices but without the baked icing. When
the slices are cold, fill with vanilla-
flavoured confectioners' custard (page 126)
instead of cream. Ice the tops with white
Glacé Icing (page 103).

🥣 **MRS BEETON'S TIP** The pastry
can be cooked and baked with royal
icing using 100 g/4 oz icing sugar, instead
of the glacé icing.

MAIDS OF HONOUR

*These cakes are supposed to date back to
Elizabethan times, when they were a great
favourite of the court. Orange flower water is a
fragrantly scented flavouring essence. It is
prepared by distilling the spring blossom of the
bitter Seville or Bigarade orange.*

Puff Pastry (page 55), using 200 g/7 oz
    flour
flour for rolling out
200 g/7 oz ground almonds
100 g/4 oz caster sugar
2 eggs, beaten
25 g/1 oz plain flour
60 ml/4 tbsp single cream
30 ml/2 tbsp orange flower water

Set the oven at 200°C/400°F gas 6. Roll
out the pastry on a lightly floured surface
and use to line twenty 7.5 cm/3 inch patty
tins.

Mix the ground almonds and sugar in a
bowl. Add the eggs, then mix in the flour,
cream and orange flower water. Put the
mixture into the pastry cases.

Bake for about 15 minutes or until the
filling is firm and golden brown.

MAKES 20

MRS BEETON'S CUSTARD TARTLETS

Puff Pastry (page 55), using 200 g/7 oz
    flour
flour for rolling out
25 g/1 oz butter
scant 75 ml/5 tbsp icing sugar
15 ml/1 tbsp plain flour
3 eggs
250 ml/8 fl oz milk
few drops of vanilla essence
30 ml/2 tbsp whole fruit strawberry or
    blackcurrant jam

Roll out the pastry on a lightly floured surface to 5 mm/¼ inch thick. Leave to rest while preparing the custard.

Cream the butter and sugar in a bowl, then mix in the flour until well blended. Whisk the eggs into the milk and add the vanilla essence. Blend the mixture gradually into the butter and sugar, breaking down any lumps. Heat gently in a heavy saucepan, stirring all the time, until the mixture reaches simmering point and thickens. Remove from the heat, cover with damp greaseproof paper and leave to cool while preparing the pastry cases. Set the oven at 190°C/375°F/gas 5.

Line twelve 7.5 cm/3 inch patty tins, about 1 cm/½ inch deep, with the pastry, pressing it in well. Put a little of the jam in the bottom of each pastry case. Spoon the custard mixture over the jam, almost filling the cases.

Bake for 20-25 minutes, until the custard is firm. Cool in the tins. Before serving, decorate each tartlet with a small dab of the jam in the centre.

MAKES 12

ECCLES CAKES

Illustrated on page 74

Flaky or Rough Puff Pastry (page 56),
    using 200 g/7 oz flour
flour for rolling out
25 g/1 oz butter or margarine
15 ml/1 tbsp sugar
75 g/3 oz currants
25 g/1 oz chopped mixed peel
1.25 ml/¼ tsp ground mixed spice
1.25 ml/¼ tsp ground nutmeg
caster sugar for dusting

Set the oven at 200°C/425°F gas 7. Roll out the pastry on a lightly floured surface to 3 mm/⅛ inch thick. Cut into rounds using a 10 cm/4 inch pastry cutter.

Cream the butter or margarine and sugar in a bowl. Add the currants, peel and spices. Place spoonfuls of the mixture in the centre of each pastry round. Gather the edges of each round together to form a ball. With the smooth side uppermost, form into a flat cake. Make 2 cuts in the top of each cake with a sharp knife. Brush with water and dust with caster sugar.

Put on a baking sheet and bake for 20 minutes or until golden brown.

MAKES 12 TO 14

Pastry Horns (page 68) and Vols-au-vent (page 69)

Eccles Cakes (page 72) and Cream Eclairs (page 81)

Eve's Pudding (page 96)

Phyllo Pastries (page 84)

Raised Pork Pies (page 87)

Nutty Plum Crumble (page 96)

Grand Marnier Soufflé (page 92)

Baked Apples (page 95)

CREAM ECLAIRS

Illustrated on page 74

fat for greasing
250 ml/8 fl oz whipping cream
25 g/1 oz caster sugar and icing sugar,
   mixed
3-4 drops of vanilla essence

CHOUX PASTRY
  100 g/4 oz plain flour
  50 g/2 oz butter or margarine
  pinch of salt
  2 whole eggs plus 1 yolk

CHOCOLATE GLACE ICING
  50 g/2 oz plain chocolate
  10 ml/2 tsp butter
  100 g/4 oz icing sugar, sifted

Lightly grease a baking sheet. Set the oven at 220°C/425°F/gas 7. To make the pastry, sift the flour on to a sheet of grease-proof paper. Put 250 ml/8 fl oz water in a saucepan and add the butter or margarine with the salt. Heat gently until the fat melts.

When the fat has melted, bring the liquid rapidly to the boil and add all the flour at once. Immediately remove the pan from the heat and stir the flour into the liquid to make a smooth paste which leaves the sides of the pan clean. Set aside to cool slightly.

Add the egg yolk and beat well. Add the whole eggs, one at a time, beating well after each addition. Continue beating until the paste is very glossy.

Put the pastry into a piping bag fitted with a 2 cm/¾ inch nozzle and pipe it in 10 cm/4 inch lengths on the prepared baking sheet. Cut off each length with a knife or scissors dipped in hot water.

Bake for 30 minutes. Do not open the oven door while baking. Reduce the oven temperature to 180°C/350°F/gas 4. Bake for a further 10 minutes. Remove the éclairs from the oven, split them open and remove any uncooked paste. Return to the oven for 5 minutes to dry. Cool completely on a wire rack.

Meanwhile, to make the glacé icing, break the chocolate into a heavy-bottomed pan. Add 15 ml/1 tbsp water and the butter. Warm gently, stirring until smooth and creamy. Stir in the icing sugar, a little at a time.

Whip the cream until it holds its shape, adding the mixed sugars gradually. Add the vanilla essence while whipping.

Fill the éclairs with the cream and close neatly. Cover the tops with the glacé icing.

MAKES 10 TO 12

VARIATION

CREAM BUNS Pipe the pastry in 5 cm/2 inch balls. Fill as above, and sift icing sugar over the tops instead of glacé icing.

☆ **FREEZER TIP** When cool, the unfilled choux éclairs or buns may be packed in sealed polythene bags and frozen. Thaw in wrappings for 1-1½ hours at room temperature, then place on baking sheets and crisp in a 180°C/350°F/gas 4 oven for 5 minutes. Cool before filling and topping.

CHEESE ECLAIRS

*Serve these savoury éclairs as cocktail snacks
or at a buffet party.*

CHOUX PASTRY
   100 g/4 oz plain flour
   50 g/2 oz butter or margarine
   pinch of salt
   2 whole eggs plus 1 yolk
   salt and pepper
   pinch of cayenne pepper

FILLING
   25 g/1 oz butter
   25 g/1 oz plain flour
   300 ml/½ pint milk
   75-100 g/3-4 oz Cheddar cheese, grated
   pinch of dry mustard

Lightly grease a baking sheet. Set the oven at 200°C/400°F/gas 6. To make the pastry, sift the flour on to a sheet of grease-proof paper. Put 250 ml/8 fl oz water in a saucepan and add the butter or margarine with the salt. Heat gently until the fat melts.

When the fat has melted, bring the liquid rapidly to the boil and add all the flour at once. Immediately remove the pan from the heat and stir the flour into the liquid to make a smooth paste which leaves the sides of the pan clean. Set aside to cool slightly.

Add the egg yolk and beat well. Add the whole eggs, one at a time, beating well after each addition. Add salt, pepper and cayenne with the final egg. Continue beating until the paste is very glossy.

Put the pastry into a piping bag fitted with a 1 cm/½ inch nozzle and pipe it in 5 cm/2 inch lengths on the prepared baking sheet. Cut off each length with a knife or scissors dipped in hot water.

Bake for 20-30 minutes until risen and browned. Split the éclairs open and remove any uncooked paste. Return to the oven for 2-3 minutes to dry.

Meanwhile to make the filling, melt the butter in a saucepan. Stir in the flour and cook over a low heat for 2-3 minutes, without colouring. Over a very low heat, gradually add the milk, stirring constantly. Bring to the boil, stirring, and simmer for 1-2 minutes until smooth and thickened. Add the cheese, mustard and salt and pepper to taste.

Cool the éclairs on a wire rack. Fill with the cheese sauce.

MAKES 20 TO 24

VARIATIONS

HAM AND EGG ECLAIRS   Omit the cheese. Add 2 chopped hard-boiled eggs, 15 ml/1 tbsp chopped tarragon and 75 g/3 oz diced cooked ham.

SMOKED SALMON ECLAIRS   Omit the cheese. Add 75 g/3 oz roughly chopped smoked salmon and 2.5 ml/½ tsp grated lemon rind. Smoked salmon offcuts are ideal: up to 100 g/4 oz may be added, depending on flavour and the saltiness of the salmon.

TURKEY ECLAIRS   Omit the cheese. Add 100 g/4 oz diced cooked turkey and 30 ml/2 tbsp chopped parsley.

———————— ◆ ————————

CROQUEMBOUCHE

This spectacular gâteau is often used as a wedding cake in France.

1 Madeira cake (20 cm/8 inches in diameter, 6 cm/2½ inches high)
200 g/7 oz Almond Paste (page 102)
Apricot Glaze (page 126)
white Glacé Icing (page 103)
marzipan flowers, to decorate

CHOUX PASTRY
butter for greasing
Choux Pastry (see Cheese Eclairs, opposite), using 225 g/8 oz flour
Confectioners' Custard (page 126) as required

CARAMEL
500 g/18 oz granulated sugar
juice of 1 lemon

If the Madeira cake is peaked, cut out a thin strip of almond paste and put it round the edge of the cake to level the top. Brush off any loose crumbs, then brush the whole cake with warmed apricot glaze. Roll out the rest of the almond paste, and use it to cover the top and sides of the cake. Place the cake on a 30 cm/12 inch serving board.

Lightly butter a baking sheet. Set the oven at 190°C/375°F/gas 5. Do not add cayenne pepper to the choux pastry. Put the choux pastry into a piping bag fitted with a 5 mm/¼ inch nozzle and pipe small choux puffs on the prepared baking sheet. Bake for about 30 minutes. Split the éclairs open and remove any uncooked paste. Return to the oven for 2-3 minutes to dry. Cool on a wire rack. When cold, fill with confectioners' custard.

Make a strong paper cone, 30 cm/12 inches high and 15 cm/6 inch diameter at the base.

To make the caramel, boil the sugar, 50 ml/2 fl oz water and the lemon juice in a heavy-bottomed pan until golden. Immediately the caramel colours, plunge the bottom of the pan into iced water to prevent further cooking and darkening.

Stick the filled choux on the cone by dipping each in caramel and pressing it on to the cone. Begin with a circle of choux at the bottom, and work upwards. At the top, stick on the decorative marzipan flowers, using dabs of caramel.

Leave the caramel to harden; then lift the cone very carefully on to the Madeira cake.

Ice the exposed sections of the Madeira cake quickly with glacé icing.

SERVES ABOUT 20

*P*HYLLO AND FETA TRIANGLES

225 g/8 oz feta cheese
5 ml/1 tsp dried oregano
1 spring onion, chopped
pepper
4 sheets of phyllo pastry
50 g/2 oz butter, melted

Set the oven at 190°C/375°F/gas 5. Mash the feta with the oregano in a bowl, then mix in the spring onion and pepper to taste.

Lay a sheet of phyllo pastry on a clean, dry surface and brush it with melted butter. Cut the sheet widthways into 9 strips. Place a little feta mixture at one end of the first strip, leaving the corner of the pastry without filling. Fold the corner over the feta to cover it in a triangular shape, then fold the mixture over and over to wrap it in several layers of pastry, making a small triangular-shaped pasty.

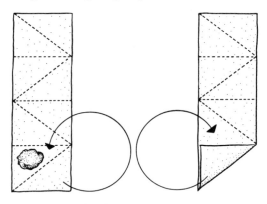

Repeat with the other strips of pastry. Cut and fill the remaining sheets in the same way to make 36 triangular pastries. Place these on baking sheets and brush any remaining butter over them.

Bake for about 10 minutes, until the phyllo pastry is crisp and golden. Transfer the triangles to a wire rack to cool. They are best served warm.

MAKES 36

SHAPES AND FILLINGS FOR PHYLLO PASTRY

The feta filling used in the triangles is a Greek speciality. A variety of other fillings may be used and the pastry may be shaped in other ways.

SHAPES

Instead of cutting strips, the pastry may be cut into squares (about 6 per sheet). The filling should be placed in the middle of the squares, then the pastry may be gathered up to form a small bundle. The butter coating keeps the bundle closed when the phyllo is pressed together. For extra strength, the squares may be used double.

Alternatively, squares of phyllo may be filled and folded into neat oblong shapes.

Oblong pieces of phyllo (about 4 per sheet) may be folded into neat squares.

FILLINGS

SPINACH AND CHEESE Thoroughly drained cooked spinach may be used with or without the cheese. Flavour plain spinach with chopped spring onion and grated nutmeg.

SARDINE Mashed canned sardines in tomato sauce make a good filling for phyllo triangles.

CHICKEN OR HAM Chopped cooked chicken or ham are both tasty fillings for phyllo. Combine them with salt, pepper and a little low-fat soft cheese.

APRICOT Apricot halves (drained canned or fresh) topped with a dot of marmalade make good sweet phyllo pastries. Dust them with icing sugar after baking.

APPLE AND ALMOND Mix some ground almonds into cold, sweetened apple purée. Use to fill triangles or squares.

APPLE STRUDEL

Anyone who has ever watched an Austrian pastrycook at work will know that the best strudel is coaxed out to the correct size by hand. Using a rolling pin is no disgrace, however, and the recipe below gives very good results.

200 g/7 oz plain flour
1.25 ml/¼ tsp salt
30 ml/2 tbsp oil
1 egg
flour for rolling out

FILLING
450 g/1 lb cooking apples
50 g/2 oz butter
50 g/2 oz soft light brown sugar
5 ml/1 tsp ground cinnamon
50 g/2 oz sultanas

To make the pastry, sift the flour and salt into a mixing bowl. Add the oil and egg, with 60 ml/4 tbsp warm water. Mix to a firm dough, cover with foil and leave in a warm place for about an hour. Set the oven at 190°C/375°F/gas 5.

Peel and core the apples. Chop them finely and put them into a bowl. Melt the butter in a small saucepan. Have the sugar, cinnamon and sultanas ready.

Lightly flour a clean tablecloth or sheet, placed on a work surface. Place the pastry on the cloth and roll it out very thinly to a rectangle measuring 25 × 50 cm/10 × 20 inches.

Brush the strudel pastry with some of the melted butter and sprinkle with the brown sugar, cinnamon and sultanas. Top with the chopped apple. Starting from a long side, roll the strudel up like a Swiss roll, using the sheet as a guide.

Slide the strudel on to a large baking sheet, turning it to a horseshoe shape if necessary. Position it so that the join is underneath. Brush the top with more melted butter.

Bake for 40 minutes or until golden brown. To serve, cut the strudel in wide diagonal slices. It is equally good hot or cold, with or without cream.

SERVES 8

VARIATION

Phyllo pastry may be used for a quick strudel. Brush each sheet generously with melted butter, covering any phyllo not in use with a clean damp tea-towel or cling film to prevent it from drying out.

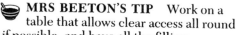 **MRS BEETON'S TIP** Work on a table that allows clear access all round if possible, and have all the filling ingredients ready before you begin.

SAVOURY STRUDEL Savoury fillings may be used instead of apples in the strudel. Chopped onion, cooked in oil or butter until soft, with shredded cabbage, a little grated carrot and grated eating apple is tasty. Diced cooked ham or lean bacon may be added and the mixture may be seasoned with a little grated nutmeg.

Alternatively, drained cooked spinach with lightly toasted pine nuts, cooked onion and crumbled Lancashire or Wensleydale cheese is delicious. A few sultanas or raisins may be added to the spinach which may be spiced with a good sprinkle of ground coriander.

———————— ◆ ————————

HOT WATER CRUST PASTRY

This pastry is used for pork, veal and ham, and raised game pies. It must be moulded while still warm.

200 g/7 oz plain flour
2.5 ml/½ tsp salt
75 g/3 oz lard
100 ml/3½ fl oz milk or water

Sift the flour and salt into a warm bowl and make a well in the centre. Keep the bowl in a warm place.

Meanwhile, heat the lard and milk or water until boiling. Add the hot mixture to the flour, mixing well with a wooden spoon until the pastry is cool enough to knead with the hands. Knead thoroughly and mould as required.

Bake at 220°C/425°F/gas 7 until the pastry is set, then reduce the oven temperature to 180°C/350°F/gas 4 until fully baked.

MAKES 350 G/12 OZ

TO MOULD A RAISED PIE

Hot Water Crust Pastry (above)
fat for greasing
flour

Use a jar, round cake tin or similar container, as a mould: grease and flour the sides and base of the mould and invert it.

Reserve one-quarter of the warm pastry for the lid and leave in the bowl in a warm place, covered with a greased polythene bag.

Roll out the remainder to about 5 mm/ ¼ inch thick, in a round or oval shape. Lay the pastry over the mould, then ease the pastry round the sides. Take care not to pull the pastry and make sure that the sides and base are of an even thickness. Leave to cool.

When cold, remove the pastry case from the mould and put in the filling. Roll out the pastry reserved for the lid, dampen the rim of the case, put on the lid, pressing the edges firmly together. Tie 3 or 4 folds of greaseproof paper round the pie to hold it in shape during baking and to prevent it becoming too brown.

MAKES ONE 13 CM/5 INCH PIE

USING A RAISED PIE MOULD Decorative pie moulds may be purchased from cookshops. Usually oval in shape, they range in size from those which provide up to 6 servings to others which make pies large enough to feed 40 people.

The two sides of the mould fit into a base and they are secured with clips. The sides should be secured and the inside of the mould should be well greased. The pastry should be rolled out to about two-thirds of the require size.

Lift the pastry into the mould and secure its edge just below the rim of the mould. Use your fingers to press the pastry into the mould, casing it upwards at the same time so that it comes above the rim of the mould when the lining is complete. The pie may be filled at once.

The sides of the mould should be removed about 15-30 minutes before the end of the cooking time. Brush the pastry with beaten egg immediately and return the pie to the oven promptly to prevent the sides collapsing.

RAISED VEAL PIE

*If preferred, these ingredients can be made into
6 individual pies. The eggs should be sliced and
divided between the smaller pies.*

Hot Water Crust Pastry (page 86), using
    400 g/14 oz flour
400 g/14 oz pie veal
400 g/14 oz lean pork
25 g/1 oz plain flour
7.5 ml/1½ tsp salt
1.25 ml/¼ tsp ground pepper
3 hard-boiled eggs
beaten egg for glazing
about 125 ml/4 fl oz well-flavoured,
    cooled and jellied stock or canned
    consommé

Set the oven at 230°C/450°F/gas 8. Line a 20 cm/8 inch round pie mould with three-quarters of the pastry, or use a round cake tin to mould the pie as described opposite. Use the remaining quarter for the lid.

Cut the meat into small pieces, removing any gristle or fat. Season the flour with the salt and pepper, then toss the pieces of meat in it. Put half the meat into the pastry case and put in the whole eggs. Add the rest of the meat and 30 ml/2 tbsp water. Put on the lid and brush with beaten egg. Make a hole in the centre to allow steam to escape. Bake for 15 minutes, then reduce the oven temperature to 140°C/275°F/gas 1. Continue baking for 2½ hours. Remove the greaseproof paper or mould for the last 30 minutes of the cooking time and brush the top and sides of the pastry with beaten egg.

Heat the stock or consommé until melted. When the pie is cooked, pour it through the hole in the lid using a funnel until the pie is full. Leave to cool.

SERVES 6

RAISED PORK PIES

Illustrated on page 77

about 400 g/14 oz pork bones
1 small onion, finely chopped
salt and pepper
300 ml/½ pint cold water or stock
Hot Water Crust Pastry (page 86), using
    400 g/14 oz flour
500 g/18 oz lean pork, minced
1.25 ml/¼ tsp dried sage
beaten egg for glazing

Simmer the pork bones, onion, salt, pepper and water or stock, covered, for 2 hours. Strain and cool. Make 1 15 cm/6 inch pie (left) or divide three-quarters of the pastry into 6 portions. Mould each piece using a jam jar, as described on page 86, keeping it about 5 mm/¼ inch thick. Use the remainder for the lids. Set the oven at 220°C/425°F/gas 7.

Season the pork with salt, pepper and sage. Divide between the prepared pie crusts and add 10 ml/2 tsp of the jellied stock to each. Put on the lids, brush with beaten egg, and make holes in the centres.

Bake for 15 minutes, then reduce the oven temperature to 180°C/350°F/gas 4. Continue baking for 45 minutes (1 hour for a large pie). Remove the greaseproof paper for the last 30 minutes and brush the top and sides of the pastry with egg.

When cooked, remove from the oven and leave to cool. Warm the remainder of the jellied stock and pour through the hole in the pastry lids using a funnel until the pies are full. Leave to cool.

SERVES 6

SOUFFLES

Many people shy away from baking soufflés yet, with a little
practice, they are not difficult to prepare. Savoury soufflés
are quick, easy and economical for family suppers as well
as making excellent dinner party starters for the
confident cook.

PREPARING A SOUFFLE DISH

1 Using a piece of string, measure
the height of the dish and its circumference.

2 Cut a strip from two thicknesses of
greaseproof paper or non-stick baking
parchment that exceeds the height of
the dish by 7.5 cm/3 inches and is long
enough to go right around the dish
with an overlap.

3 Tie the paper around the dish with
string. If the dish has sloping sides or
a projecting rim, secure the paper
above and below the rim with gummed
tape or pins. Make sure the paper has
no creases and forms a neat round
shape.

4 For a hot soufflé, it is not essential
to add a collar because the mixture
sets and holds its shape as it cooks.
However some cooks prefer using a
collar for an 'even' shape. Grease the
inside of the dish and paper collar with
clarified butter or oil.

SAVOURY SOUFFLE

Individual hot soufflés make a very good starter, light main course or savoury finish to a meal. The quantity of mixture below will make 6 individual soufflés in 200 ml/7 fl oz dishes, and will take 20 minutes to bake.

fat for greasing
50 g/2 oz butter
25 g/1 oz plain flour
250 ml/8 fl oz milk
100-150 g/4-5 oz Cheddar cheese, grated,
    or 75-100 g/3-4 oz mixed grated
    Parmesan and Gruyère cheese
salt and pepper
2.5 ml/½ tsp dry mustard
pinch of cayenne pepper
4 eggs, separated, plus 1 egg white

Prepare a 1 litre/1¾ pint soufflé dish (page 88). Set the oven at 190°C/375°F/gas 5.

Melt the butter in a saucepan, stir in the flour and cook over a low heat for 2-3 minutes without colouring, stirring all the time. Over a very low heat, gradually add the milk, stirring constantly. Bring to the boil, stirring, and simmer 1-2 minutes more until smooth and thickened. Remove from the heat and beat hard until the sauce comes away cleanly from the sides of the pan. Cool slightly and put into a bowl. Stir in the cheese, salt, pepper, mustard and cayenne.

Beat the yolks into the mixture one by one. In a clean, grease-free bowl, whisk all the egg whites until stiff. Using a metal spoon, stir one spoonful of the whites into the mixture to lighten it, then fold in the rest until evenly distributed.

Spoon the mixture into the prepared dish and bake for 30-35 minutes, until well risen and browned. Serve immediately with hot buttered toast.

SERVES 4

> **MRS BEETON'S TIP** The flavour of some soufflés, such as those made with fish or white meat, can be bland, so it is a good idea to infuse the milk with plenty of flavouring as when making a white sauce (see Stuffed Baked Cannelloni, page 46).

VARIATIONS

CHEESE AND ONION SOUFFLE Add 50 g/2 oz very finely chopped onion cooked in the butter for 2-3 minutes until transparent, to the cheese.

CHEESE AND WATERCRESS SOUFFLE Chop the leaves from half a bunch of watercress and add to the cheese.

LAYERED CHEESE SOUFFLE Put half the soufflé mixture into the dish and add a layer of 75 g/3 oz sautéed mushrooms, or 100 g/4 oz cooked flaked fish, or 45 ml/3 tbsp spinach purée and then the remaining mixture.

OEUFS MOLLETS EN SOUFFLE Soft boil 4 small eggs. Put one-third of the soufflé mixture into the dish. Arrange the eggs on top. Add the remainder of the mixture and bake.

CHICKEN SOUFFLE Add 200 g/7 oz cooked minced chicken, 25 g/1 oz chopped sautéed onion, 30 ml/2 tbsp lemon juice and 5 ml/1 tsp chopped parsley.

POTATO SOUFFLE

butter for greasing
500 g/18 oz potatoes
3 eggs, separated, plus 1 egg white
100 g/4 oz Cheddar cheese, finely grated
salt and pepper
grated nutmeg
50 g/2 oz butter
125 ml/4 fl oz top of the milk
30 ml/2 tbsp chopped parsley

Prepare a 1 litre/1¾ pint soufflé dish (page 88). Cook the potatoes in a saucepan of boiling salted water for about 20 minutes.

Set the oven at 190°C/375°F/gas 5. Mash the potatoes and put them through a sieve. Add a generous amount of salt, pepper and nutmeg. Stir in the rest of the ingredients except the egg whites. Beat well with a wooden spoon until smooth.

In a clean, grease-free bowl, whisk all the egg whites until stiff. Using a metal spoon, stir one spoonful of the whites into the potato mixture to lighten it, then fold in the rest until evenly distributed. Spoon the mixture into the prepared dish.

Bake for 30-35 minutes, until well risen and browned. Serve at once.

SERVES 4

VARIATION

FISH AND POTATO SOUFFLE Make as for Potato Soufflé using 350 g/12 oz potatoes. Poach 200 g/7 oz white fish, cod or haddock, for 10 minutes in the milk. Drain, remove any skin or bone from the fish, then flake the flesh. Omit the cheese and add the flaked fish, the milk made up to 125 ml/4 fl oz if necessary, and a few drops of anchovy essence, if liked.

SPINACH SOUFFLE

Accompany this colourful soufflé with biscuits or cheese straws.

fat for greasing
25 g/1 oz butter
30 ml/2 tbsp plain flour
125 g/4½ oz spinach purée
125 ml/4 fl oz single cream
50 g/2 oz cheese, finely grated
salt and pepper
4 eggs, separated, plus 1 egg white
grated Parmesan cheese, to garnish
   (optional)

Prepare a 1 litre/1¾ pint soufflé dish (page 88). Set the oven at 190°C/375°F/ gas 5.

Melt the butter in a saucepan, stir in the flour and cook over a low heat for 2-3 minutes without colouring, stirring all the time. Stir in the spinach purée and add the cream gradually, still stirring. Cook for 1-2 minutes more, still stirring. Remove from the heat, stir in the cheese, then beat hard until the sauce comes away cleanly from the sides of the pan. Cool slightly and put into a bowl. Add salt and pepper to taste.

Beat the yolks into the mixture one by one. In a clean, grease-free bowl, whisk all the egg whites until stiff. Using a metal spoon, stir one spoonful of the whites into the mixture to lighten it, then fold in the rest until evenly distributed. Spoon the mixture into the prepared dish.

Bake for 30-35 minutes until well risen and browned. Sprinkle with grated Parmesan cheese, if liked. Serve immediately.

SERVES 4

PARSNIP SOUFFLE

butter for greasing
200 g/7 oz parsnips
65 g/2½ oz butter
30 ml/2 tbsp grated onion
45 ml/3 tbsp plain flour
100 ml/3½ fl oz vegetable stock or parsnip
    cooking water
100 ml/3½ fl oz milk
30 ml/2 tbsp chopped parsley
salt and pepper
pinch of grated nutmeg
4 eggs, separated
125 ml/4 fl oz sauce (see Stuffed Baked
    Cannelloni, page 46)

Prepare a 1 litre/1¾ pint soufflé dish
(page 88). Cook the parsnips in a saucepan
with a little boiling salted water for about
30 minutes until tender. Mash and sieve
them, working into a smooth purée. Measure out 150 g/5 oz purée, and keep the rest
on one side.

Melt 15 g/½ oz of the butter in a frying
pan and gently cook the onion until soft.
Mix it with the parsnip purée.

Set the oven at 190°C/375°F/gas 5. Melt
the remaining butter in a saucepan, stir in
the flour and cook over a low heat for 2-3
minutes, without colouring, stirring all the
time. Mix the stock or water and the milk.
Over a very low heat, gradually add the
liquid to the pan, stirring constantly. Bring
to the boil, stirring, and simmer for 1-2
minutes until smooth and thickened. Stir in
the parsnip purée and parsley. Add salt,
pepper and nutmeg to taste. Cool slightly
and put into a bowl.

Beat the yolks into the mixture one by
one. In a clean, grease-free bowl, whisk all
the egg whites until stiff. Using a metal
spoon, fold into the mixture. Spoon the
mixture into the prepared dish. Bake for
25-30 minutes, until risen and set.

Meanwhile, mix the remaining purée
with the Béchamel sauce, and heat gently.
Serve separately in a warmed sauce-boat.

SERVES 4

CHEESE RAMEKINS

*Serve these individual savoury soufflés as a
spectacular start to a special meal.*

butter for greasing
about 50 ml/2 fl oz milk
about 25 g/1 oz fresh white breadcrumbs
25 g/1 oz Parmesan cheese, grated
25 g/1 oz Cheshire cheese, finely grated
25 g/1 oz unsalted butter, softened
1 egg, separated
salt and pepper
pinch of ground mace

Grease 4 small ovenproof pots or ramekins. Set the oven at 200°C/400°F/gas 6.

Heat the milk and pour just enough over
the breadcrumbs to cover them. Leave to
stand for 5-10 minutes. Stir in the cheeses
and butter. Beat the yolk into the cheese
mixture. Add salt, pepper and mace to
taste. In a clean, grease-free bowl, whisk
the egg white until stiff. Using a metal
spoon, stir one spoonful of the white into
the cheese mixture to lighten it, then fold
in the rest. Spoon into the prepared pots
or ramekins.

Bake for 15-20 minutes until risen and
slightly browned. Serve immediately.

SERVES 4

VANILLA SOUFFLE

fat for greasing
40 g/1½ oz butter
40 g/1½ oz plain flour
250 ml/8 fl oz milk
4 eggs, separated, plus 1 egg white
50 g/2 oz caster sugar
2.5 ml/½ tsp vanilla essence
caster or icing sugar for dredging

Prepare a 1 litre/1¾ pint soufflé dish (page 88). Set the oven at 180°C/350°F/gas 4.

Melt the butter in a saucepan, stir in the flour and cook slowly for 2-3 minutes without colouring, stirring all the time. Add the milk gradually and beat until smooth. Cook for 1-2 minutes more, still stirring. Remove from the heat and beat hard until the sauce comes away cleanly from the sides of the pan. Cool slightly and put into a bowl.

Beat the yolks into the flour mixture one by one. Beat in the sugar and vanilla.

In a clean, grease-free bowl, whisk all the egg whites until stiff. Using a metal spoon, stir one spoonful of the whites into the mixture to lighten it, then fold in the rest until evenly distributed.

Spoon into the prepared dish and bake for 45 minutes until well risen and browned. Dredge with caster or icing sugar and serve immediately with a jam sauce.

SERVES 4 TO 6

VARIATIONS

ALMOND SOUFFLE   Add 100 g/4 oz ground almonds, 15 ml/1 tbsp lemon juice and a few drops of ratafia essence to the mixture before adding the egg yolks. Reduce the sugar to 40 g/1½ oz. Omit the vanilla essence.

COFFEE SOUFFLE   Add 30 ml/2 tbsp instant coffee dissolved in a little hot water before adding the egg yolks, or use 125 ml/4 fl oz strong black coffee and only 125 ml/4 fl oz milk. Omit the vanilla essence.

GINGER SOUFFLE   Add a pinch of ground ginger and 50 g/2 oz chopped preserved stem ginger before adding the egg yolks. Omit the vanilla essence. Serve each portion topped with double cream and a spoonful of ginger syrup.

LEMON SOUFFLE   Add the thinly grated rind and juice of 1 lemon before adding the egg yolks. Omit the vanilla essence. Serve with lemon sauce, if liked.

LIQUEUR SOUFFLE   Add 30 ml/2 tbsp Cointreau, kirsch or curaçao instead of vanilla essence and make as for Soufflé au Grand Marnier below. Serve with sweetened cream flavoured with the liqueur.

ORANGE SOUFFLE   Thinly pare the rind of 2 oranges. Put in a saucepan with the milk and bring slowly to the boil. Remove from the heat, cover, and leave to stand for 10 minutes, then remove the rind. Make up the sauce using the flavoured milk. Reduce the sugar to 40 g/1½ oz and omit the vanilla essence. Add the strained juice of ½ orange.

SOUFFLE AU GRAND MARNIER   Add 30-45 ml/2-3 tbsp Grand Marnier to the orange soufflé mixture. Serve with an orange sauce made by boiling 125 ml/4 fl oz orange juice and a few drops of liqueur with 50 g/2 oz caster sugar until syrupy. Add very fine strips of orange rind.

SOUFFLE AMBASSADRICE   Crumble 2 Almond Macaroons (page 110); soak them in 30 ml/2 tbsp rum with 50 g/2 oz chopped blanched almonds. Stir into a vanilla soufflé mixture.

SOUFFLE ROTHSCHILD   Rinse 50 g/2 oz mixed glacé fruit in hot water to remove any excess sugar. Chop the fruit and soak it in 30 ml/2 tbsp brandy or kirsch for 2 hours. Make up 1 quantity vanilla soufflé mixture. Put half the vanilla soufflé mixture into the dish, add the fruit, and then the rest of the soufflé mixture.

FRUIT SOUFFLES

For fruit-flavoured soufflés a thick, sweet purée is added to the basic vanilla soufflé. It is important that the purée should have a strong flavour, otherwise the taste will not be discernible. If extra purée is added, the soufflé will be heavy and will not rise.

APPLE SOUFFLE Add 125 ml/ 4 fl oz thick sweet apple purée, 15 ml/ 1 tbsp lemon juice, and a pinch of powdered cinnamon to the soufflé before adding the egg yolks. Dust with cinnamon before serving.

APRICOT SOUFFLE Before adding the egg yolks, add 125 ml/4 fl oz thick apricot purée and 15 ml/1 tbsp lemon juice, if using fresh apricots. If using canned apricots (1 × 397 g/14 oz can yields 125 ml/4 fl oz purée) use half milk and half can syrup for the sauce. A purée made from dried apricots makes a delicious soufflé.

PINEAPPLE SOUFFLE Before adding the egg yolks, add 125 ml/ 4 fl oz crushed pineapple or 75 g/3 oz chopped fresh pineapple, and make the sauce using half milk and half pineapple juice.

RASPBERRY SOUFFLE Before adding the egg yolks, add 125 ml/ 4 fl oz raspberry purée (1 × 397 g/ 14 oz can yields 125 ml/4 fl oz purée) and 10 ml/2 tsp lemon juice.

STRAWBERRY SOUFFLE Before adding the egg yolks, add 125 ml/ 4 fl oz strawberry purée. Make the sauce using half milk and half single cream. Add a little pink food colouring, if necessary.

CHOCOLATE DREAM

fat for greasing
100 g/4 oz plain chocolate
400 ml/14 fl oz milk
50 g/2 oz caster sugar
50 g/2 oz plain flour
15 ml/1 tbsp butter
3 eggs, separated, plus 1 egg white
icing sugar for dusting

Prepare a 1.1 litre/2 pint soufflé dish (page 88). Set the oven at 180°C/350°F/gas 4.

Break the chocolate into pieces and put into a saucepan. Reserve 60 ml/4 tbsp of the milk in a mixing bowl and pour the rest into the pan with the chocolate. Add the sugar and warm over a low heat until the chocolate begins to melt. Remove from the heat and leave to stand until the chocolate is completely melted, stirring occasionally.

Add the flour to the bowl containing the milk and stir to a smooth paste. Stir in the chocolate-flavoured milk, return the mixture to the clean pan and bring to the boil. Cook for 1-2 minutes, stirring all the time, then remove from the heat and add the butter. Stir well, then set aside to cool slightly.

Beat the egg yolks into the chocolate mixture one at a time. In a clean, grease-free bowl, whisk the egg whites until stiff. Stir one spoonful of the egg whites into the chocolate mixture to lighten it, then fold in the rest until evenly blended.

Spoon into the prepared dish and bake for 45 minutes. Dust with icing sugar and serve immediately.

SERVES 4

PUDDINGS

The selection of baked puddings on offer in this chapter includes some of the best of British baking, with heart-warming recipes such as Eve's Pudding and old favourites like Rice Pudding or Queen of Puddings. They are the perfect endings for winter meals.

ACCOMPANIMENTS FOR PUDDINGS

Cream   Single, whipping or double cream may be poured over puddings. Whipping and double creams may be whipped until thickened or canned aerated dairy cream may be served. Look out for low-fat creams and non-dairy creams.

Yogurt   Plain low-fat yogurt makes a tangy accompaniment for rich puddings. Creamy Greek yogurt is richer and thicker. Combine low-fat yogurt with whipped whipping cream for a light topping.

Fromage Frais   Available with different fat contents, this very soft, lightly fermented cheese is an alternative to cream.

Sweet Butters   Unsalted butter beaten with icing sugar (between half and three-quarters its weight) may be flavoured with brandy, rum or citrus rind and juice, then used to top sponge puddings.

Chocolate Sauce   Simply melt dark plain chocolate with golden syrup (about 60 ml/ 4 tbsp syrup to 225 g/8 oz chocolate) and a knob of butter to make a rich sauce. Add a dash of brandy, rum or some grated orange rind. Good with sponge puddings.

Jam Sauces   Warmed jam thinned with a little boiling water makes a quick sauce for baked sponges or milk puddings. Raspberry, strawberry, apricot or plum jam are just a few examples.

VANILLA CUSTARD

Adding cornflour stabilizes the custard and makes it less inclined to curdle.

10 ml/2 tsp cornflour
500 ml/17 fl oz milk
25 g/1 oz caster sugar
2 eggs
vanilla essence

In a bowl, mix the cornflour to a smooth paste with a little of the cold milk. Heat the rest of the milk in a saucepan and when hot pour it on to the blended cornflour, stirring.

Return the mixture to the saucepan, bring to the boil and boil for 1-2 minutes, stirring all the time, to cook the cornflour. Remove from the heat and stir in the sugar. Leave to cool.

Beat the eggs together lightly in a small bowl. Add a little of the cooked cornflour mixture, stir well, then pour into the saucepan. Heat gently for a few minutes until the custard has thickened, stirring all the time. Do not boil. Stir in a few drops of vanilla essence.

Serve hot or cold as an accompaniment to a pudding or pie.

MAKES ABOUT 600 ML/1 PINT

———————— ◇ ————————

BAKED APPLES

Illustrated on page 80

6 cooking apples
75 g/3 oz sultanas, chopped
50 g/2 oz demerara sugar

Set the oven at 180°C/350°F/gas 4. Wash and core the apples. Cut around the skin of each apple with the tip of a sharp knife two-thirds of the way up from the base. Put the apples into an ovenproof dish, and fill the centres with the chopped sultanas.

Sprinkle the demerara sugar on top of the apples and pour 75 ml/5 tbsp water around them. Bake for 45-60 minutes, depending on the cooking quality and size of the apples.

Serve with Vanilla Custard (opposite), ice cream, brandy butter or with whipped cream.

SERVES 6

VARIATIONS

Fill the apple cavities with a mixture of 50 g/2 oz Barbados or other raw sugar and 50 g/2 oz butter, or use blackcurrant, raspberry, strawberry or apricot jam, or marmalade. Instead of sultanas, chopped stoned dates, raisins or currants could be used. A topping of toasted almonds looks effective and tastes delicious.

☀ **MICROWAVE TIP** Baked apples cook superbly in the microwave. Prepare as suggested above, but reduce the amount of water to 30 ml/2 tbsp. Cook for 10-12 minutes on High.

APPLE CHARLOTTE

butter for greasing
400 g/14 oz cooking apples
grated rind and juice of 1 lemon
100 g/4 oz soft light brown sugar
pinch of ground cinnamon
50-75 g/2-3 oz butter
8-10 large slices white bread, about
    5 mm/¼ inch thick
15 ml/1 tbsp caster sugar

Generously grease a 1 litre/1¾ pint charlotte mould or 15 cm/6 inch cake tin with butter. Set the oven at 180°C/350°F/gas 4. Peel and core the apples. Slice them into a saucepan and add the lemon rind and juice. Stir in the brown sugar and cinnamon and simmer until the apples soften to a thick purée. Leave to cool.

Melt the butter in a saucepan, then pour into a shallow dish. Cut the crusts off the bread, and dip 1 slice in the butter. Cut it into a round to fit the bottom of the mould or tin. Fill any spaces with extra butter-soaked bread, if necessary. Dip the remaining bread slices in the butter. Use 6 slices to line the inside of the mould. The slices should touch one another to make a bread case.

Fill the bread case with the cooled apple purée. Complete the case by fitting the top with more bread slices. Cover loosely with greased greaseproof paper or foil, and bake for 40-45 minutes. To serve the charlotte, turn out and dredge with caster sugar. Serve with bramble jelly and cream.

SERVES 6

🥣 **MRS BEETON'S TIP** The mould or tin may be lined with slices of bread and butter, placed buttered side out.

EVE'S PUDDING

Illustrated on page 75

fat for greasing
450 g/1 lb cooking apples
grated rind and juice of 1 lemon
75 g/3 oz demerara sugar
75 g/3 oz butter or margarine
75 g/3 oz caster sugar
1 egg, beaten
100 g/4 oz self-raising flour
icing sugar for dusting

Grease a 1 litre/1¾ pint pie dish. Set the oven at 180°C/350°F/gas 4. Peel and core the apples and slice them thinly into a large bowl. Add the lemon rind and juice, with the demerara sugar. Stir in 15 ml/1 tbsp water, then tip the mixture into the prepared pie dish.

In a mixing bowl, cream the butter or margarine with the caster sugar until light and fluffy. Beat in the egg. Fold in the flour lightly and spread the mixture over the apples.

Bake for 40-45 minutes until the apples are soft and the sponge is firm. Dust with icing sugar. Serve with melted apple jelly and single cream or Greek yogurt.

SERVES 4

VARIATIONS

Instead of apples use 450 g/1 lb apricots, peaches, gooseberries, rhubarb, raspberries or plums.

NUTTY PLUM CRUMBLE

Illustrated on page 78

Tangy plums and toasted hazelnuts make a tasty combination in this tempting pudding. Apples, rhubarb, gooseberries, or a mixture of fruit may be used instead of the plums.

675 g/1½ lb plums, halved and stoned
50 g/2 oz sugar

TOPPING
175 g/6 oz plain flour
75 g/3 oz butter or margarine
25 g/1 oz demerara sugar
5 ml/1 tsp ground cinnamon
75 g/3 oz hazelnuts, toasted and chopped

Set the oven at 180°C/350°F/gas 4. Place the plums in an ovenproof dish and sprinkle with the sugar.

Make the topping. Sift the flour into a mixing bowl and rub in the butter or margarine until the mixture resembles fine breadcrumbs. Stir in the sugar, cinnamon and hazelnuts.

Sprinkle the topping evenly over the plums, pressing it down very lightly. Bake the crumble for about 45 minutes, until the topping is golden brown and the plums are cooked. Serve with custard, cream or vanilla ice cream.

SERVES 4 TO 6

BAKED SPONGE PUDDING

fat for greasing
100 g/4 oz butter or margarine
100 g/4 oz caster sugar
2 eggs, beaten
150 g/5 oz plain flour
5 ml/1 tsp baking powder
1.25 ml/¼ tsp vanilla essence
about 30 ml/2 tbsp milk

Grease a 1 litre/1¾ pint pie dish. Set the oven at 180°C/350°F/gas 4. In a mixing bowl, cream the butter or margarine with the sugar until light and fluffy. Gradually beat in the eggs. Sift the flour and baking powder together into a bowl, then fold them into the creamed mixture. Add the vanilla essence and enough milk to form a soft dropping consistency.

Spoon the mixture into the prepared pie dish and bake for 30-35 minutes until well risen and golden brown.

Serve from the dish with Vanilla Custard (page 94) or any sweet sauce.

SERVES 4 TO 6

VARIATIONS

JAM SPONGE   Put 30 ml/2 tbsp jam in the base of the dish before adding the sponge mixture. Serve with a jam sauce made with the same type of jam.
ORANGE OR LEMON SPONGE   Add the grated rind of 1 orange or lemon to the creamed mixture. Serve with a lemon sauce, if liked.
SPICY SPONGE   Sift 5 ml/1 tsp mixed spice, ground ginger, grated nutmeg or cinnamon with the flour. Serve with Vanilla Custard (page 94).
COCONUT SPONGE   Substitute 25 g/1 oz desiccated coconut for 25 g/1 oz flour. Serve with an apricot jam sauce.

CHOCOLATE SPONGE Substitute 50 g/2 oz cocoa for 50 g/2 oz flour.

HONESTY PUDDING

fat for greasing
50 g/2 oz fine oatmeal
15 ml/1 tbsp plain flour
750 ml/1¼ pints milk
1 egg, beaten
pinch of salt
2.5 ml/½ tsp grated orange rind

Grease a 750 ml/1¼ pint pie dish. Set the oven at 180°C/350°F/gas 4. Put the oatmeal and flour in a bowl and mix to a smooth paste with a little of the milk. Bring the rest of the milk to the boil in a saucepan, then pour it over the oatmeal mixture, stirring all the time.

Return the mixture to the clean pan and cook over a low heat for 5 minutes, stirring all the time. Remove from the heat, and cool for 5 minutes.

Beat the egg into the cooled oatmeal mixture. Flavour with the salt and orange rind. Pour the mixture into the prepared pie dish, and bake for 35-40 minutes.

Serve hot from the dish, with cream and brown sugar.

SERVES 4

CASTLE PUDDINGS

fat for greasing
100 g/4 oz butter or margarine
100 g/4 oz caster sugar
2 eggs
1.25 ml/¼ tsp vanilla essence
100 g/4 oz plain flour
5 ml/1 tsp baking powder

Grease 6-8 dariole moulds. Set the oven at 180°C/350°F/gas 4.

In a mixing bowl, cream the butter or margarine with the sugar until light and creamy. Beat in the eggs and vanilla essence. Sift the flour and baking powder into a bowl, then fold into the creamed mixture.

Three-quarters fill the prepared dariole moulds. Bake for 20-25 minutes, until set and well risen. Serve with Vanilla Custard (page 94) or a jam sauce.

SERVES 6 TO 8

VARIATION

SOMERSET PUDDINGS Serve the puddings cold, with the inside of each scooped out, and the cavity filled with stewed apple or jam. Serve with whipped cream.

ALMOND CASTLES

fat for greasing
75 g/3 oz butter
75 g/3 oz caster sugar
3 eggs, separated
45 ml/3 tbsp single cream or milk
15 ml/1 tbsp brandy
150 g/5 oz ground almonds

Grease 8 dariole moulds. Set the oven at 160°C/325°F/gas 3.

In a mixing bowl, cream the butter and sugar until light and fluffy. Stir in the egg yolks, cream or milk, brandy and ground almonds.

In a clean, grease-free bowl, whisk the egg whites until just stiff, and fold lightly into the mixture. Three-quarters fill the dariole moulds and bake for 20-25 minutes, until the puddings are firm in the centre and golden brown.

Turn out on to individual plates and serve with Vanilla Custard (page 94).

SERVES 8

COTTAGE PUDDING

butter for greasing
200 g/7 oz plain flour
pinch of salt
10 ml/2 tsp baking powder
100 g/4 oz butter or margarine
75 g/3 oz soft light brown sugar
100 g/4 oz raisins
1 egg, beaten
45-75 ml/3-5 tbsp milk

Grease a 25 × 20 cm/10 × 8 inch baking dish. Set the oven at 190°C/375°F/gas 5.

Sift the flour, salt and baking powder into a mixing bowl. Rub in the butter or margarine and add the sugar and raisins. Stir in the egg, with enough milk to make a soft dropping consistency.

Spoon the mixture into the prepared baking dish and bake for 35-40 minutes until firm in the centre and golden brown.

Serve with Vanilla Custard (page 94).

SERVES 6

COLLEGE PUDDINGS

fat for greasing
100 g/4 oz plain flour
2.5 ml/½ tsp baking powder
pinch of salt
1.25 ml/¼ tsp mixed spice
100 g/4 oz dry white breadcrumbs
75 g/3 oz shredded suet
75 g/3 oz caster sugar
50 g/2 oz currants
50 g/2 oz sultanas
2 eggs, beaten
100-125 ml/3½-4 fl oz milk

Grease 6-8 dariole moulds. Set the oven at 190°C/375°F/gas 5.

Sift the flour, baking powder, salt and spice into a mixing bowl. Add the crumbs, suet, sugar, currants and sultanas, and mix well. Stir in the eggs with enough milk to form a soft dropping consistency.

Half fill the prepared dariole moulds with the mixture and bake for 20-25 minutes.

Turn out and serve with a fruit sauce, if liked.

SERVES 6 TO 8

EXETER PUDDING

butter for greasing
100 g/4 oz dry white breadcrumbs
25 g/1 oz small Almond Macaroons
    (page 112)
75 g/3 oz shredded suet
50 g/2 oz sago
75 g/3 oz caster sugar
grated rind and juice of 1 lemon
3 eggs
30 ml/2 tbsp milk
2 individual sponge cakes or trifle
    sponges, sliced
75 g/3 oz jam (any type)

Grease a 1 litre/1¾ pint pie dish. Coat with some of the crumbs, and cover the base with half the macaroons. Set the oven at 180°C/350°F/gas 4.

Put the remaining crumbs into a mixing bowl with the suet, sago, sugar, lemon rind and juice. In a separate bowl, beat together the eggs and milk. Stir the liquid mixture into the dry ingredients.

Spoon a layer of the suet mixture into the prepared pie dish and cover with some of the slices of sponge cake. Add a layer of jam and some of the remaining ratafias. Repeat the layers until all the ingredients are used, finishing with a layer of suet mixture.

Bake for 45-60 minutes. Serve with a jam sauce using the same jam as that used in the recipe.

SERVES 6

ARANYGALUSKA BORSODOVAL

These tempting baked golden dumplings from Hungary are served with a white wine sauce.

fat for greasing
400 g/14 oz plain flour
pinch of salt
30 ml/2 tbsp caster sugar
100 g/4 oz softened butter
400 ml/14 fl oz milk
15 g/½ oz fresh yeast or 10 ml/2 tsp dried
   yeast
3 egg yolks
flour for rolling out
100 g/4 oz apricot jam
100 g/4 oz ground walnuts

SAUCE
2 eggs
50 g/2 oz caster sugar
5 ml/1 tsp plain flour
250 ml/8 fl oz medium-sweet white wine

Lightly grease a 25 cm/10 inch cake tin. Sift together the flour, salt and sugar, reserving 2.5 ml/½ tsp, into a large bowl. Rub in half the softened butter. Warm one-third of the milk until lukewarm.

Blend the fresh yeast to a thin paste with the reserved sugar and the likewarm milk. Set aside in a warm place until frothy – about 5 minutes. Sprinkle dried yeast over the lukewarm milk and set aside until frothy, then stir well.

Pour the yeast mixture, egg yolks and the rest of the milk into the flour mixture, then mix to a soft dough. Turn on to a floured surface and knead for about 10 minutes or until the dough is smooth, elastic and no longer sticky. Return to the bowl and cover with cling film. Leave in a warm place until the dough has doubled in volume – this will take up to 2 hours, or longer.

Roll out the dough on a floured surface to about 1 cm/½ inch thickness. Cut out circles with a 5 cm/2 inch pastry cutter. Melt the remaining butter and dip the dough circles in it until completely coated. Place them about 2.5 cm/1 inch apart in the prepared cake tin. Brush the tops with a layer of jam and sprinkle with walnuts.

Place the cake tin in a large, lightly oiled polythene bag and leave in a warm place for about 30 minutes or until the circles have joined together and are light and puffy. Set the oven at 180°C/350°F/gas 4. Bake for 35 minutes until golden brown.

Prepare the sauce 5 minutes before the dumplings are cooked. Whisk together the eggs, sugar and flour in a large heatproof bowl. When the mixture has thickened, place the bowl over a pan of simmering water or pour the sauce into a double saucepan over heat. Slowly add the wine. Continue whisking until the sauce is light and fluffy. Pour immediately over the dumplings and serve hot.

SERVES 8

RICE PUDDING

This basic recipe works equally well with flaked rice, sago or flaked tapioca.

butter for greasing
100 g/4 oz pudding rice
1 litre/1¾ pints milk
pinch of salt
50-75 g/2-3 oz caster sugar
15 g/½ oz butter (optional)
1.25 ml/¼ tsp grated nutmeg

Butter a 1.75 litre/3 pint pie dish. Wash the rice in cold water, drain and put it into the dish with the milk. Leave to stand for 30 minutes.

Set the oven at 150°C/300°F/gas 2. Stir the salt and sugar into the milk mixture and sprinkle with flakes of butter, if used, and nutmeg.

Bake for 2-2½ hours or until the pudding is thick and creamy, and brown on the top. The pudding is better if it cooks even more slowly, at 120°C/250°F/gas ½ for 4-5 hours.

SERVES 4 TO 6

PRESSURE COOKER TIP Bring all the ingredients to the boil in the open cooker, stirring. Reduce the heat so that the milk just bubbles. Put the lid on and bring to 15 lb pressure without increasing the heat. Cook for 12 minutes. Reduce pressure slowly.

QUEEN OF PUDDINGS

butter for greasing
75 g/3 oz fresh white breadcrumbs
400 ml/14 fl oz milk
25 g/1 oz butter
10 ml/2 tsp grated lemon rind
2 eggs, separated
75 g/3 oz caster sugar
30 ml/2 tbsp red jam

Grease a 750 ml/1¼ pint pie dish. Set the oven at 160°C/325°F/gas 3. Spread the breadcrumbs out on a baking sheet and put into the oven to dry off slightly.

Warm the milk and butter with the lemon rind in a saucepan. Meanwhile put the egg yolks in a bowl and stir in 25 g/1 oz of the sugar. Pour on the warmed milk mixture, stirring thoroughly. Add the breadcrumbs, mix thoroughly and pour into the prepared pie dish. Leave to stand for 30 minutes.

Bake the pudding for 40-50 minutes until lightly set, then remove from the oven. Reduce the oven temperature to 120°C/250°F/gas ½. Warm the jam in a small saucepan until runny, then spread it over the top of the pudding.

In a clean, grease-free bowl, whisk the egg whites until stiff. Add half the remaining sugar and whisk again. Fold in all but 30 ml/2 tbsp of the remaining sugar. Spoon the meringue around the edge of the jam, drawing it up into peaks at regular intervals to resemble a crown. Sprinkle with the rest of the sugar.

Return the pudding to the oven and bake for 40-45 minutes more, until the meringue is set.

SERVES 4

CAKES AND BISCUITS

This chapter concentrates on the classic cakes and biscuits that form the basis for many more elaborate variations, from plain Victoria Sandwich cake to Dundee Cake or Rich Fruit Cake and melt-in-the-mouth Shortbread. A couple of recipes for savoury biscuits are included at the end of the chapter.

BUTTERCREAM

100 g/4 oz butter, softened
15 ml/1 tbsp milk or fruit juice
225 g/8 oz icing sugar, sifted

In a mixing bowl, cream the butter with the milk or juice and gradually work in the icing sugar. Beat the icing until light and fluffy. Alternatively, work all the ingredients in a food processor, removing the plunger for the final mixing to allow air to enter the buttercream mixture.

SUFFICIENT TO FILL AND TOP A 20 CM/ 8 INCH CAKE

VARIATIONS

CHOCOLATE BUTTERCREAM Grate 50 g/2 oz block plain chocolate. Place it in a basin over hot water with 15 ml/1 tbsp milk, stir until dissolved, then cool. Use instead of the milk or fruit juice.
COFFEE BUTTERCREAM Dissolve 5 ml/1 tsp instant coffee in 15 ml/1 tbsp hot water. Cool before use. Use instead of the milk or fruit juice.
LEMON OR ORANGE BUTTERCREAM Use 15 ml/1 tbsp juice and a little grated rind.
VANILLA BUTTERCREAM Add 2.5 ml/½ tsp vanilla essence with the milk.
WALNUT BUTTERCREAM Add 25 g/1 oz chopped walnuts.

ALMOND PASTE

225 g/8 oz ground almonds
100 g/4 oz caster sugar
100 g/4 oz icing sugar
5 ml/1 tsp lemon juice
few drops of almond essence
1 egg, beaten

Using a coarse sieve, sift the almonds, caster sugar and icing sugar into a mixing bowl. Add the lemon juice, almond essence and sufficient egg to bind the ingredients together. Knead lightly with the fingertips until smooth.

Wrap in cling film and overwrap in foil or a plastic bag to prevent the paste drying out. Store in a cool place until required.

MAKES ABOUT 450 G/1 LB

> **MRS BEETON'S TIP** Don't knead the paste too much: this can draw the oils from the almonds and make the paste greasy. It will then be unsuitable as a base for icing.

VICTORIA SANDWICH CAKE

The original Victoria Sandwich was oblong, filled with jam or marmalade and cut into fingers or sandwiches. Now, the basic mixture is used with many different flavourings and fillings and is served as a single, round cake. For a softer centred cake, bake the mixture in a 20 cm/8 inch round cake tin, then split and fill. All loose crumbs must be brushed off before filling. Keep the filling fairly firm – if it is too moist, it will seep into the cake.

fat for greasing
150 g/5 oz butter or margarine
150 g/5 oz caster sugar
3 eggs, beaten
150 g/5 oz self-raising flour or plain flour
   and 5 ml/1 tsp baking powder
pinch of salt
raspberry or other jam for filling
caster sugar for dredging

Line and grease two 18 cm/7 inch sandwich tins. Set the oven at 180°C/350°F/gas 4.

In a mixing bowl cream the butter or margarine with the sugar until light and fluffy. Add the eggs gradually, beating well after each addition. Sift the flour, salt and baking powder, if used, into a bowl. Stir into the creamed mixture, lightly but thoroughly, until evenly mixed.

Divide between the tins and bake for 25-30 minutes. Cool on a wire rack, then sandwich together with jam. Sprinkle the top with caster sugar or spread with Glacé Icing (page 103).

MAKES ONE 18 CM/7 INCH CAKE

ONE-STAGE VICTORIA SANDWICH

fat for greasing
150 g/5 oz self-raising flour
pinch of salt
150 g/5 oz soft margarine
150 g/5 oz caster sugar
3 eggs

Line and grease two 18 cm/7 inch sandwich tins. Set the oven at 180°C/350°F/gas 4.

Put all the ingredients in a mixing bowl and stir. Beat until smooth, allowing 2-3 minutes by hand or 1-1½ minutes with an electric mixer.

Divide the mixture evenly between the tins and level each surface. Bake for 25-30 minutes. Cool on a wire rack, then fill and top as desired.

MAKES ONE 18 CM/7 INCH CAKE

GLACÉ ICING

100 g/4 oz icing sugar, sifted
food colouring, optional

Place the icing sugar in a bowl. Using a wooden spoon gradually stir in sufficient warm water (about 15 ml/1 tbsp) to create icing whose consistency will thickly coat the back of the spoon. Take care not to add too much liquid or the icing will be too runny. At first the icing will seem quite stiff, but it slackens rapidly as the icing sugar absorbs the water. Stir in 1-2 drops of food colouring, if required.

SPONGE CAKE

fat for greasing
flour for dusting
3 eggs
75 g/3 oz caster sugar
75 g/3 oz plain flour
pinch of salt
pinch of baking powder

Grease an 18 cm/7 inch round cake tin or two 15 cm/6 inch sandwich tins. Dust with sifted flour, tapping out the excess. Set the oven at 180°C/350°F/gas 4.

Whisk the eggs and sugar together in a bowl over a saucepan of hot water, taking care that the base of the bowl does not touch the water. Continue whisking for 10-15 minutes until the mixture is thick and creamy. Remove the bowl from the pan. Whisk until cold.

Sift the flour, salt and baking powder into a bowl. Add to the creamed mixture, using a metal spoon. Do this lightly, so that the air incorporated during whisking is not lost. Pour the mixture into the prepared tins.

Bake a single 18 cm/7 inch cake for 40 minutes; two 15 cm/6 inch cakes for 25 minutes. Leave the sponge in the tins for a few minutes, then cool on a wire rack. Fill and top as desired.

MAKES ONE 18 CM/7 INCH CAKE OR TWO 15 CM/6 INCH LAYERS

> **MRS BEETON'S TIP** If an electric mixer is used there is no need to place the bowl over hot water. Whisk at high speed for about 5 minutes until thick. Fold in the flour by hand.

GENOESE SPONGE

For an 18 cm/7 inch square or 15 × 25 cm/6 × 10 inch oblong cake, use 75 g/3 oz flour, pinch of salt, 50 g/2 oz clarified butter or margarine, 3 eggs and 75 g/3 oz caster sugar.

fat for greasing
100 g/4 oz plain flour
2.5 ml/½ tsp salt
75 g/3 oz Clarified Butter (page 18) or margarine
4 eggs
100 g/4 oz caster sugar

Line and grease a 20 × 30 cm/8 × 12 inch Swiss roll tin. Set the oven at 180°C/350°F/gas 4.

Sift the flour and salt into a bowl and put in a warm place. Melt the clarified butter or margarine without letting it get hot.

Whisk the eggs lightly in a mixing bowl. Add the sugar and place the bowl over a saucepan of hot water. Whisk for 10-15 minutes until thick. Take care that the base of the bowl does not touch the water. Remove from the heat and continue whisking until at blood-heat. The melted butter should be at the same temperature.

Sift half the flour over the eggs, then pour in half the melted butter or margarine in a thin stream. Fold in gently. Repeat, using the remaining flour and fat. Spoon gently into the prepared tin and bake for 30-40 minutes. Cool on a wire rack.

MAKES ONE 20 × 30 CM/ 8 × 12 INCH CAKE

> **MICROWAVE TIP** Melt the clarified butter or margarine in a bowl on High for 45 seconds-1 minute.

SWISS ROLL

Illustrated on page 116

fat for greasing
3 eggs
75 g/3 oz caster sugar
75 g/3 oz plain flour
2.5 ml/½ tsp baking powder
pinch of salt
about 60 ml/4 tbsp jam for filling
caster sugar for dusting

Line and grease a 20 × 30 cm/8 × 12 inch Swiss roll tin. Set the oven at 220°C/425°F/gas 7.

Combine the eggs and sugar in a heat-proof bowl. Set the bowl over a pan of hot water, taking care that the bottom of the bowl does not touch the water. Whisk for 10-15 minutes until thick and creamy, then remove from the pan and continue whisking until the mixture is cold.

Sift the flour, baking powder and salt into a bowl, then lightly fold into the egg mixture. Pour into the prepared tin and bake for 10 minutes. Meanwhile warm the jam in a small saucepan.

When the cake is cooked, turn it on to a large sheet of greaseproof paper dusted with caster sugar. Peel off the lining paper. Trim off any crisp edges. Spread the cake with the warmed jam and roll up tightly from one long side. Dredge with caster sugar and place on a wire rack, with the join underneath, to cool.

MAKES ONE 30 CM/12 INCH SWISS ROLL

CHOCOLATE ROLL

fat for greasing
3 eggs
75 g/3 oz caster sugar
65 g/2½ oz plain flour
30 ml/2 tbsp cocoa
2.5 ml/½ tsp baking powder
pinch of salt
Chocolate Buttercream (page 102) for filling
caster sugar for dusting

Line and grease a 20 × 30 cm/8 × 12 inch Swiss roll tin. Set the oven at 220°C/425°F/gas 7.

Combine the eggs and sugar in a heat-proof bowl. Set the bowl over a pan of hot water, taking care that the bottom of the bowl does not touch the water. Whisk for 10-15 minutes until thick and creamy, then remove from the pan and continue whisking until the mixture is cold.

Sift the flour, cocoa, baking powder and salt into a bowl, then lightly fold into the egg mixture. Pour into the prepared tin and bake for 10 minutes.

When the cake is cooked, turn it on to a large sheet of greaseproof paper dusted with caster sugar. Peel off the lining paper. Trim off any crisp edges. Place a second piece of greaseproof paper on top of the cake and roll up tightly from one long side, with the paper inside. Cool completely on a wire rack.

When cold, unroll carefully, spread with the buttercream and roll up again. Dust with caster sugar.

MAKES ONE 30 CM/12 INCH SWISS ROLL

DUNDEE CAKE

Illustrated on page 113

fat for greasing
200 g/7 oz plain flour
2.5 ml/½ tsp baking powder
1.25 ml/¼ tsp salt
150 g/5 oz butter
150 g/5 oz caster sugar
4 eggs, beaten
100 g/4 oz glacé cherries, quartered
150 g/5 oz currants
150 g/5 oz sultanas
100 g/4 oz seedless raisins
50 g/2 oz cut mixed peel
50 g/2 oz ground almonds
grated rind of 1 lemon
50 g/2 oz blanched split almonds

Line and grease an 18 cm/7 inch round cake tin. Set the oven at 180°C/350°F/gas 4. Sift the flour, baking powder and salt into a bowl. In a mixing bowl, cream the butter and sugar together well, and beat in the eggs. Fold the flour mixture, cherries, dried fruit, peel and ground almonds into the creamed mixture. Add the lemon rind and mix well.

Spoon into the prepared tin and make a slight hollow in the centre. Bake for 20 minutes, by which time the hollow should have filled in. Arrange the split almonds on top.

Return the cake to the oven, bake for a further 40-45 minutes, then reduce the temperature to 160°C/325°F/gas 3 and bake for another hour. Cool on a wire rack.

MAKES ONE 18 CM/7 INCH CAKE

CLASSIC MADEIRA CAKE

fat for greasing
150 g/5 oz butter or margarine
150 g/5 oz caster sugar
4 eggs, beaten
200 g/7 oz plain flour
10 ml/2 tsp baking powder
pinch of salt
grated rind of 1 lemon
caster sugar for dredging
1 thin slice candied or glacé citron peel

Line and grease a 15 cm/6 inch round cake tin. Set the oven at 180°C/350°F/gas 4.

In a mixing bowl, cream the butter or margarine with the sugar until light and fluffy. Gradually add the eggs, beating well after each addition. Sift the flour, baking powder and salt together into a second bowl, then fold into the creamed mixture. Stir in the lemon rind and mix well. Spoon into the prepared tin. Dredge the top with caster sugar.

Bake for 20 minutes, then lay the slice of peel on top. Bake for a further 45-50 minutes or until cooked through and firm to the touch. Cool on a wire rack.

MAKES ONE 15 CM/6 INCH CAKE

MRS BEETON'S TIP If you do not have a sugar dredger, place a small amount of sugar in a tea strainer and pass it over the top of the cake.

*B*ATTENBURG CAKE

Illustrated on page 116

fat for greasing
100 g/4 oz self-raising flour
pinch of salt
100 g/4 oz butter or margarine
100 g/4 oz caster sugar
2 eggs
pink food colouring
Apricot Glaze (page 126)
200 g/7 oz Almond Paste (page 102)

Line and grease a 23 × 18 cm/9 × 7 inch battenburg tin, which has a metal divider down the centre; or use a 23 × 18 cm/9 × 7 inch tin and cut double greaseproof paper to separate the mixture into 2 parts. Set the oven at 190°C/375°F/gas 5. Mix the flour and salt in a bowl.

In a mixing bowl, cream the butter or margarine and sugar together until light and fluffy. Add the eggs, one at a time with a little flour. Stir in, then beat well. Stir in the remaining flour lightly but thoroughly.

Place half the mixture in one half of the tin. Tint the remaining mixture pink, and place it in the other half of the tin. Smooth both mixtures away from the centre towards the outside of the tin.

Bake for 25-30 minutes. Leave the cakes in the tin for a few minutes, then transfer them to a wire rack and peel off the paper. Leave to cool completely.

To finish the Battenburg, cut each slab of cake lengthways into 3 strips. Trim off any crisp edges and rounded surfaces so that all 6 strips are neat and of the same size. Arrange 3 strips with 1 pink strip in the middle. Where the cakes touch, brush with the glaze and press together lightly. Make up the other layer in the same way, using 2 pink strips with 1 plain strip in the middle. Brush glaze over the top of the base layer and place the second layer on top.

Roll out the almond paste thinly into a rectangle the same length as the strips and wide enough to wrap around them. Brush it with glaze and place the cake in the centre. Wrap the paste around the cake and press the edges together lightly. Turn so that the join is underneath; trim the ends. Mark the top of the paste with the back of a knife to make a criss-cross pattern.

MAKES ONE 23 × 18 CM/9 × 7 INCH CAKE

MICROWAVE TIP Almond paste that has hardened will become soft and malleable again if heated in the microwave for a few seconds on High.

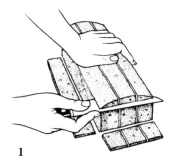

1

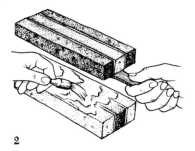

2

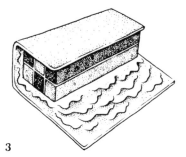

3

DATE AND WALNUT CAKE

fat for greasing
200 g/7 oz self-raising flour or 200 g/7 oz
    plain flour and 10 ml/2 tsp baking
    powder
pinch of grated nutmeg
75 g/3 oz margarine
75 g/3 oz dates, stoned and chopped
25 g/1 oz walnuts, chopped
75 g/3 oz soft light brown sugar
2 small eggs
about 125 ml/4 fl oz milk

Line and grease a 15 cm/6 inch tin. Set the oven at 180°C/350°F/gas 4.

Mix the flour and nutmeg in a mixing bowl, and rub in the margarine until the mixture resembles fine breadcrumbs. Add the dates and walnuts with the sugar and baking powder, if used.

In a bowl, beat the eggs with the milk and stir into the dry ingredients. Mix well.

Spoon the mixture into the cake tin and bake for 1¼-1½ hours or until cooked through and firm to the touch. Cool on a wire rack.

MAKES ONE 15 CM/6 INCH CAKE

☀ **MICROWAVE TIP**   Dried dates in a compact slab are often difficult to chop. Soften them by heating for 30-40 seconds on Defrost and the job will be made much easier.

PLAIN CHOCOLATE LOAF

Serve this simple loaf sliced, with a chocolate and hazelnut spread for those who like to gild the lily.

fat for greasing
175 g/6 oz plain flour
50 g/2 oz cocoa
10 ml/2 tsp baking powder
2.5 ml/½ tsp bicarbonate of soda
1.25 ml/¼ tsp salt
150 g/5 oz sugar
2 eggs, beaten
75 g/3 oz butter or margarine, melted
250 ml/8 fl oz milk

Line and grease a 23 × 13 × 7.5 cm/9 × 5 × 3 inch loaf tin. Set the oven at 180°C/350°F/gas 4. Sift the flour, cocoa, baking powder, bicarbonate of soda and salt into a mixing bowl. Stir in the sugar.

In a second bowl beat the eggs with the melted butter or margarine and milk. Pour the milk mixture into the dry ingredients and stir lightly but thoroughly.

Spoon into the prepared tin and bake for 40-50 minutes until cooked through and firm to the touch. Cool on a wire rack.

MAKES ONE 23 × 13 × 7.5 CM/9 × 5 × 3 INCH LOAF

SIMNEL CAKE

fat for greasing
200 g/7 oz plain flour
2.5 ml/½ tsp baking powder
1.25 ml/¼ tsp salt
150 g/5 oz butter
150 g/5 oz caster sugar
4 eggs
100 g/4 oz glacé cherries, halved
150 g/5 oz currants
150 g/5 oz sultanas
100 g/4 oz seedless raisins
50 g/2 oz chopped mixed peel
50 g/2 oz ground almonds
grated rind of 1 lemon

DECORATION
    double quantity Almond Paste (page 102)
      or 450 g/1 lb marzipan
    30 ml/2 tbsp smooth apricot jam (see
      method)
    1 egg, beaten
    white Glacé Icing (page 103) using 50 g/
      2 oz icing sugar
    Easter decorations

Line and grease an 18 cm/7 inch cake tin. Set the oven at 180°C/350°F/gas 4.

Sift the flour, baking powder and salt into a bowl. In a mixing bowl, cream the butter and sugar together well and beat in the eggs, adding a little of the flour mixture if necessary. Fold the flour mixture, cherries, dried fruit, peel and ground almonds into the creamed mixture. Add the lemon rind and mix well.

Spoon half the mixture into the prepared tin. Cut off one third of the almond paste and roll it to a pancake about 1 cm/½ inch thick and slightly smaller than the circumference of the tin. Place it gently on top of the cake mixture and spoon the remaining cake mixture on top.

Bake for 1 hour, then reduce the oven temperature to 160°C/325°F/gas 3 and bake for 1½ hours more. Cool in the tin, then turn out on a wire rack.

Warm, then sieve the apricot jam. When the cake is cold, divide the remaining almond paste in half. Roll one half to a round slightly narrower than the circumference of the cake. Brush the top of the cake with apricot jam and press the almond paste lightly on to it. Trim the edge neatly.

Make 11 small balls with the remaining paste and place them around the edge of the cake. Brush the balls with the beaten egg and brown under the grill. Pour the glacé icing into the centre of the cake and decorate with chickens and Easter eggs.

MAKES ONE 18 CM/7 INCH CAKE

RICH FRUIT CAKE

fat for greasing
200 g/7 oz plain flour
1.25 ml/¼ tsp salt
5-10 ml/1-2 tsp mixed spice
200 g/7 oz butter
200 g/7 oz caster sugar
6 eggs, beaten
30-60 ml/2-4 tbsp brandy or sherry
100 g/4 oz glacé cherries, chopped
50 g/2 oz preserved ginger, chopped
50 g/2 oz walnuts, chopped
200 g/7 oz currants
200 g/7 oz sultanas
150 g/5 oz seedless raisins
75 g/3 oz chopped mixed peel

Line and grease a 20 cm/8 inch round cake tin. Use doubled greaseproof paper and tie a strip of brown paper around the outside. Set the oven at 160°C/325°F/gas 3.

Sift the flour, salt and spice into a bowl. In a mixing bowl, cream the butter and sugar together until light and fluffy. Gradually beat in the eggs and the brandy or sherry, adding a little flour if the mixture starts to curdle. Add the cherries, ginger and walnuts. Stir in the dried fruit, peel and flour mixture. Spoon into the prepared tin and make a slight hollow in the centre.

Bake for 45 minutes, then reduce the oven temperature to 150°C/300°F/gas 2 and bake for a further hour. Reduce the temperature still further to 140°C/275°F/gas 1, and continue cooking for 45-60 minutes until cooked through and firm to the touch. Cool in the tin.

MAKES ONE 20 CM/8 INCH CAKE

ENGLISH MADELEINES

Illustrated on page 117

fat for greasing
100 g/4 oz self-raising flour
pinch of salt
100 g/4 oz butter or margarine
100 g/4 oz caster sugar
2 eggs, beaten

DECORATION
45 ml/3 tbsp smooth apricot jam
25 g/1 oz desiccated coconut
glacé cherries, halved
20 angelica leaves

Thoroughly grease 10 dariole moulds. Set the oven at 180°C/350°F/gas 4. Mix the flour and salt in a bowl.

In a mixing bowl cream the butter or margarine with the sugar until light and fluffy. Beat in the eggs, then lightly stir in the flour and salt. Divide the mixture evenly between the prepared moulds and bake for 15-20 minutes until golden brown. Cool on a wire rack.

Trim off the rounded ends of the cakes, if necessary, and stand upright. Warm the jam in a small saucepan, then brush the cakes all over. Toss in coconut. Decorate the top of each with a glacé cherry or angelica leaves or both.

MAKES 10

BUTTERFLY CAKES

Illustrated on page 117

fat for greasing
100 g/4 oz self-raising flour
pinch of salt
100 g/4 oz butter or margarine
100 g/4 oz caster sugar
2 eggs, beaten

DECORATION
150 ml/¼ pint double cream
5 ml/1 tsp caster sugar
1.25 ml/¼ tsp vanilla essence
icing sugar for dusting

Grease 12-14 bun tins. Set the oven at 180°C/350°F/gas 4. Mix the flour and salt in a bowl.

In a mixing bowl, cream the butter or margarine with the sugar until light and fluffy. Beat in the eggs, then lightly stir in the flour and salt. Divide the mixture evenly between the prepared bun tins, and bake for 15-20 minutes until golden brown. Cool on a wire rack.

In a bowl, whip the cream with the caster sugar and vanilla essence until stiff. Transfer to a piping bag fitted with a large star nozzle.

When the cakes are cold, cut a round off the top of each. Cut each round in half to create two 'butterfly wings'. Pipe a star of cream on each cake, then add the 'wings', placing them cut side down, and slightly apart. Dust with icing sugar.

MAKES 12 TO 14

FAIRY CAKES

fat for greasing (optional)
100 g/4 oz self-raising flour
pinch of salt
100 g/4 oz butter or margarine
100 g/4 oz caster sugar
2 eggs, beaten

Grease 12-14 bun tins or support an equivalent number of paper cases in dry bun tins. Set the oven at 180°C/350°F/gas 4. Mix the flour and salt in a bowl.

In a mixing bowl, cream the butter or margarine with the sugar until light and fluffy. Beat in the eggs, then lightly stir in the flour and salt.

Divide the mixture evenly between the prepared paper cases or bun tins, and bake for 15-20 minutes until golden brown. Cool on a wire rack.

MAKES 12 TO 14

RASPBERRY BUNS

fat for greasing
200 g/7 oz self-raising flour
1.25 ml/¼ tsp salt
75 g/3 oz margarine
75 g/3 oz sugar
1 egg
milk (see method)
60-75 ml/4-5 tbsp raspberry jam
beaten egg for brushing
caster sugar for sprinkling

Thoroughly grease 2 baking sheets. Set the oven at 200°C/400°F/gas 6.

Sift the flour and salt into a mixing bowl. Rub in the margarine until the mixture resembles fine breadcrumbs. Stir in the sugar. Put the egg into a measuring jug and add enough milk to make up to 125 ml/4 fl oz. Add the liquid to the dry ingredients and mix with a fork to a sticky stiff mixture that will support the fork.

Divide the mixture into 12-14 portions. Form into 12-14 balls with lightly floured hands. Make a deep dent in the centre of each and drop 5 ml/1 tsp raspberry jam inside. Close the bun mixture over the jam. Brush with egg and sprinkle with sugar, then arrange on the prepared sheets, allowing about 2 cm/¾ inch between each for spreading. Bake for 15-20 minutes or until each bun is firm to the touch on the base. Cool on a wire rack.

MAKES 12 TO 14

ALMOND MACAROONS

fat for greasing
2 egg whites
150 g/5 oz caster sugar
100 g/4 oz ground almonds
10 ml/2 tsp ground rice
split almonds or halved glacé cherries

Grease 2 baking sheets and cover with rice paper. Set the oven at 160°C/325°F/gas 3.

In a clean dry bowl, whisk the egg whites until frothy but not stiff. Stir in the sugar, ground almonds and ground rice. Beat until thick and white.

Put small spoonfuls of the mixture 5 cm/2 inches apart on the prepared baking sheets or pipe them on. Place a split almond or halved glacé cherry on each macaroon. Bake for 20 minutes or until pale fawn in colour. Cool slightly on the baking sheets, then finish cooling on wire racks.

FLAPJACKS

fat for greasing
50 g/2 oz margarine
50 g/2 oz soft light brown sugar
30 ml/2 tbsp golden syrup
100 g/4 oz rolled oats

Grease a 28 × 18 cm/11 × 7 inch baking tin. Set the oven at 160°C/325°F/gas 3. Melt the margarine in a large saucepan. Add the sugar and syrup, and warm gently. Remove from the heat and stir in the oats.

Press into the prepared tin, then bake for 25 minutes or until firm. Cut into fingers while still warm and leave in the tin to cool.

MAKES ABOUT 20

Dundee Cake (page 106)

Basic White Bread and Wholemeal Bread (pages 132 and 133)

A selection of bread rolls (page 135)

Battenburg Cake (page 107) and Swiss Roll (page 105)

English Madeleines (page 110) and Butterfly Cakes (page 111)

Saffron Bread (page 140) and Brioches (page 144)

Croissants (page 145)

Florentines and Brandy Snaps (both on page 123)

MERINGUES

This basic meringue mixture – Swiss or Chantilly meringue – may be used for a wide variety of dishes, from individual meringues of various sizes to shells, cases and toppings. Provided the cooked meringues are dried out thoroughly, they will keep for 1-2 weeks in an airtight tin.

4 egg whites
pinch of salt
200 g/7 oz caster sugar, plus extra for
**   dusting**
1.25 ml/¼ tsp baking powder (optional)
whipped cream to fill (optional)

Line a baking sheet with oiled grease-proof paper or with non-stick baking parchment. Set the oven at 110°C/225°F/gas ¼.

Combine the egg whites and salt in a mixing bowl and whisk until the whites are very stiff and standing in points. They must be completely dry or the meringues will break down in baking. Gradually add half the caster sugar, 15 ml/1 tbsp at a time, whisking after each addition until stiff. If the sugar is not thoroughly blended in it will form droplets of syrup which will brown, spoiling the appearance of the meringues and making them difficult to remove from the paper.

When half the sugar has been whisked in, sprinkle the rest over the surface of the mixture and, using a metal spoon, fold it in very lightly with the baking powder, if used. Put the meringue mixture into a piping bag fitted with a large nozzle and pipe into rounds on the paper. Alternatively, shape the mixture using two wet tablespoons. Take up a spoonful of the mixture and smooth it with a palette knife, bringing it up into a ridge in the centre. Slide it out with the other spoon on to the prepared baking sheet, with the ridge on top.

Dust the meringues lightly with caster sugar, then dry off in the oven for 3-4 hours, until they are firm and crisp but still white. If the meringues begin to brown, prop the oven door open a little. When they are crisp on the outside, lift the meringues carefully off the sheet, using a palette knife. Turn them on to their sides and return to the oven until the bases are dry. Cool on a wire rack and, if liked, sandwich them together with whipped cream. Filled meringues should be served within 1 hour or they will soften.

MAKES 24 TO 30 MEDIUM MERINGUES

> **MRS BEETON'S TIP** It is vital that the egg whites have been separated with great care. The fat in even a trace of egg yolk would prevent the whites from whisking properly. For the same reason, the bowl and whisk must be dry and absolutely clean and grease-free.

PIPED ALMOND RINGS

fat for greasing
175 g/6 oz butter
100 g/4 oz caster sugar
1 egg, beaten
225 g/8 oz self-raising flour
50 g/2 oz ground almonds
1-2 drops vanilla essence
about 10 ml/4 tsp milk

Thoroughly grease 1-2 baking sheets. In a mixing bowl, cream the butter and sugar until light and fluffy. Add the beaten egg, beating thoroughly and adding a little of the flour if the mixture begins to curdle. Blend in the remaining flour and ground almonds gradually. Add the vanilla essence and enough milk to give a piping consistency. Leave the mixture to stand for about 20 minutes in a cool place.

Set the oven at 200°C/400°F/gas 6. Put the biscuit mixture into a piping bag fitted with a medium star nozzle, and pipe small rings on to the prepared baking sheets. Bake for 10 minutes or until golden. Leave to stand for a few minutes, then cool on a wire rack.

MAKES ABOUT 24

> 🥣 **MRS BEETON'S TIP** An oil well is a useful aid when greasing baking sheets. The device consists of a clear spill-resistant oil reservoir with a built-in brush.

SHORTBREAD

fat for greasing
100 g/4 oz plain flour
1.25 ml/¼ tsp salt
50 g/2 oz rice flour, ground rice or
    semolina
50 g/2 oz caster sugar
100 g/4 oz butter

Invert a baking sheet, then grease the surface now uppermost. Set the oven at 180°C/350°F/gas 4.

Mix all the dry ingredients in a mixing bowl. Rub in the butter until the mixture binds together to a dough. Shape into a large round about 1 cm/½ inch thick. Pinch up the edges to decorate. Place on the prepared baking sheet, and prick with a fork. Bake for 40-45 minutes. Cut into wedges while still warm.

MAKES 8 WEDGES

*B*RANDY SNAPS

Illustrated on page 120

These may be filled with fresh whipped cream or Confectioners' Custard (page 126). Use either a small spoon or a piping bag fitted with a large star nozzle.

fat for greasing
50 g/2 oz plain flour
5 ml/1 tsp ground ginger
50 g/2 oz margarine
50 g/2 oz soft dark brown sugar
30 ml/2 tbsp golden syrup
10 ml/2 tsp grated lemon rind
5 ml/1 tsp lemon juice

Grease two or three 20 × 25 cm/8 × 10 inch baking sheets. Also grease the handles of several wooden spoons, standing them upside down in a jar until required. Set the oven at 180°C/350°F/gas 4.

Sift the flour and ginger into a bowl. Melt the margarine in a saucepan. Add the sugar and syrup and warm gently, but do not allow to become hot. Remove from the heat and add the sifted ingredients with the lemon rind and juice. Mix well.

Put small spoonfuls of the mixture on to the prepared baking sheets, spacing well apart to allow for spreading. Do not put more than 6 spoonfuls on a baking sheet. Bake for 8-10 minutes.

Remove from the oven and leave to cool for a few seconds until the edges begin to firm. Lift one of the biscuits with a palette knife and roll loosely around the greased handle of one of the wooden spoons. Allow to cool before removing the spoon handle. Repeat with the remaining biscuits.

MAKES 14 TO 18

*F*LORENTINES

Illustrated on page 120

oil for greasing
25 g/1 oz glacé cherries, chopped
100 g/4 oz finely chopped mixed peel
50 g/2 oz flaked almonds
100 g/4 oz chopped almonds
25 g/1 oz sultanas
100 g/4 oz butter or margarine
100 g/4 oz caster sugar
30 ml/2 tbsp double cream
100 g/4 oz plain or couverture chocolate

Line 3 or 4 baking sheets with oiled greaseproof paper. Set the oven at 180°C/350°F/gas 4.

In a bowl, mix the cherries and mixed peel with the flaked and chopped almonds and the sultanas. Melt the butter or margarine in a small saucepan, add the sugar and boil for 1 minute. Remove from the heat and stir in the fruit and nuts. Whip the cream in a separate bowl, then fold it in.

Place small spoonfuls of the mixture on to the prepared baking sheets, leaving room for spreading. Bake for 8-10 minutes. After the biscuits have been cooking for about 5 minutes, neaten the edges by drawing them together with a plain biscuit cutter. Leave the cooked biscuits on the baking sheets to firm up slightly before transferring to a wire rack to cool completely.

To finish, melt the chocolate in a bowl over hot water and use to coat the flat underside of each biscuit. Mark into wavy lines with a fork as the chocolate cools.

MAKES 20 TO 24

OATCAKES

fat for greasing
50 g/2 oz bacon fat or dripping
100 g/4 oz medium oatmeal
1.25 ml/¼ tsp salt
1.25 ml/¼ tsp bicarbonate of soda
fine oatmeal for rolling out

Grease 2 baking sheets. Set the oven at 160°C/325°F/gas 3.

Melt the bacon fat or dripping in a large saucepan. Remove from the heat and stir in the dry ingredients, then add enough boiling water to make a stiff dough.

When cool enough to handle, knead the dough thoroughly, then roll out on a surface dusted with fine oatmeal, to a thickness of 5 mm/¼ inch. Cut into wedge-shaped pieces and transfer to the prepared baking sheets. Bake for 20-30 minutes. Cool on a wire rack.

MAKES ABOUT 16

CRISP CRACKERS

These plain crackers are the ideal accompaniment for cheese. If you use very small cutters to cut the dough, then the crackers can be used as a base for making little canapés – top them with piped smooth pâté or cream cheese, olives and parsley.

fat for greasing
225 g/8 oz plain flour
2.5 ml/½ tsp salt
about 100 ml/4 fl oz milk
1 egg yolk, beaten

Grease 2 baking sheets. Set the oven at 180°C/350°F/gas 4. Sift the flour and salt into a bowl, then make a well in the middle and add about half the milk. Add the egg yolk to the milk and gradually work in the flour to make a firm dough, adding more milk as necessary.

Turn the dough out on to a lightly floured surface and knead it briefly until it is perfectly smooth. Divide the piece of dough in half and wrap one piece in cling film to prevent it from drying out while you roll out the other piece.

Roll out the dough very thinly and use a 7.5 cm/3 inch round cutter to stamp out crackers. Gather up the trimmings and re-roll them. Place the crackers on the prepared baking sheets. Bake for 12-18 minutes, until they are golden. Transfer the crackers to a wire rack to cool.

MAKES ABOUT 24

GÂTEAUX

Gâteaux are the elaborate cakes befitting of grand occasions. For special coffee mornings or tea-time gatherings to dinner party desserts, gâteaux may be light, creamy and filled with fruit or dark, smooth and irresistibly rich.

FINISHING TOUCHES

It is often the finishing touches that distinguish a gâteau from a cake – a coating applied to the sides, piping around the top edge or a glossy glaze on fresh fruit decorations.

Coating the Sides Chopped or flaked nuts, crushed biscuits, grated chocolate or vermicelli are often used to coat the sides of a gâteau. Do this before adding any topping to the gâteau. Spread a thin layer of cream around the cake. Sprinkle the coating ingredient on a sheet of greaseproof paper, then roll the cake in it. Alternatively, use a palette knife to press the coating on the cake.

Adding Toppings and Edgings The choice of topping determines whether it is added before or after the edging. Creams are spread over the top before the edging is added. Fruit is arranged on top before the edging is added. A thin glaze to be flooded over the top may be poured on after creating a piped edge.

Grated chocolate, chocolate caraque or small pieces of fruit (such as cherries) may be added to the gâteau just before it is served, as a topping or an edging.

Piping Piping on gâteaux is usually luscious and lavish. A piping bag fitted with a medium or large star nozzle is used. Whipped cream or buttercream may be piped, or sweetened low-fat soft cheese, thinned if necessary with a little plain yogurt, may be used.

Fit the nozzle and fill the bag. Keep your hands and utensils as cool as possible. Hold the bag firmly and pipe one swirl or shell at a time.

On a round cake, it helps to pipe four swirls opposite each other, then fill in the gaps rather than risk ending with either a very large or very small decoration because of bad spacing.

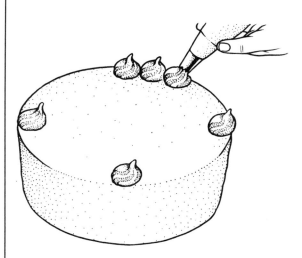

The most difficult part of piping a shell edging is adding the last shell. Using a sharp kitchen knife to cut the cream down into the space is easier than trying to finish the shell by pressing down with the piping bag.

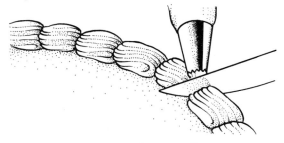

Use small stars, evenly spaced, to cover up a small mistake – particularly useful if the last shell looks a little messy. Do not be tempted to ruin a simple edge by finishing off a small amount of cream and adding lots of over-fussy piping.

APRICOT GLAZE

225 g/8 oz apricot jam

Warm the jam with 30 ml/2 tbsp water in a small saucepan over a low heat until the jam has melted. Sieve the mixture and return the glaze to the clean saucepan. Bring slowly to the boil. Allow to cool slightly before use.

MICROWAVE TIP Melt the jam with the water in a bowl on High. Sieve into a small basin and heat the syrup on High. Cool slightly before use.

CONFECTIONERS' CUSTARD

300 ml/½ pint milk
1 vanilla pod or a few drops of vanilla essence
2 egg yolks
50 g/2 oz caster sugar
25 g/1 oz plain flour

Place the milk and vanilla pod, if used, in a small saucepan and bring to the boil over a low heat. Remove from the heat and leave to one side, adding the essence, if used.

Whisk the egg yolks with the sugar in a bowl until thick and creamy, then add the flour. Remove the vanilla pod and very gradually add the milk to the egg mixture, beating constantly until all has been incorporated. Pour the mixture back into the saucepan and stir over a low heat for 1-2 minutes to cook the flour. The custard should be thick, smooth and shiny.

Pour the custard into a clean bowl, cover and leave to cool. Beat well, then cover again and chill until required.

MAKES ABOUT 300 ML/½ PINT

VARIATIONS

CHOCOLATE CUSTARD Stir 25 g/ 1 oz grated chocolate into the custard while still hot.
CREME ST HONORE Whisk 2 egg whites with 10 ml/2 tsp of caster sugar until stiff. Fold into cold custard. Use for choux pastry or for gâteaux.
CREME FRANGIPANE Omit the vanilla flavouring. Add 40 g/1½ oz finely chopped butter to final cooking. When cold, fold in 75 g/3 oz crushed almond macaroons or 50 g/2 oz ground almonds and a few drops of almond essence.

SACHER TORTE

Invented by Franz Sacher, this is one of the most delectable (and calorific) cakes imaginable. Serve it solo, or with whipped cream. The icing owes its gloss to glycerine, which is available from chemists.

butter for greasing
175 g/6 oz butter
175 g/6 oz icing sugar, sifted
6 eggs, separated
175 g/6 oz plain chocolate, in squares
2-3 drops vanilla essence
150 g/5 oz plain flour, sifted
about 125 ml/4 fl oz apricot jam, warmed
    and sieved, for filling and glazing

ICING
150 g/5 oz plain chocolate, in squares
125 g/4½ oz icing sugar, sifted
12.5 ml/2½ tsp glycerine

Line and grease a 20 cm/8 inch loose-bottomed cake tin. Set the oven at 180°C/350°F/gas 4.

In a mixing bowl, beat the butter until creamy. Add 100 g/4 oz of the icing sugar, beating until light and fluffy. Add the egg yolks, one at a time, beating after each addition.

Melt the chocolate with 30 ml/2 tbsp water in a heatproof bowl over hot water. Stir into the cake mixture with the vanilla essence.

In a clean, grease-free bowl, whisk the egg whites to soft peaks. Beat in the remaining icing sugar and continue beating until stiff but not dry. Fold into the chocolate mixture alternately with the sifted flour, adding about 15 ml/1 tbsp of each at a time.

Spoon the mixture into the prepared cake tin and set the tin on a baking sheet.

With the back of a spoon, make a slight depression in the centre of the cake to ensure even rising. Bake for 1-1¼ hours or until a skewer inserted in the centre of the cake comes out clean.

Leave the cake in the tin for a few minutes, then turn out on to a wire rack. Cool to room temperature.

Split the cake in half and brush the cut sides with warmed apricot jam. Sandwich the layers together again and glaze the top and sides of the cake with apricot jam. Set aside.

Make the icing. Melt the chocolate with 75 ml/5 tbsp water in a heatproof bowl over hot water. Stir in the icing sugar and whisk in the glycerine, preferably using a balloon whisk.

Pour the icing over the cake, letting it run down the sides. If necessary, use a metal spatula, warmed in hot water, to smooth the surface. Avoid touching the icing too much at this stage, or the gloss will be lost. Serve when the icing has set.

SERVES 12

MRS BEETON'S TIP Do not refrigerate this cake after baking; chilling would spoil the glossy appearance of the icing.

BLACK FOREST GATEAU

fat for greasing
150 g/5 oz butter or margarine
150 g/5 oz caster sugar
3 eggs, beaten
few drops of vanilla essence
100 g/4 oz self-raising flour or plain flour
    and 5 ml/1 tsp baking powder
25 g/1 oz cocoa
pinch of salt

FILLING AND TOPPING
    250 ml/8 fl oz double cream
    125 ml/4 fl oz single cream
    1 × 540 g/18 oz can Morello cherries
    kirsch (see method)
    25 g/1 oz plain chocolate, grated

Line and grease a 20 cm/8 inch cake tin. Set the oven at 180°C/350°F/gas 4.

In a mixing bowl, cream the butter or margarine with the sugar until light and fluffy. Add the eggs gradually, beating well after each addition. Stir in the vanilla essence.

Sift the flour, cocoa, salt and baking powder, if used, into a bowl. Stir into the creamed mixture, lightly but thoroughly, until evenly mixed.

Spoon into the tin and bake for 40 minutes. Cool on a wire rack. When quite cold, carefully cut the cake into three layers, brushing all loose crumbs off the cut sides.

Make the filling. Combine the creams in a bowl and whip until stiff. Place half the whipped cream in another bowl.

Drain the cherries, reserving the juice. Set aside 11 whole cherries and halve and stone the remainder. Gently fold the halved cherries into one of the bowls of cream. Set aside. Strain the reserved cherry juice into a measuring jug and add kirsch to taste.

Prick the cake layers and sprinkle with the cherry juice and kirsch until well saturated. Sandwich the layers together with the whipped cream and cherries. When assembled, cover with the remaining plain cream and use the whole cherries to decorate the top. Sprinkle the grated chocolate over the cream.

SERVES 10 TO 12

— ◈ —

COFFEE GATEAU

fat for greasing
20 ml/4 tsp instant coffee
150 g/5 oz butter
150 g/5 oz caster sugar
3 eggs, beaten
150 g/5 oz self-raising flour

COFFEE BUTTERCREAM
    30 ml/2 tbsp instant coffee
    150 g/5 oz butter
    450 g/1 lb icing sugar

DECORATION
    50-75 g/2-3 oz walnuts, chopped
    10-12 walnut halves

Line and grease two 20 cm/8 inch sandwich tins. Set the oven at 160°C/325°F/gas

3. In a cup, mix the instant coffee with 20 ml/4 tsp boiling water. Set aside to cool.

In a mixing bowl, cream the butter with the sugar until light and fluffy. Beat in the cooled coffee. Add the eggs gradually, beating well after each addition.

Sift the flour and fold it into the creamed mixture, using a metal spoon. Divide between the tins and bake for 35-40 minutes or until well risen, firm and golden brown. Leave in the tins for 2-3 minutes, then cool on a wire rack.

Make the buttercream. In a cup, mix the instant coffee with 30 ml/2 tbsp boiling water and leave to cool. Cream the butter with half the icing sugar in a bowl. Beat in the cooled coffee, then add the rest of the icing sugar. Beat to a creamy mixture.

Using about a quarter of the buttercream, sandwich the cake layers together. Spread about half the remaining buttercream on the sides of the cake, then roll in the chopped walnuts. Spread most of the remaining buttercream on top of the cake and mark with a fork in a wavy design. Spoon any remaining buttercream into a piping bag fitted with a small star nozzle and pipe 10-12 rosettes on top of the cake. Decorate each rosette with a walnut half.

SERVES 8 TO 12

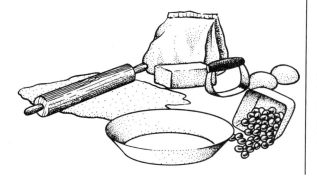

AUSTRIAN HAZELNUT LAYER

fat for greasing
200 g/7 oz hazelnuts
5 eggs, separated
150 g/5 oz caster sugar
grated rind of ½ lemon
flour for dusting
whole hazelnuts to decorate

FILLING
250 ml/8 fl oz double cream
vanilla essence

Grease and flour two 25 cm/10 inch springform or loose-bottomed cake tins. Set the oven at 180°C/350°F/gas 4.

Spread the hazelnuts out on a baking sheet and roast for 10 minutes or until the skins start to split. While still warm, rub them in a rough cloth to remove the skins. Grind the nuts in a nut mill or process briefly in a blender.

Combine the egg yolks and sugar in a bowl and beat until light and creamy. Mix in the ground nuts and lemon rind. Whisk the egg whites in a clean, grease-free bowl, until stiff but not dry. Fold the egg whites quickly and gently into the nut mixture. Divide between the prepared tins and bake for 1 hour, until well risen, firm and slightly shrunk from the tin. Cool on wire racks, removing the tins after a few minutes.

To make the filling, whip the cream with a few drops of vanilla essence until stiff. When the cake layers are cold, sandwich them together with some of the cream, and cover the top with the remainder. Decorate with a few whole hazelnuts.

SERVES 12

PAVLOVA

Make the pavlova shell on the day when it is to be eaten, as it does not store well unless frozen. Fill it just before serving.

3 egg whites
150 g/5 oz caster sugar
2.5 ml/½ tsp vinegar
2.5 ml/½ tsp vanilla essence
10 ml/2 tsp cornflour
glacé cherries and angelica to decorate

FILLING
250 ml/8 fl oz double cream
caster sugar (see method)
2 peaches, skinned and sliced

Line a baking sheet with greaseproof paper or non-stick baking parchment. Draw a 20 cm/8 inch circle on the paper and very lightly grease the greaseproof paper, if used. Set the oven at 150°C/300°F/gas 2.

In a large bowl, whisk the egg whites until very stiff. Continue whisking, gradually adding the sugar until the mixture stands in stiff peaks. Beat in the vinegar, vanilla essence and cornflour.

Spread the meringue over the circle, piling it up at the edges to form a rim, or pipe the circle and rim from a piping bag fitted with a large star nozzle.

Bake for about 1 hour or until the pavlova is crisp on the outside and has the texture of marshmallow inside. It should be pale coffee in colour. Leave to cool, then carefully remove the paper and put on a large serving plate.

Make the filling by whipping the cream in a bowl with caster sugar to taste. Add the sliced peaches and pile into the pav-lova shell. Decorate with glacé cherries and angelica and serve as soon as possible.

SERVES 4

VARIATIONS

FRUIT AND LIQUEUR Add 15-30 ml/1-2 tbsp liqueur to the cream when whipping it. Stir in prepared fruit of your choice (pineapple, apricots, grapes, kiwi fruit, strawberries or raspberries). Pile into the pavlova case.

BANANAS AND BRANDY Thinly slice 4 bananas into a bowl. Add 30 ml/2 tbsp brandy and chill for 1 hour, turning the fruit from time to time. In a second bowl, lightly whip 250 ml/8 fl oz double cream. Fold in the bananas and add 100 g/4 oz halved, stoned fresh or maraschino cherries. Pile into the pavlova case and sprinkle generously with grated chocolate and nuts.

☆ **FREEZER TIP** The crisp, cooled pavlova shell may be frozen without the filling. It is best packed in a rigid freezer container for protection and it may be stored, frozen, for several months. If you do not have a suitable container, open freeze the pavlova, then pack it in several layers of foil. The pavlova may be filled while frozen and allowed to stand for about 1 hour before serving.

YEASTED BREADS

The aroma of freshly baked bread is unmistakable and appetizing, and the results are worth the effort. This chapter offers an excellent selection of recipes, from plain white or wholemeal loaves to specialist international breads.

The choice of ingredients for making yeast mixtures is important. Strong flour is used because of its high gluten content. Gluten is the strengthening agent which forms the elastic dough during kneading, to trap the bubbles of gas given off by the yeast during proving. This makes the dough rise and gives the light result.

YEAST

There are various options and all work well.

Fresh Yeast Available from bakers who cook on the premises – small bread shops, hot bread shops or the hot bread counters at larger supermarkets.

Fresh yeast should be pale, firm and slightly crumbly in texture. It should smell fresh. Yeast that is very broken, dark, soft or sour smelling is old and should not be used. Wrapped in polythene, fresh yeast will keep for several days in the refrigerator or it may be frozen. Freeze 25 g/1 oz portions ready for use.

Cream fresh yeast with a little sugar and lukewarm liquid to make a paste. Add a little extra liquid, then place the mixture in a warm place until it becomes frothy. This process gives the yeast a good start so that it is very active when mixed with the other ingredients. It is also a good way of checking that the yeast is fresh and working.

There has been some controversy over whether the yeast should be creamed with sugar or just with water. The addition of sugar was thought to give a strong 'yeasty' flavour to the finished baking but as long as the quantities in recipes are followed, and the liquid is not left too long, the results using sugar are better than without.

Other methods of starting the yeast include sponging it – mixing it to a paste, then adding all the liquid and enough flour to make a batter. This is left to rise and bubble before mixing the ingredients to a dough.

Sometimes the yeast liquid may be poured into a well in the dry ingredients and allowed to ferment, usually sprinkled with a little flour.

Dried Yeasts There are two types, so always read the manufacturer's instructions and follow them.

The first is a granular product that is sprinkled over warm liquid and left to dissolve, then ferment until frothy before being stirred and mixed with the remaining ingredients. Usually the granules contain enough food for the yeast to work without having to add extra sugar.

The second, newer and now more popular, type is a finer grained dried yeast which should be added to the dry ingredients. Slightly hotter liquid is used to mix the dough and only one rising, or proving, is necessary.

TECHNIQUES

Kneading The kneading is important as it mixes the yeast evenly with the other ingredients and it develops the gluten in the flour to make the dough elastic. Once the dough is toughened, it traps the bubbles of gas produced by the yeast and rises.

Proving This is the process of rising. The dough must be left in a warm place until it has doubled in size. It must be covered to keep in moisture and prevent a skin forming on the dough (polythene, cling film or a damp cloth may be used). The warmer the place, the faster the rising but if the dough becomes hot the yeast will be killed. Dough may be left overnight in the refrigerator to rise slowly, or in a cool place for many hours. In a warm room dough will rise in a couple of hours.

Except when using fast-action dried yeast (the type combined with dry ingredients), most doughs are proved twice.

Knocking Back After the first proving, the dough is very lightly kneaded to knock out the gas, then it is shaped and allowed to prove for a second time. The second kneading is known as knocking back.

STORING

Breads should be stored in a clean airtight container. If kept in a polythene bag, they should be placed in a cool place (but not the refrigerator which tends to promote staling) to prevent them from sweating.

FREEZING

Yeasted goods freeze well, they should be cooked and cooled, then packed and frozen promptly. Most breads freeze well for up to 2 months. Loaves should be left to thaw for several hours at room temperature, rolls and small items thaw within a couple of hours at room temperature.

BASIC WHITE BREAD

Illustrated on page 114

fat for greasing
800 g/1¾ lb strong white flour
10 ml/2 tsp salt
25 g/1 oz lard
25 g/1 oz fresh yeast or 15 ml/1 tbsp dried yeast
2.5 ml/½ tsp sugar
flour for kneading
beaten egg or milk for glazing

Grease two 23 × 13 × 7.5 cm/9 × 5 × 3 inch loaf tins. Sift the flour and salt into a large bowl. Rub in the lard. Measure 500 ml/17 fl oz lukewarm water.

Blend the fresh yeast to a thin paste with the sugar and a little of the warm water. Set aside in a warm place until frothy – about 5 minutes. Sprinkle dried yeast over all the warm water and set aside until frothy, then stir well.

Add the yeast liquid and remaining water to the flour mixture and mix to a soft dough. Turn on to a floured surface and knead for about 8 minutes or until the dough is smooth, elastic and no longer sticky. Return to the bowl and cover with cling film. Leave in warm place until the dough has doubled in volume – this will take up to 2 hours, or longer.

Knead the dough again until firm. Cut into 2 equal portions and form each into a loaf shape. Place the dough into the prepared loaf tins and brush the surface with beaten egg or milk. Place the tins in a large, lightly oiled polythene bag. Leave in a warm place for about 45 minutes or until the dough has doubled in volume. Set the oven at 230°C/450°F/gas 8.

Bake for 35-40 minutes, until the loaves are crisp and golden brown, and sound hollow when tapped on the bottom.

MAKES TWO 800 G/1¾ LB LOAVES

VARIATIONS

MILK BREAD Substitute lukewarm milk for the lukewarm water.

WHOLEMEAL BREAD Mix wholemeal flour instead of stong white flour with 15 ml/1 tbsp salt.

FRENCH BREAD

flour for dusting and kneading
350 g/12 oz plain white flour
50 g/2 oz cornflour
5 ml/1 tsp salt
15 g/½ oz fresh yeast or 10 ml/2 tsp dried
   yeast
2.5 ml/½ tsp sugar
beaten egg for glazing

Well flour a baking sheet. Sift the flours and salt into a large bowl. Measure 250 ml/ 8 fl oz lukewarm water.

Blend the fresh yeast to a thin paste with the sugar and a little of the warm water. Set aside in a warm place until frothy – about 5 minutes. Sprinkle dried yeast over all the warm water and set aside until frothy, then stir well.

Stir the yeast liquid and remaining water into the flours and mix to a firm dough. Turn on to a floured surface and knead for about 4 minutes or until the dough is smooth and no longer sticky. Return to the bowl and cover with cling film. Leave in a warm place until the dough has doubled in volume – this will take up to 2 hours, or longer.

Cut the dough into 2 equal portions. On a floured surface, roll out one piece to an oval 40 cm/16 inches in length. Roll up like a Swiss roll and place on the prepared baking sheet. With a sharp knife, slash the top surface at intervals. Brush the surface with beaten egg. Repeat with the other piece of dough. Leave both, *uncovered*, in a warm place for about 30 minutes or until doubled in volume.

Meanwhile, place a pan of hot water in the bottom of the oven. (This is to provide steam to make the French bread expand fully before using dry heat to form the typical crisp crust.) Set the oven at 220°C/ 425°F/gas 7. Bake for 15 minutes, remove the pan of water, then continue baking for 15-20 minutes until the sticks are very crisp and well browned.

MAKES 2 FRENCH STICKS

 MRS BEETON'S TIP The dough is left uncovered to rise for the second time, so that the surface dries out and a very crisp crust is obtained after the loaf has been 'blown up' by steam heat in the oven. This can be done only when the volume of dough is as small as it is here, otherwise the bread splits open on baking.
   Strong flour is not suitable for this bread.

SHAPING YEAST DOUGHS

Yeast doughs of all types may be shaped in many ways to make attractive breads. The following ideas may be used for making 2 loaves from the dough recipes on pages 132-133.

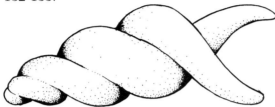

TWIST Divide the dough in half and roll each piece into a strip. Pinch the 2 ends of the strips together on a greased baking sheet, then twist the strips together, tucking the ends under neatly and pinching them in place.

RING Make a long, fairly slim twist, then shape it in a ring on a greased baking sheet.

PLAIT Divide the dough for one loaf into 3 equal portions and roll them into long strips. Pinch the ends of the strips together on a greased baking sheet, then plait the strips neatly. Fold the ends under at the end of the plait, pinching them underneath to secure the plait.

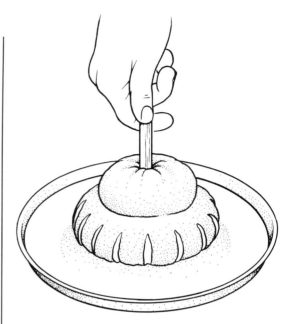

COTTAGE LOAF Shape two-thirds of the dough into a round loaf and place on a greased baking sheet. Shape the remaining dough into a ball. Make an indentation in the middle of the round loaf, then dampen the dough in the middle and place the ball on top. Make a deep indentation with your fingers or a wooden spoon handle down through the ball of dough and the round base. Before baking, score several slits down the side of the base of the loaf.

TOPPINGS FOR BREADS

Before baking, the risen dough may be glazed with beaten egg or milk for a golden crust. Brushing with water makes a crisp crust. Then the dough may be sprinkled with any of the following:

■ Poppy seeds – dark or white.

■ Sesame seeds – black or white, for flavour as well as texture and appearance.

■ Cracked wheat – good on wholemeal loaves.

■ Caraway, fennel or cumin seeds – when used generously these all contribute flavour.

FANCY ROLL SHAPES

Divide the risen Basic White Bread dough (page 132) into 50 g/2 oz pieces and shape as below:

MAKES 26

SMALL PLAITS Divide each piece of dough into 3 equal portions; then shape each of these into a long strand. Plait the 3 strands together, pinching the ends securely.

SMALL TWISTS Divide each piece of dough into 2 equal portions, and shape into strands about 12 cm/4½ inches in length. Twist the 2 strands together, pinching the ends securely.

'S' ROLLS Shape each piece of dough into a roll about 15 cm/6 inches in length, and form it into an 'S' shape.

COTTAGE ROLLS Cut two-thirds off each piece of dough and shape into a ball. Shape the remaining third in the same way. Place the small ball on top of the larger one and push a hole through the centre of both with one finger, dusted with flour, to join the 2 pieces firmly together.

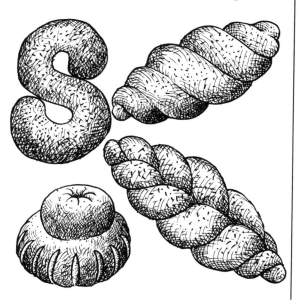

DINNER ROLLS

fat for greasing
800 g/1¾ lb strong white flour
10 ml/2 tsp sugar
400 ml/14 fl oz milk
25 g/1 oz fresh yeast or 15 ml/1 tbsp dried yeast
10 ml/2 tsp salt
100 g/4 oz butter or margarine
2 eggs
flour for kneading
beaten egg for glazing

Grease 2 baking sheets. Sift about 75 g/3 oz of the flour and all the sugar into a large bowl. Warm the milk until lukewarm, then blend in the fresh yeast or stir in the dried yeast. Pour the yeast liquid into the flour and sugar and beat well. Leave the bowl in a warm place for 20 minutes.

Sift the remaining flour and the salt into a bowl. Rub in the butter or margarine. Beat the eggs into the yeast mixture and stir in the flour mixture. Mix to a soft dough. Turn on to a lightly floured surface and knead for about 6 minutes or until the dough is smooth and no longer sticky. Return to the bowl and cover with cling film. Leave in a warm place until the dough has doubled in volume – this will take up to 2 hours, or longer.

Knead the dough again until firm. Cut into 50 g/2 oz pieces, then shape each piece into a ball. Place on the prepared baking sheets 5-7.5 cm/2-3 inches apart. Brush with beaten egg. Cover with sheets lightly oiled polythene. Leave in a warm place for about 20 minutes or until the rolls have doubled in volume. Set the oven at 220°C/425°F/gas 7.

Bake for 12-15 minutes until the rolls are golden brown.

MAKES 34 TO 38

ENRICHED BREAD

fat for greasing
800 g/1¾ lb strong white flour
10 ml/2 tsp sugar
400 ml/14 fl oz milk
25 g/1 oz fresh yeast or 15 ml/1 tbsp dried
    yeast
10 ml/2 tsp salt
100 g/4 oz butter or margarine
2 eggs
flour for kneading
milk for glazing

Grease two 23 × 13 × 7.5 cm/9 × 5 × 3 inch loaf tins. Sift about 75 g/3 oz of the flour and all the sugar into a large bowl. Warm the milk until lukewarm, then blend in the fresh yeast or stir in the dried yeast. Pour the yeast liquid into the flour and sugar and beat well. Leave the bowl in a warm place for 20 minutes.

Sift the remaining flour and the salt into a bowl. Rub in the butter or margarine. Beat the eggs into the yeast mixture and stir in the flour mixture. Mix to soft dough. Turn on to a lightly floured surface and knead for about 6 minutes or until the dough is smooth and no longer sticky. Return to the bowl and cover with cling film. Leave in a warm place until the dough has doubled in volume – this will take up to 2 hours, or longer.

Knead the dough again until firm. Cut into 2 equal portions and form each into a loaf shape. Place the dough in the prepared loaf tins. Place the tins in a large, lightly oiled polythene bag. Leave in a warm place for about 30 minutes or until the dough has doubled in volume. Set the oven at 220°C/425°F/gas 7.

Brush the surface of the dough with milk. Bake for 35-40 minutes until the loaves are golden brown and sound hollow when tapped on the bottom.

MAKES TWO 800 G/1¾ LB LOAVES

VARIATIONS

BREAD PLAIT   Make as for Enriched Bread. Cut the risen dough into 2 equal portions. Cut one of these into 3 equal pieces. Roll each piece into a strand 25-30 cm/10-12 inches long and plait the strands together. Repeat, using the second portion. Place the plaits on a greased baking sheet. Cover, rise and bake as for Enriched Bread.

CHEESE BREAD PLAIT   Make as for Bread Plait but add 200 g/7 oz grated Cheddar cheese to the dry ingredients.

CARAWAY BREAD   Make as for Enriched Bread but add 10 ml/2 tsp sage, 5 ml/1 tsp grated nutmeg and 15 ml/1 tbsp caraway seeds to the dry ingredients.

FRUIT BREAD   Make as for Enriched Bread but add 200 g/7 oz sultanas, currants or raisins to the dough when kneading for the second time.

NUT BREAD   Make as for Enriched Bread but add 200 g/7 oz chopped nuts, such as walnuts or peanuts, to the dough when kneading for the second time.

POPPY SEED BREAD   Make as for Enriched Bread but sprinkle poppy seeds thickly over the dough before baking.

BRIDGE ROLLS   Make as for Enriched Bread but cut the risen dough into 50 g/2 oz pieces. Roll each piece into a finger shape about 10 cm/4 inches long. Place on a greased baking sheet so that the rolls almost touch each other. Dust the surface of the rolls with flour. Cover and leave to rise for about 20 minutes or until the rolls have joined together. Bake as for Enriched Bread but reduce the baking time to 12-15 minutes.

MAKES 34-38

SHORT-TIME WHITE BREAD

This dough is best made with fresh yeast rather than dried. Ascorbic acid (vitamin C) tablets are available from chemists.

fat for greasing
800 g/1¾ lb strong white flour
10 ml/2 tsp salt
10 ml/2 tsp sugar
25 g/1 oz lard
25 mg tablet ascorbic acid
25 g/1 oz fresh yeast
flour for kneading
beaten egg or milk for glazing

Grease two 23 × 13 × 7.5 cm/9 × 5 × 3 inch loaf tins. Sift together the flour and salt into a large bowl. Rub in the lard. Measure 500 ml/17 fl oz lukewarm water.

Crush the ascorbic acid tablet into the warm water, then stir in the fresh yeast. Pour the yeast liquid on to the flour mixture and mix to a soft dough. Turn on to a floured surface and knead for about 8 minutes or until the dough is smooth and elastic and no longer sticky.

Cut the dough into 2 equal portions and form each into a loaf shape. Place in the prepared loaf tins and brush the surface with beaten egg or milk. Place the tins in a large, lightly oiled polythene bag. Leave in a warm place for about 45 minutes or until the dough has doubled in volume. Set the oven at 230°C/450°F/gas 8.

Bake for 35-40 minutes, until the loaves are crisp and golden brown, and sound hollow when tapped on the bottom.

MAKES TWO 800 G/1¾ LB LOAVES

WHEATMEAL BREAD

fat for greasing
400 g/14 oz wholemeal flour
400 g/14 oz strong white flour
10 ml/2 tsp spoon salt
25 g/1 oz lard
25 g/1 oz fresh yeast or 15 ml/1 tbsp dried yeast
2.5 ml/½ tsp sugar
flour for kneading
salted water

Grease two 23 × 13 × 7.5 cm/9 × 5 × 3 inch loaf tins. Mix the flours and salt in a large bowl. Rub in the lard. Measure 500 ml/17 fl oz lukewarm water.

Blend the fresh yeast to a thin paste with the sugar and a little of the warm water. Set aside in a warm place until frothy – about 5 minutes. Sprinkle dried yeast over all the warm water and set aside until frothy, then stir well.

Add the yeast liquid and remaining water to the flour mixture and mix to a soft dough. Turn on to a floured surface and knead for about 4 minutes or until the dough is smooth and no longer sticky.

Cut the dough into 2 equal portions and form each into a loaf shape. Place the dough in the prepared loaf tins, then brush the surface with salted water. Place the tins in a large, lightly oiled polythene bag. Leave in a warm place for about 50 minutes or until the dough has doubled in volume. Set the oven at 230°C/450°F/gas 8.

Bake for 30-40 minutes, until the loaves are golden brown and crisp, and sound hollow when tapped lightly on the bottom.

MAKES TWO 800 G/1¾ LB LOAVES

MALTED BROWN BREAD

fat for greasing
800 g/1¾ lb wholemeal flour
15 ml/1 tbsp salt
25 g/1 oz fresh yeast or 15 ml/1 tbsp dried
    yeast
2.5 ml/½ tsp sugar
30 ml/2 tbsp malt extract
flour for kneading

Grease two 23 × 13 × 7.5 cm/9 × 5 × 3 inch loaf tins. Mix the flour and salt in a large bowl. Measure 500 ml/17 fl oz luke-warm water.

Blend the fresh yeast to a thin paste with the sugar and a little of the warm water. Set aside in a warm place until frothy – about 5 minutes. Sprinkle dried yeast over all the warm water and set aside until frothy.

Stir the malt extract into the yeast liquid and remaining water. Add to the flour and mix to a soft dough. Turn on to a lightly floured surface and knead for about 4 minutes or until the dough is smooth, elastic and no longer sticky. Return to the bowl and cover with cling film. Leave in a warm place until the dough has doubled in volume – this takes 2 hours, or longer.

Knead the dough again until firm. Cut into 2 equal portions and form each into a loaf shape. Place the dough in the prepared loaf tins. Place the tins in a large, lightly oiled polythene bag. Leave in a warm place for about 45 minutes or until the dough has doubled in volume. Set the oven at 230°C/450°F/gas 8.

Bake for 35-45 minutes, until the loaves are golden brown and crisp, and sound hollow when tapped on the bottom.

MAKES TWO 800 G/1¾ LB LOAVES

SCOTTISH BROWN BREAD

fat for greasing
600 g/1 lb 5 oz wholemeal flour
200 g/7 oz fine or medium oatmeal
15 ml/1 tbsp salt
25 g/1 oz fresh yeast or 15 ml/1 tbsp dried
    yeast
2.5 ml/½ tsp sugar
5 ml/1 tsp bicarbonate of soda
flour for kneading

Grease two 23 × 13 × 7.5 cm/9 × 5 × 3 inch loaf tins. Mix the flour, oatmeal and salt in a large bowl. Measure 500 ml/17 fl oz lukewarm water.

Blend the fresh yeast to a thin paste with the sugar and a little of the warm water. Set aside in a warm place until frothy – about 5 minutes. Sprinkle dried yeast over all the warm water and set aside until frothy, then stir well.

Add the bicarbonate of soda to the yeast liquid and remaining water, then stir this into the flour mixture to form a soft dough. Turn on to a lightly floured surface and knead for about 4 minutes or until the dough is smooth and no longer sticky. Return to the bowl and cover with cling film. Leave in a warm place until the dough has doubled in volume – this will take up to 2 hours, or longer.

Knead to dough again until firm. Cut into 2 equal portions and form each into a loaf shape. Place the dough in the prepared loaf tins. Place the tins in a large, lightly oiled polythene bag. Leave in a warm place for about 45 minutes or until the dough has doubled in volume. Set the oven at 230°C/450°F/gas 8.

Bake for 20 minutes, then reduce the oven temperature to 190°C/375°F/gas 5.

Continue baking for 25-35 minutes, until the loaves are crisp and golden brown, and sound hollow when tapped on the bottom.

MAKES TWO 800 G/1¾ LB LOAVES

GRANT LOAF

fat for greasing
800 g/1¾ lb wholemeal flour
15 ml/1 tbsp salt
25 g/1 oz fresh yeast or 15 ml/1 tbsp dried
    yeast
2.5 ml/½ tsp sugar

Grease three 20 × 10 × 6 cm/8 × 4 × 2½ inch loaf tins. Mix the flour and salt in a large bowl. Measure 700 ml/scant 1¼ pints lukewarm water.

Blend the fresh yeast to a thin paste with the sugar and a little of the warm water. Set aside in a warm place until frothy – about 5 minutes. Sprinkle dried yeast over all the warm water and set aside until frothy, then stir well.

Pour the yeast liquid and remaining water into the flour and stir until the flour is evenly wetted. The resulting dough should be wet and slippery. Spoon it into the prepared loaf tins. Place the tins in a large, lightly oiled polythene bag. Leave in a warm place until the dough has risen by a third. Set the oven at 190°C/375°F/ gas 5.

Bake for 50-60 minutes, until the loaves are golden brown and crisp, and sound hollow when tapped on the bottom.

MAKES THREE 400 G/14 OZ LOAVES

GRANARY BREAD

fat for greasing
800 g/1¾ lb granary flour or meal
10 ml/2 tsp salt
10 ml/2 tsp molasses
25 g/1 oz fresh yeast or 15 ml/1 tbsp dried
    yeast
10 ml/2 tsp corn oil
flour for kneading
15 ml/1 tbsp cracked wheat

Grease two 23 × 13 × 7.5 cm/9 × 5 × 3 inch loaf tins. Mix the flour and salt in a large bowl. Measure 500 ml/17 fl oz luke-warm water. Stir in the molasses.

Blend the fresh yeast to a thin paste with a little of the warm water and molasses. Set aside in a warm place until frothy – about 5 minutes. Sprinkle dried yeast over all the warm water and molasses and set aside until frothy, then stir well. Add the yeast liquid, remaining liquid and the oil to the flour and mix to a soft dough. Turn on to a floured surface and knead for about 4 minutes or until the dough is smooth, elastic and no longer sticky. Return to the bowl and cover with cling film. Leave in a warm place until doubled in volume – this will take about 2 hours, or longer.

Knead the dough again until firm. Cut into 2 equal portions and form each into a loaf shape. Place the dough in the prepared loaf tins, brush the surface with salted water and sprinkle with the cracked wheat. Place the tins in a large, lightly oiled poly- thene bag. Leave in a warm place for about 45 minutes or until the dough has doubled. Set the oven at 230°C/450°F/gas 8.

Bake for 30-40 minutes, until the loaves are browned and crisp, and sound hollow when tapped on the bottom.

MAKES TWO 800 G/1¾ LB LOAVES

RYE COBS

fat for greasing
900 g/2 lb strong white flour
25 g/1 oz fresh yeast or 15 ml/1 tbsp dried
    yeast
2.5 ml/½ tsp sugar
450 g/1 lb coarse rye flour
500 ml/17 fl oz skimmed milk
20 ml/4 tsp salt
60 ml/4 tbsp molasses
60 ml/4 tbsp cooking oil
flour for kneading

Grease a baking sheet or four 15 cm/6 inch sandwich tins. Sift the white flour into a large bowl. Measure 250 ml/8 fl oz lukewarm water.

Blend the fresh yeast to a thin paste with the sugar and a little of the warm water. Set aside in a warm place until frothy – about 5 minutes. Sprinkle dried yeast over all the warm water and set aside until frothy, then stir well.

Mix the rye flour into the white flour. Add the yeast liquid, remaining water, skimmed milk, salt, molasses and oil, then knead to a soft dough. Cover the bowl with cling film. Leave in a warm place until the dough has doubled in volume – this will take at least 2 hours, or longer. (Rye bread is slow to rise.)

When risen, shape into 4 round loaves. Place on the prepared baking sheet or press into the sandwich tins. Place in a large, lightly oiled polythene bag. Leave to rise for 30-45 minutes. Set the oven at 190°C/375°F/gas 5.

Sprinkle the dough with warm water. Bake for about 40 minutes, until the loaves sound hollow when tapped on the bottom.

MAKES 4 LOAVES

SAFFRON BREAD

Illustrated on page 118

fat for greasing
400 g/14 oz strong white flour
5 ml/1 tsp salt
125 ml/4 fl oz milk
75 g/3 oz butter
large pinch of powdered saffron
75 g/3 oz caster sugar
1 egg
25 g/1 oz fresh yeast or 15 ml/1 tbsp dried
    yeast
50 g/2 oz ground almonds
flour for kneading
50 g/2 oz chopped mixed peel
50 g/2 oz currants
50 g/2 oz raisins
beaten egg for glazing
10 ml/2 tsp granulated sugar
4 blanched almonds, roughly chopped

Grease a 23 × 13 × 7.5 cm/9 × 5 × 3 inch loaf tin. Sift the flour and salt together. Measure 100 ml/3½ fl oz lukewarm water. Warm the milk and butter together until the butter has melted. Transfer to a bowl, add the saffron and leave to stand for 10 minutes. Beat in the caster sugar, reserving 25 ml/½ tsp if using fresh yeast, and egg.

Blend the fresh yeast to a thin paste with the reserved sugar and a little of the warm water. Set aside in a warm place until frothy – about 5 minutes. Sprinkle dried yeast over all the warm water and set aside until frothy, then stir well.

Add the yeast liquid and remaining water to the milk and saffron mixture and stir in a third of the flour. Leave in a warm place for 20 minutes.

Work in the rest of the flour and ground almonds to form a very soft dough. Turn on to a well floured surface and knead for about 5 minutes or until the dough is smooth. Return to the bowl and cover with cling film. Leave in a warm place until the dough has doubled in volume – this will take at least 2 hours, or longer.

Work in the dried fruit and form the dough into a loaf shape. Place the dough in the prepared loaf tin. Brush the top with beaten egg. Sprinkle on the granulated sugar and almonds. Place the tin in a large, lightly oiled polythene bag. Leave in a warm place for about 45 minutes or until the dough has doubled in volume. Set the oven at 220°C/425°F/gas 7.

Bake for 10 minutes, then reduce the oven temperature to 190°C/375°F/gas 5. Continue baking for a further 30 minutes, until golden brown.

MAKES ONE 800 G/1¾ LB LOAF

VARIATION

KULICH Make as for Saffron Bread. After working the fruit into the dough, divide into 2 equal pieces. Well grease two 450-500 g/1 lb circular empty cans. For example, large fruit or coffee cans may be used. They should be washed and dried before use. Shape the pieces of dough to fit the tins and put the dough in them. Place the tins in a large, lightly oiled polythene bag. Leave in a warm place for about 35 minutes or until the dough has reached the top of the tins. Set the oven at 220°C/425°F/gas 7. Bake for 35-40 minutes, until golden brown. When cold, ice with Glacé Icing (page 103).

MAKES TWO 400 G/14 OZ KULICH

NAAN

fat for greasing
25 g/1 oz fresh yeast or 15 g/½ oz dried yeast
5 ml/1 tsp sugar
450 g/1 lb strong white flour
5 ml/1 tsp salt
150 ml/¼ pint plain yogurt
flour for kneading
50 g/2 oz butter, melted

Grease 4 baking sheets. Sift the flour and salt into a bowl. Measure 150 ml/¼ pint lukewarm water. Blend the fresh yeast with the sugar and a little lukewarm water, then stir in the remaining water and set aside until frothy. For dried yeast, sprinkle it over all the water, then set aside until frothy.

Make a well in the centre of the dry ingredients and pour in the yogurt with the yeast liquid. Gradually mix in the dry ingredients to make a firm dough. Knead the dough on a lightly floured surface until smooth and elastic – about 10 minutes. Place the dough in a clean bowl, cover with cling film and leave in a warm place until doubled in size.

Set the oven at 250°C/475°F/gas 9. Knead about a third of the dough again, then divide it into four. Stretch each portion of dough into a large, thin oblong, about 20 cm/8 inches long. Heat the prepared baking sheets in the oven then slap the thin breads on them. Brush the breads with melted butter.

Bake for 5-7 minutes, until bubbling and well browned. Shape a second batch of naan while the first breads are baking, then place them straight on to the hot sheets. Transfer to a wire rack when cooked.

MAKES FOUR NAAN

PRINCESS ROLLS

fat for greasing
400 g/14 oz strong white flour
250 ml/8 fl oz milk
15 g/½ oz fresh yeast or 10 ml/2 tsp dried
    yeast
15 ml/1 tbsp caster sugar
50 g/2 oz margarine
5 ml/1 tsp salt
flour for kneading
about 150 g/5 oz butter

Grease a baking sheet. Sift the flour into a large bowl. Warm the milk until lukewarm. Blend the fresh yeast to a thin paste with 2.5 ml/½ tsp of the sugar and half of the warm milk. Set aside in a warm place until frothy. Sprinkle dried yeast over the warm milk and set aside until frothy.

Add the margarine, remaining sugar and salt to the remaining milk, and heat until the fat has melted. Leave until lukewarm. Stir with the yeast liquid into the flour and mix to a soft dough. Turn on to a lightly floured surface and knead until smooth. Return the dough to the bowl and cover with cling film. Leave in a warm place until doubled in volume.

Lightly knead the dough again. Roll out on a floured surface to 8 mm/⅓ inch thickness. Cut into rounds, using a plain 7.5 cm/3 inch cutter. Place a small piece of butter on one half of each round. Fold over the other half and pinch the edges firmly together. Place the rolls on the prepared baking sheet. Put the sheet in a large, lightly oiled polythene bag. Leave in a warm place for about 30 minutes or until the rolls have almost doubled in size. Set the oven at 220°C/425°F/gas 7. Bake for 10-15 minutes, until golden brown.

MAKES 18

CHALLAH

fat for greasing
800 g/1¾ lb strong white flour
10 ml/2 tsp sugar
25 g/1 oz fresh yeast or 15 ml/1 tbsp dried
    yeast
10 ml/2 tsp salt
100 g/4 oz butter or margarine
2 eggs
flour for kneading
beaten egg for glazing

Grease 2 baking sheets. Sift about 75 g/3 oz of the flour and all the sugar into a large bowl. Measure 400 ml/14 fl oz lukewarm water. Blend the fresh yeast into the water or stir in the dried yeast. Pour the yeast liquid into the flour and sugar and beat well. Leave the bowl in a warm place for 20 minutes.

Sift the remaining flour and the salt into a bowl. Rub in the butter or margarine. Beat the eggs into the yeast mixture and stir in the flour mixture. Mix to a soft dough. Turn on to a lightly floured surface and knead for about 6 minutes or until the dough is smooth and no longer sticky. Return to the bowl and cover with cling film. Leave in a warm place until the dough has doubled in volume – this will take up to 2 hours, or longer.

Knead the dough again until firm. Cut into 2 equal portions. Cut one of these into 2 equal pieces and roll these into long strands 30-35 cm/12-14 inches in length. Arrange the 2 strands in a cross on a flat surface. Take the 2 opposite ends of the bottom strand and cross them over the top strand in the centre. Repeat this, using the other strand. Cross each strand alternately, building up the plait vertically, until all the dough is used up. Gather the short ends together and pinch firmly. Lay the challah on its side and place on the prepared baking sheet. Brush with beaten egg. Repeat, using the second portion. Cover with lightly oiled polythene. Leave in a warm place for about 30 minutes or until the dough has doubled in volume. Set the oven at 220°C/425°F/gas 7.

Bake for 35-40 minutes, until the loaves are golden brown and sound hollow when tapped on the bottom.

MAKES TWO 800 G/1¾ LB LOAVES

---------------◇---------------

BAGELS

These ring buns are poached in water before baking. The result is a close-textured, moist bread with a deep-golden coloured crust which is quite thick but not hard. It is worth making a large batch and freezing them.

fat for greasing
400 g/14 oz strong white flour
5 ml/1 tsp salt
30 ml/2 tbsp sugar
50 g/2 oz margarine
15 g/½ oz fresh yeast or 10 ml/2 tsp dried
   yeast
1 egg, separated
flour for kneading
poppy seeds

Grease a baking sheet. Sift the flour into a large bowl. Measure 250 ml/5 fl oz lukewarm water. Put the salt, sugar, re-

serving 2.5 ml/½ tsp if using fresh yeast, the margarine and half the water in a saucepan and warm gently until the fat has melted. Leave until lukewarm.

Blend the fresh yeast to a thin paste with the reserved sugar and the remaining warm water. Set aside in a warm place until frothy – abut 5 minutes. Sprinkle dried yeast over the warm water and set aside until frothy, then stir well.

Whisk the egg white lightly, then add to the flour with the cooled margarine mixture and the yeast liquid. Mix to a soft dough. Cover the bowl with cling film. Leave in a warm place until the dough has almost doubled in volume – this will take up to 2 hours, or longer.

Knead the dough again until firm. Cut into 25 g/1 oz pieces. Roll each piece into a sausage shape 15-20 cm/6-8 inches in length; then form this into a ring, pinching the ends securely together. Place the rings on a floured surface and leave for 10 minutes or until they begin to rise.

Heat a saucepan of water deep enough to float the bagels, to just under boiling point. Drop in the bagels, a few at a time. Cook them on one side for 2 minutes, then turn them over and cook on the other side for about 2 minutes or until they are light and have risen slightly. Place on the prepared baking sheet. Set the oven at 190°C/375°F/gas 5.

Beat the egg yolk, brush it over the top surface of the bagels and sprinkle with poppy seeds. Bake for 20-30 minutes, until golden brown and crisp.

MAKES 28

---------------◇---------------

BRIOCHES

Illustrated on page 118

fat for greasing
400 g/14 oz strong white flour
5 ml/1 tsp salt
50 g/2 oz butter
15 g/½ oz fresh yeast or 10 ml/2 tsp dried
   yeast
2.5 ml/½ tsp sugar
2 eggs
flour for kneading
beaten egg for glazing

Grease twenty-two 7.5 cm/3 inch brioche or deep bun tins. Sift the flour and salt into a large bowl. Rub in the butter.

Blend the fresh yeast with the sugar and 40 ml/8 tsp lukewarm water. Set aside in a warm place until frothy. Sprinkle dried yeast over the warm water and set aside until frothy.

Beat the eggs into the yeast liquid and stir into the flour to form a soft dough. Turn on to a floured surface and knead for about 5 minutes or until the dough is smooth and no longer sticky. Return to the bowl and cover with cling film. Leave in a warm place for about 45 minutes or until doubled.

Knead the dough again until firm. Cut into 22 equal pieces. Cut off one-quarter of each piece used. Form the larger piece into a ball and place in a prepared tin. Firmly press a hole in the centre and place the remaining quarter as a knob in the centre. Place the tins on a baking sheet and cover with a large, lightly oiled polythene bag. Leave in a warm place for about 30 minutes or until the dough is light and puffy. Set the oven at 230°C/450°F/gas 8. Brush with beaten egg. Bake for 15-20 minutes, until golden brown.

MAKES 12

SALLY LUNN

Sally Lunn was a cake seller in Bath during the 18th century and her cake, or bun, became very famous.

fat for greasing
400 g/14 oz strong white flour
5 ml/1 tsp salt
50 g/2 oz butter
150 ml/¼ pint milk
15 g/½ oz fresh yeast or 10 ml/2 tsp dried
   yeast
2.5 ml/½ tsp sugar
1 egg
15 ml/1 tbsp caster sugar for glazing

Grease two 15 cm/6 inch round cake tins. Sift the flour and salt into a large bowl. Rub in the butter. Warm the milk until lukewarm.

Blend the fresh yeast to a thin paste with the sugar and warm milk. Set aside in a warm place until frothy – about 5 minutes. Sprinkle dried yeast over the warm milk and set aside until frothy, then stir well.

Beat the egg into the yeast liquid and stir into the flour mixture to form a very soft dough. Beat well. Pour the mixture into the prepared cake tins.

Place the tins in a large, lightly oiled polythene bag. Leave in a warm place until the dough has doubled in volume – this will take up to 2 hours, or longer. Set the oven at 220°C/425°F/gas 7.

Bake for 20-25 minutes, until golden brown.

To make the glaze, boil together 15 ml/ 1 tbsp water and the sugar until syrupy. Brush the hot glaze over the top of the Sally Lunns.

To serve, split each Sally Lunn cross-ways into 3 rounds and toast each piece lightly on both sides. Butter thickly or fill with clotted cream, re-form the cake, and cut into slices or wedges.

MAKES TWO 15 CM/6 INCH SALLY LUNNS

———— ◇ ————

CROISSANTS

Illustrated on page 119

Rich, flaky French croissants make the perfect breakfast, especially when homemade.

fat for greasing
400 g/14 oz strong white flour
5 ml/1 tbsp salt
100 g/4 oz lard
25 g/1 oz fresh yeast or 15 ml/1 tbsp dried
    yeast
2.5 ml/½ tsp sugar
1 egg, beaten
flour for kneading
75 g/3 oz unsalted butter
beaten egg for glazing

Grease a baking sheet. Sift the flour and salt into a large bowl. Rub in 25 g/1 oz of the lard. Measure 200 ml/7 fl oz lukewarm water.

Blend the fresh yeast to a thin paste with the sugar and a little of the warm water. Set aside in a warm place until frothy – about 5 minutes. Sprinkle dried yeast over all the warm water and set aside until frothy, then stir well.

Stir the egg, yeast liquid and remaining water into the flour and mix to a soft dough. Turn on to a lightly floured surface and knead for about 8 minutes or until the dough is smooth and no longer sticky. Return the dough to the bowl and cover with cling film. Leave at room temperature for 15 minutes.

Meanwhile, beat together the rest of the lard and the butter until well mixed; then chill. On a lightly floured surface, roll out the dough carefully into an oblong 50 × 20 cm/30 × 8 inches. Divide the chilled fat into three. Use one-third to dot over the top two-thirds of the dough, leaving a small border. Fold the dough into three by bringing the bottom third up and the top third down. Seal the edges together by pressing with the rolling pin. Give the dough a quarter turn and repeat the rolling and folding twice, using the other 2 portions of fat. Place the dough in a large, lightly oiled polythene bag. Leave in a cool place for 15 minutes.

Repeat the rolling and folding 3 more times. Rest the dough in the polythene bag in a cool place for 15 minutes. Roll out to an oblong 23 × 35 cm/9 × 14 inches and then cut it into six 13 cm/5 inch squares. Cut each square into triangles. Brush the surface of the dough with beaten egg and roll each triangle loosely, towards the point, finishing with the tip underneath. Curve into a crescent shape. Place on the prepared baking sheet and brush with beaten egg. Place the sheet in the polythene bag again. Leave in a warm place for about 30 minutes or until the dough is light and puffy. Set the oven at 220°C/425°F/gas 7.

Bake for 15-20 minutes, until golden brown and crisp.

MAKES 12

SWEET YEAST DOUGHS

**Yeasted tea breads and buns are the perfect weekend treat,
and they are sure to be superior if you make them at home.
This chapter includes instructions for making Danish
pastries too – they are the perfect batch baking and freezer
candidates.**

Sweet yeast doughs differ from plain breads in that they are enriched as well as sweetened. All the information on flour, yeast and the techniques used for bread making applies to the recipes in this chapter.

UNDERSTANDING RICH DOUGHS

Even more so than when making plain breads, patience plays a vital role when handling rich yeasted mixtures. Although a little sugar is used to speed up the initial action of yeast, when it is added to doughs in quantity, it tends to have the opposite effect, so sweet doughs usually take longer to rise.

The addition of extra fat and eggs to enrich the dough also tends to slow down the action of the yeast. Therefore it is important to allow plenty of time for sweet breads to rise. As well, some of the very rich mixtures (for example, Danish pastries) are best left in a cool place to rise over a long period so that their high butter content does not melt.

ADAPTING BASIC RECIPES

Sweet yeast doughs may be used as the basic for making many exciting breads. Ready-to-eat dried fruits, apricots, apples and peaches as well as raisins, sultanas and dates, are all ideal for kneading into sweet breads. Nuts may be added too – chopped walnuts, hazel nuts, Brazils or pistachios make loaves or buns quite different. With imagination, sweet doughs can be swirled with rich fillings – grated chocolate, ground almonds and icing sugar combine well; cinnamon, brown sugar, chopped walnuts and butter may be used; or chopped candied citron peel mixed with honey and chopped almonds makes a tempting combination. Roll out the dough, spread the filling in the middle, then roll it up and place it in a tin. Or flatten small pieces of dough and fill them, then shape them into buns.

Place shaped round buns in a square tin, slightly apart, so that they rise together into a bubbly loaf. Drizzle with melted butter and sprinkle with sugar for a golden glaze when baked.

STORING AND FREEZING

Allow the breads to cool on a wire rack before storing them in airtight containers. When cool, most sweet breads freeze well. However, remember not to add icing or glazes before freezing, but apply them after the bread has thawed.

If sweet breads do become stale they may be toasted and served hot and buttered. Stale bun loaves make good bread and butter pudding. Soak other sweet breads in eggs and milk, then bake them slowly before topping with jam and meringue and browning (rather like Queen of Puddings).

DANISH PASTRIES

200 g/7 oz plain flour
pinch of salt
25 g/1 oz lard
15 g/½ oz fresh yeast or 10 ml/2 tsp dried
    yeast
2.5 ml/½ tsp caster sugar
1 egg, beaten
flour for dusting
125 g/4½ oz softened butter

Sift the flour and salt into a bowl. Rub in the lard.

Blend the fresh yeast to a thin paste with the sugar and 75 ml/3 fl oz lukewarm water. Set aside in a warm place until frothy – about 5 minutes. Sprinkle dried yeast over the warm water and set aside until frothy, then stir well. Add the beaten egg.

Pour the yeast liquid into the flour mixture and mix to a soft dough. Turn on to a floured surface and knead lightly until smooth. Return the dough to the bowl and cover with cling film. Leave in a cool place for 10 minutes.

Shape the butter into a long rectangle about 1 cm/½ inch thick. Roll out the dough to about 25 cm/10 inches square. Place the butter down the centre. Fold the sides of the dough over the middle to overlap about 1 cm/½ inch only. Roll the dough into a strip 45 × 15 cm/18 × 6 inches. Fold it evenly into three. Place the dough in a large, lightly oiled polythene bag. Leave for 10 minutes. Roll and fold the dough in the same way twice more, letting it rest for 10 minutes each time. The dough is now ready for making the pastry shapes. Set the oven at 220°C/425°F/gas 7, while shaping and proving the pastries.

MAKES 16 PASTRIES

WINDMILLS   Roll out half the dough to about 20 × 40 cm/8 × 16 inches. Cut into eight 10 cm/4 inch squares and place the squares on a baking sheet. Put a little Almond Paste (page 102) in the centre of each square (about 50 g/2 oz in all). Brush the paste lightly with beaten egg. Make a cut from the corners of each square towards the middle. Fold the corners of each triangular piece towards the centre, then press the points into the almond paste firmly. Brush with beaten egg. Cover the pastries with oiled polythene and leave in a warm place for about 10-15 minutes until puffy. (It is important not to have the temperature too warm or the butter will run out.) Bake for 12-15 minutes. When cool, place a little raspberry jam in the centre of each pastry.

MAKES 8

FRUIT SNAILS   Cream together 50 g/2 oz butter, 50 g/2 oz caster sugar and 10 ml/2 tsp ground cinnamon. Roll out the second half of the dough into a rectangle 15 × 40 cm/6 × 16 inches. Spread with the spiced butter and scatter 25 g/1 oz sultanas over it. Roll up from the short side to make a fat roll. Cut in into 8 slices and place on a baking sheet. Flatten slightly. Prove and bake as above. Decorate with a little white Glacé Icing (page 103) when cold.

MAKES 8

COCKSCOMBS   Roll out the dough and cut it into squares as for windmills. Spread the middle of each square with a little bought chocolate hazelnut spread and top with a thin sausage shape of Almond Paste (page 102). Fold each square in half and pinch the edges together to seal in the filling. Make 4 or 5 cuts into the pastries, then place on a baking sheet, curving them slightly to open the slits. Prove and bake as for windmills. Brush with Apricot Glaze (page 126) when cool.

MAKES 8

CORNISH SPLITS

Illustrated on page 154

fat for greasing
400 g/14 oz strong white flour
50 g/2 oz sugar
125 ml/4 fl oz milk
15 g/½ oz fresh yeast or 10 ml/2 tsp dried
    yeast
5 ml/1 tsp salt
50 g/2 oz butter
flour for kneading

Grease a baking sheet. Sift about 75 g/3 oz of the flour and 5 ml/1 tsp of the sugar into a large bowl. Warm the milk and 125 ml/4 fl oz water until lukewarm. Blend in the fresh yeast or sprinkle on the dried yeast. Pour the yeast liquid into the flour and sugar, then beat well. Leave the bowl in a warm place for 20 minutes.

Sift the rest of the flour and sugar and the salt together in a bowl. Rub in the butter. Stir into the yeast mixture and mix to form a soft dough. Turn on to a lightly floured surface and knead for about 6 minutes or until the dough is smooth and no longer sticky. Return to the bowl and cover with cling film. Leave in a warm place until the dough has doubled in volume – this will take up to 2 hours, or longer.

Knead the dough again until firm. Divide into 50 g/2 oz pieces and form each into a round bun. Place the buns on the prepared baking sheet. Place the sheet in a large, lightly oiled polythene bag. Leave in a warm place for about 30 minutes or until the buns have doubled in size. Set the oven at 220°C/425°F/gas 7.

Bake for 15-20 minutes, until golden brown. Serve cold, split and spread with cream and jam.

MAKES 14

BUN LOAF

400 g/14 oz strong white flour
5 ml/1 tsp sugar
125 ml/4 fl oz milk
25 g/1 oz fresh yeast or 15 ml/1 tbsp dried
    yeast
5 ml/1 tsp salt
7.5 ml/1½ tsp ground mixed spice
2.5 ml/½ tsp ground cinnamon
2.5 ml/½ tsp grated nutmeg
50 g/2 oz butter
50 g/2 oz caster sugar
100 g/4 oz currants
50 g/2 oz chopped mixed peel
1 egg
flour for kneading

GLAZE
30 ml/2 tbsp milk
40 g/1½ oz caster sugar

Grease a 23 × 13 × 7.5 cm/9 × 5 × 3 inch loaf tin. Sift about 75 g/3 oz of the flour and the 5 ml/1 tsp sugar into a large bowl. Warm the milk and 75 ml/3 fl oz water until lukewarm. Blend in the fresh yeast or sprinkle on the dried yeast. Pour the yeast liquid into the flour and sugar, then beat well. Leave the bowl in a warm place for 20 minutes.

Sift the rest of the flour, the salt and spices into a bowl. Rub in the butter. Add the caster sugar and dried fruit. Beat the egg into the yeast mixture and add the flour, fat and fruit mixture. Mix to a soft dough. Turn on to a lightly floured surface and knead for about 5 minutes until the dough is smooth and no longer sticky. Return to the bowl and cover with cling film. Leave in a warm place until the dough has almost doubled in volume – this will take up to 2 hours, or longer.

Knead the dough again until firm. Shape into a loaf and place in the prepared loaf tin. Place the tin in a large, lightly oiled polythene bag. Leave for about 45 minutes until the dough has doubled in volume. Set the oven at 220°C/425°F/gas 7.

Bake for 30-40 minutes until golden brown. For the glaze, boil the milk, sugar and 30 ml/2 tbsp water together for 6 minutes. Brush the surface with the glaze.

MAKES ABOUT 12 SLICES

◇

SWEET ALMOND BREAD

A layer of almond paste is baked into this bread.

fat for greasing
200 g/7 oz strong white flour
5 ml/1 tsp sugar
100 ml/3½ fl oz milk
15 g/½ oz fresh yeast or 10 ml/2 tsp dried
     yeast
2.5 ml/½ tsp salt
25 g/1 oz butter or margarine
1 egg
flour
milk for glazing
sifted icing sugar for dredging

ALMOND PASTE
75 g/3 oz icing sugar, sifted
75 g/3 oz ground almonds
5 ml/1 tsp lemon juice
few drops of almond essence
beaten egg white

Grease a baking sheet. Sift about 50 g/2 oz of the flour and the sugar into a bowl. Warm the milk until lukewarm. Blend in the fresh yeast or sprinkle on the dried yeast. Pour the yeast liquid into the flour and sugar, then beat well. Leave the bowl in a warm place for 20 minutes.

Sift the remaining flour and salt into a bowl. Rub in the butter or margarine. Beat the egg into the yeast mixture and stir in the flour and fat mixture. Mix to a soft dough. Turn on to a lightly floured surface and knead for about 5 minutes or until the dough is smooth and no longer sticky. Return to the bowl and cover with cling film. Leave in a warm place until the dough has doubled in volume – this will take about 40 minutes, or longer.

To make the almond paste, mix the icing sugar, ground almonds, lemon juice and almond essence with enough egg white to bind the mixture together.

Roll out the dough on a lightly floured surface to a 25 cm/10 inch round.

Spread the almond paste on to half the dough round. Fold the uncovered half of the dough over to cover the paste. Press the edges of dough firmly together. Brush the surface with milk. Place on the prepared baking sheet and cover with oiled polythene. Leave for about 30 minutes to rise. Set the oven at 220°C/425°F/gas 7.

Bake for 10 minutes, then reduce the oven temperature to 190°C/375°F/gas 5. Continue baking for 15-25 minutes, until golden brown. When cold, dredge with a little sifted icing sugar.

MAKES ONE 400 G/14 OZ LOAF

◇

CHERRY BREAD

Illustrated on page 153

fat for greasing
200 g/7 oz strong white flour
5 ml/1 tsp sugar
100 ml/3½ fl oz milk
15 g/½ oz fresh yeast or 10 ml/2 tsp dried
   yeast
2.5 ml/½ tsp salt
25 g/1 oz butter or margarine
1 egg
flour for kneading
75 g/3 oz glacé cherries
milk for glazing

Grease a 15 cm/6 inch cake tin. Sift about 50 g/2 oz of the flour and the sugar into a bowl. Warm the milk until lukewarm. Blend in the fresh yeast or sprinkle on the dried yeast. Pour the yeast liquid into the flour and sugar, then beat well. Leave the bowl in a warm place for 20 minutes.

Sift the remaining flour and salt into a bowl. Rub in the butter or margarine. Beat the egg into the yeast mixture and stir in the flour and fat mixture. Mix to a soft dough. Turn on to a lightly floured surface and knead for about 5 minutes or until the dough is smooth and no longer sticky. Return to the bowl and cover with cling film. Leave in a warm place until the dough has doubled in volume – this will take about 40 minutes, or longer.

Chop the cherries roughly and squeeze them into the risen dough until well distributed. Press the dough into the prepared cake tin and brush the surface with a little milk. Place the tin in a large, lightly oiled polythene bag. Leave in a warm place for about 30 minutes or until the dough reaches just above the edge of the tin. Set the oven at 220°C/425°F/gas 7.

Bake for 10 minutes, then reduce the oven temperature to 190°C/375°F/gas 5. Continue baking for 15-25 minutes, until golden brown.

MAKES ONE 400 G/14 OZ LOAF

———————— ◇ ————————

BARA BRITH

Illustrated on page 153

This fruit loaf is a Welsh speciality and is still sold in most parts of Wales today.

oil for greasing
450 g/1 lb strong plain flour
75 g/3 oz lard or butter
50 g/2 oz chopped mixed peel
150 g/5 oz seedless raisins
50 g/2 oz currants
75 g/3 oz soft brown sugar
5 ml/1 tsp ground mixed spice
pinch of salt
250 ml/8 fl oz milk
25 g/1 oz fresh yeast
5 ml/1 tsp sugar
1 egg, beaten
flour for kneading
honey for glazing

Grease a 20 × 13 × 7.5 cm/8 × 5 × 3 inch loaf tin. Sift the flour into a bowl and rub in the lard or butter. Stir in the peel, raisins, currants, brown sugar, mixed spice and salt. Warm the milk to lukewarm.

Blend the fresh yeast to a thin paste with the sugar and milk. Set aside in a warm place until frothy – about 5 minutes.

Make a well in the centre of the dry ingredients and add the yeast mixture and the beaten egg. Mix to a soft dough, then cover the bowl with cling film. Leave in a warm place until the dough has doubled in volume – this will take about 2 hours, or longer.

Turn out the dough on to a floured board and knead well. Place in the prepared loaf tin, pressing it well into the corners. Place the tin in a large, lightly oiled polythene bag. Leave for a further 30 minutes to rise. Set the oven at 200°C/400°F/gas 6.

Bake for 15 minutes, then reduce the oven temperature to 160°C/325°F/gas 3. Continue baking for about 1¼ hours. Turn out on to a wire rack. Brush the top with clear warm honey while still warm. Serve sliced, spread with butter.

MAKES 12 SLICES

WHOLEMEAL FRUIT BREAD

fat for greasing
400 g/14 oz wholemeal flour
7.5 ml/1½ tsp salt
15 g/½ oz lard
15 g/½ oz fresh yeast or 10 ml/2 tsp dried
   yeast
2.5 ml/½ tsp sugar
flour for kneading
100 g/4 oz stoned prunes
grated rind of 1 orange
25 g/1 oz sugar

Grease a 23 × 13 × 7.5 cm/9 × 5 × 3 inch loaf tin. Mix the flour and salt in a large bowl. Rub in the lard. Measure 250 ml/8 fl oz lukewarm water.

Blend the fresh yeast to a thin paste with the sugar and a little of the warm water. Set aside in a warm place until frothy – about 5 minutes. Sprinkle dried yeast over all the warm water and set aside until frothy, then stir well.

Add the yeast liquid and remaining water to the flour mixture and mix to a soft dough. Turn on to a floured surface and knead for about 4 minutes or until the dough is smooth and elastic and no longer sticky. Return to the bowl and cover with cling film. Leave in a warm place until the dough has doubled in volume – this will take up to 2 hours, or longer.

Meanwhile, chop the prunes roughly. Knead the dough again until firm, incorporating the prunes, orange rind and 25 g/1 oz sugar. Place the dough in the prepared loaf tin. Place the tin in a large, lightly oiled polythene bag. Leave in a warm place for about 1 hour or until the dough has doubled in volume. Set the oven at 230°C/450°F/gas 8.

Bake for 30-40 minutes, until the loaf is golden brown and crisp, and sounds hollow when tapped on the bottom.

MAKES ONE 800 G/1¾ LB LOAF

CHELSEA BUNS

Illustrated on page 155

fat for greasing
400 g/14 oz strong white flour
5 ml/1 tsp sugar
200 ml/7 fl oz milk
25 g/1 oz fresh yeast or 15 ml/1 tbsp dried
    yeast
5 ml/1 tsp salt
50 g/2 oz butter
1 egg
flour for kneading
15 ml/1 tbsp butter
150 g/5 oz currants
50 g/2 oz chopped mixed peel
100 g/4 oz soft brown sugar
honey for glazing

Grease a baking sheet. Sift about 75 g/ 3 oz of the flour and the sugar into a large bowl. Warm the milk until lukewarm. Blend in the fresh yeast or sprinkle on the dried yeast. Pour the yeast liquid into the flour and sugar, then beat well. Leave the bowl in a warm place for 20 minutes.

Sift the remaining flour and the salt into a bowl. Rub in the 50 g/2 oz butter. Beat the egg into the yeast mixture and add the flour and fat mixture. Mix to a soft dough. Turn on to a lightly floured surface and knead for about 6 minutes or until the dough is smooth and no longer sticky. Return to the bowl and cover with cling film. Leave in a warm place until the dough has doubled in volume.

On a floured surface, roll out the dough to a 50 cm/20 inch square. Melt the ·remaining butter and brush it all over the surface of the dough. Sprinkle with the dried fruit and sugar. Roll up the dough like a Swiss roll. Cut the roll into 16 equal pieces. Place the buns, about 2.5 cm/1 inch apart, on the prepared baking sheet with the cut side uppermost. Place the baking sheet in a large, lightly oiled polythene bag. Leave in a warm place for about 30 minutes or until the buns have joined together and are light and puffy. Set the oven at 220°C/425°F/gas 7.

Bake for 15-20 minutes, until golden brown. While still hot, brush with honey.

MAKES 16

VARIATIONS

Use this classic recipe as a basis for making rolled buns with different fillings. Try chopped ready-to-eat dried apricots with chopped walnuts and a little honey; chopped dates combined with orange marmalade and some grated cooking apple; or chocolate cooking chips with chopped hazelnuts and chopped mixed peel.

> **MRS BEETON'S TIP** Chelsea buns should be arranged in a square shape on the baking tray so that they join together when risen and cooked. A square deep cake tin may be used instead of a baking tray.

Bara Brith and Cherry Bread (both on page 150)

Cornish Splits (page 148)

Hot Cross Buns (page 161) and Chelsea Buns (page 152)

Irish Soda Bread and Texas Corn Bread (both on page 166)

Plum Slice (page 187)

Italian-style Ham and Egg Pizza (pages 182 and 185)

Calzone (page 183)

Empanada (page 186)

HOT CROSS BUNS

Illustrated on page 155

400 g/14 oz strong white flour
5 ml/1 tsp sugar
125 ml/4 fl oz milk
25 g/1 oz fresh yeast or 15 ml/1 tbsp dried
    yeast
5 ml/1 tsp salt
7.5 ml/1½ tsp ground mixed spice
2.5 ml/½ tsp ground cinnamon
2.5 ml/½ tsp grated nutmeg
50 g/2 oz butter
50 g/2 oz caster sugar
100 g/4 oz currants
50 g/2 oz chopped mixed peel
1 egg
flour for kneading

GLAZE
30 ml/2 tbsp milk
40 g/1½ oz caster sugar

Sift about 75 g/3 oz of the flour and the 5 ml/1 tsp sugar into a large bowl. Warm the milk and 75 ml/3 fl oz water until lukewarm. Blend in the fresh yeast or sprinkle on the dried yeast. Pour the yeast liquid into the flour and sugar, then beat well. Leave the bowl in a warm place for 20 minutes.

Sift the rest of the flour, the salt and spices into a bowl. Rub in the butter. Add the caster sugar and dried fruit. Beat the egg into the frothy yeast mixture and add the flour, fat and fruit mixture. Mix to a soft dough. Turn on to a lightly floured surface and knead for about 5 minutes. Return to the bowl and cover with cling film. Leave in a warm place until the dough has almost doubled in volume.

Knead the dough again until firm. Cut into 12 equal pieces and shape each into a round bun. Place on a floured baking sheet. With a sharp knife, slash a cross on the top of each bun, or make crosses with pastry trimmings. Cover with oiled polythene. Leave for about 35 minutes until the dough has doubled in volume. Set the oven at 220°C/425°F/gas 7. Bake for 15-20 minutes, until golden. Boil the milk, sugar and 30 ml/2 tbsp water for 6 minutes. Brush over the hot buns.

MAKES 12

LARDY CAKE

¼ quantity risen Basic White Bread
    dough, about 350 g/12 oz (page 132)
flour for rolling out
125 g/4½ oz lard
100 g/4 oz caster sugar
100 g/4 oz sultanas or currants
5 ml/1 tsp ground mixed spice
10 ml/2 tsp caster sugar for glazing

Roll out the dough on a floured surface to a strip 2 cm/¾ inch thick. Place a third of the lard in small pats over the surface of the dough. Sprinkle one-third of the sugar, dried fruit and spice over it. Fold the dough into three by bringing the bottom third up and the top third down. Repeat the rolling and folding twice more.

Roll out to fit a 20 cm/8 inch square slab cake tin or baking tin. Score diamond shapes in the surface of the dough with a sharp knife. Place the tin in a large, lightly oiled polythene bag. Leave in a warm place for about 45 minutes or until risen by half. Set the oven at 200°C/400°F/gas 6.

Bake for 40 minutes, until golden. To make the glaze, boil the sugar and 15 ml/1 tbsp water in a saucepan until syrupy, then brush over the warm cake.

MAKES 18-20 SLICES

REVEL BUNS

These take a day to prove.

large pinch of powdered saffron
125 ml/4 fl oz milk
20 g/¾ oz fresh yeast
100 g/4 oz caster sugar
450 g/1 lb plain flour
2.5 ml/½ tsp ground cinnamon
pinch of salt
100 g/4 oz butter
150 ml/5 fl oz double cream
2 eggs, beaten
100 g/4 oz currants
fat for greasing
beaten egg for glazing

Put the saffron in a heatproof jug. Warm the milk until steaming and pour it over the saffron. Leave to infuse for 30 minutes.

Strain 60 ml/4 tbsp of the milk and leave until lukewarm. Blend the yeast to a thin paste with 2.5 ml/½ tsp of the sugar and the strained warm milk. Set aside in a warm place until frothy – about 5 minutes.

Sift the flour with the cinnamon and salt into a bowl. Rub in the butter. Strain the remaining saffron-flavoured milk and mix in the cream. Pour the milk and cream into the dry ingredients, with the eggs and yeast mixture. Mix thoroughly, then add the currants. Knead well. Cover and chill in the refrigerator overnight.

Next day, grease a baking sheet. Shape the mixture into 12 buns. Place on the prepared baking sheet and leave to rise for 20-30 minutes. Set the oven at 190°C/375°F/gas 5.

Brush the tops with beaten egg and sprinkle with the remaining sugar. Bake for about 15 minutes. Serve warm or cold with butter, for tea.

MAKES 12

BATH BUNS

fat for greasing
400 g/14 oz strong white flour
5 ml/1 tsp sugar
125 ml/4 fl oz milk
25 g/1 oz fresh yeast or 15 ml/1 tbsp dried
    yeast
5 ml/1 tsp salt
50 g/2 oz butter
50 g/2 oz caster sugar
150 g/5 oz sultanas
50 g/2 oz chopped mixed peel
2 eggs
beaten egg for glazing
50 g/2 oz sugar nibs or lump sugar,
    coarsely crushed

Grease a baking sheet. Sift about 75 g/3 oz of the flour and the 5 ml/1 tsp sugar into a large bowl. Warm the milk and 75 ml/3 fl oz water until lukewarm. Blend in the fresh yeast or sprinkle on the dried yeast. Pour the yeast liquid into the flour and sugar, then beat well. Leave the bowl in a warm place for 20 minutes.

Sift the rest of the flour and the salt into a bowl. Rub in the butter. Add the caster sugar and dried fruit. Beat the eggs into the yeast mixture and add the flour, fat and fruit mixture. Mix to a very soft dough. Beat with a wooden spoon for 3 minutes. Cover the bowl with cling film. Leave in a warm place until the dough has almost doubled in volume – this will take about 45 minutes, or longer.

Beat the dough again for 1 minute. Place 15 ml/1 tbsp spoonfuls of the mixture on the prepared baking sheet, leaving plenty of space between them. Place the sheet in a large, lightly oiled polythene bag. Leave in a warm place for about 20 minutes or until the buns have almost doubled in size. Set the oven at 220°C/425°F/gas 7.

Brush the surface of each bun with beaten

egg and sprinkle with the sugar nibs or lump sugar. Bake for 15-20 minutes, until golden brown.

MAKES 12

———————— ◈ ————————

CHRISTMAS STOLLEN

This is the classic German Christmas bread.

butter for greasing
1 kg/2¼ lb plain flour
75 g/3 oz fresh yeast
200 ml/7 fl oz lukewarm milk
350 g/12 oz butter
juice and grated rind of 1 lemon
250 g/9 oz caster sugar
2 egg yolks
5 ml/1 tsp salt
500 g/18 oz seedless raisins
225 g/8 oz sultanas
150 g/5 oz blanched slivered almonds
100 g/4 oz chopped mixed peel
flour for dusting
100 g/4 oz unsalted butter
icing sugar for dusting

Butter a baking sheet. Sift the flour into a bowl. Blend the yeast with the warm milk and 50 g/2 oz of the flour. Set aside until frothy.

Meanwhile, melt the butter. Cool slightly, then blend into the remaining flour with the lemon juice. Add the milk and yeast liquid, together with the lemon rind, sugar, egg yolks and salt. Beat well together. Knead the dough until it is very firm and elastic, and leaves the sides of the bowl. Cover with cling film. Leave in a warm place until the dough has doubled in size. This will take about 2 hours.

Meanwhile, mix the dried fruit with the nuts and mixed peel. Knead the dough again, pull the sides to the centre, turn it over and cover once more. Leave to rise for a further 30 minutes. When the dough has doubled in size again, turn it on to a floured surface and knead in the fruit and nut mixture.

Divide the dough in half and roll each half into a pointed oval shape. Lay each on the prepared baking sheet. Place a rolling pin along the length of each piece of the dough in the centre. Roll half the dough lightly from the centre outwards. Brush the thinner rolled half with a little water and fold the other half over it, leaving a margin of about 5 cm/2 inches all around which allows the dough to rise. Press well together; the water will bind it. Cover the stollen and leave to rise in a warm place until doubled in size again. Set the oven at 190°C/375°F/ gas 5.

Melt 50 g/2 oz of the unsalted butter and brush it over the stollen. Bake for about 1 hour, until golden. When baked, melt the remaining unsalted butter, brush it over the stollen, then sprinkle with sifted icing sugar. Keep for a day before cutting.

The stollen will remain fresh for many weeks if well wrapped in foil or greaseproof paper and stored in an airtight tin.

MAKES 2 LOAVES, ABOUT 24 SLICES EACH

———————— ◈ ————————

BREADS WITHOUT YEAST

A short section of doughs that rely on alternative raising agents, including Irish Soda Bread and Eastern-European style bread risen with sour dough.

SOUR DOUGH RYE BREAD

Prepare the starter paste four days before proceeding with the bread recipe.

500 g/18 oz rye flour
200 g/7 oz strong white flour
10 ml/2 tsp salt
15 ml/1 tbsp sugar
15 ml/1 tbsp oil
fat for greasing

STARTER PASTE
100 g/4 oz strong white flour
50 g/2 oz sugar
175 ml/6 fl oz milk

To make the starter paste, sift the flour and sugar in a bowl. Warm the milk until hand-hot, then stir into the flour. Beat to a smooth paste. Place the starter paste in a screw-topped jar and leave in a warm place *for 4 days.*

Grease two 23 × 13 × 7.5 cm/9 × 5 × 3 inch loaf tins. Put the flours, salt and sugar in a large bowl. Add the starter paste, 375 ml/13 fl oz warm water and the oil, then mix to a slack dough. Beat with a wooden spoon for 3 minutes. Place the dough in the prepared loaf tins. Cover with a large, lightly oiled polythene bag. Leave at room temperature for about 24 hours or until the dough reaches the top of the tins. Set the oven at 230°C/450°F/gas 8.

Bake for 10 minutes, then reduce the oven temperature to 190°C/375°F/gas 5. Continue baking for 30-35 minutes, until the loaves are well browned and sound hollow when tapped on the bottom.

MAKES TWO 800 G/1¾ LB LOAVES

MRS BEETON'S TIP To reduce the second rising of the dough to 2 hours, 15 g/½ oz fresh yeast or 10 ml/2 tsp dried yeast can be added when mixing the dough. The fresh yeast should be blended into the warm water or the dried yeast sprinkled over the water.

BASIC QUICK BREAD

fat for greasing
400 g/14 oz self-raising flour or a mixture
  of white and brown self-raising flours
  or 400 g/14 oz plain flour and 20 ml/4
  tsp baking powder
5 ml/1 tsp salt
50 g/2 oz margarine or lard
250 ml/8 fl oz milk or water or a mixture
  as preferred
flour for kneading

Grease a baking sheet. Set the oven at 200°C/400°F/gas 6. Sift the flour, baking powder (if used) and salt into a large bowl. Rub in the margarine or lard. Mix in enough liquid to make a soft dough.

Turn the dough on to a floured surface and knead lightly for 1 minute. Shape the dough into 2 rounds and place them on the prepared baking sheet. Make a cross in the top of each with the back of a knife.

Bake for 30-40 minutes. Cool on a wire rack.

MAKES 2 BUN LOAVES

VARIATIONS

WHOLEMEAL QUICK BREAD Substitute 400 g/14 oz wholemeal flour for the plain flour in the basic recipe. Note that wholemeal flour will give a closer-textured loaf.
NUT BREAD Make Wholemeal Quick Bread. Add 75 g/3 oz chopped nuts and 50 g/2 oz sugar to the dry ingredients, and add 1 beaten egg to the liquid.
APRICOT AND WALNUT LOAF Make the Quick Bread Mixture but use butter as the fat. Add 100 g/4 oz dried and soaked chopped apricots and 50 g/2 oz chopped walnuts to the dry ingredients, and add 1 beaten egg to the liquid.

BASIC SOURED MILK QUICK BREAD

fat for greasing
400 g/14 oz plain flour
5 ml/1 tsp salt
10 ml/2 tsp bicarbonate of soda
10 ml/2 tsp cream of tartar
about 250 ml/8 fl oz soured milk or
  buttermilk

Grease a baking sheet. Set the oven at 220°C/425°F/gas 7. Sift the flour, salt, bicarbonate of soda and cream of tartar into a large bowl. Mix to a light spongy dough with the milk.

Divide the dough into 2 equal pieces and form each into a round cake. Slash a cross on the top of each loaf with a sharp knife. Place on the prepared baking sheet.

Bake for about 30 minutes, until golden brown. Cool on a wire rack.

MAKES 2 LOAVES

MRS BEETON'S TIP The keeping quality of this bread is improved by rubbing 50 g/2 oz lard into the sifted flour.

IRISH SODA BREAD

Illustrated on page 156

fat for greasing
750 g/scant 1¾ lb plain flour
5 ml/1 tsp bicarbonate of soda
5 ml/1 tsp salt
5 ml/1 tsp cream of tartar (if using fresh
  milk)
300 ml/½ pint buttermilk or soured milk
  or fresh milk
flour for dusting

Grease a baking sheet. Set the oven at
190-200°C/375-400°F/gas 5-6. Mix all the
dry ingredients in a bowl, then make a well
in the centre. Add enough milk to make a
fairly slack dough, pouring it in almost all
at once, not spoonful by spoonful. Mix with
a wooden spoon, lightly and quickly.

With floured hands, place the mixture
on a lightly floured surface and flatten the
dough into a round about 2.5 cm/1 inch
thick. Turn on to the prepared baking
sheet. Make a large cross in the surface
with a floured knife to make it heat through
evenly.

Bake for about 40 minutes. Pierce the
centre with a thin skewer to test for readi-
ness; it should come out clean. Wrap the
loaf in a clean tea-towel to keep it soft until
required.

MAKES ONE 750 G/1¾ LB LOAF

TEXAS CORNBREAD

Illustrated on page 156

*This golden bread makes an ideal
accompaniment to soups, stews and casseroles.*

fat for greasing
125 g/4½ oz bacon fat or beef dripping
125 g/4½ oz cornmeal (polenta)
50 g/2 oz plain flour
5 ml/1 tsp salt
5 ml/1 tsp baking powder
2.5 ml/½ tsp bicarbonate of soda
200 ml/7 fl oz buttermilk or fresh milk
  with a squeeze of lemon juice
2 eggs, beaten

Grease a 20 cm/8 inch cake tin. Set the
oven at 230°C/450°F/gas 8. Melt the bacon
fat or dripping, then leave to cool slightly.

Mix the cornmeal, flour, salt, baking
powder and bicarbonate of soda in a bowl.
Add the buttermilk or milk, eggs and melted
fat or dripping. Mix well. Turn into the
prepared cake tin.

Bake for 30 minutes. The bread should
be firm to the touch when done. Serve
warm.

MAKES ABOUT 225 G/8 OZ

TEABREADS AND MUFFINS

Many of these recipes are quick to mix and bake but equally as delicious as yeasted doughs requiring lengthy proving. As a rule, teabreads are not as sweet as cakes and they tend to be less messy too – ideal for lunch boxes and picnics.

BRAN BAKING POWDER MUFFINS

fat for greasing
150 g/5 oz plain flour
5 ml/1 tsp baking powder
2.5 ml/½ tsp salt
50 g/2 oz sugar
100 g/4 oz natural wheat bran
5 ml/1 tsp bicarbonate of soda
200 ml/7 fl oz milk
25 g/1 oz butter
30 ml/2 tbsp golden syrup
1 egg, beaten

Grease twenty 5-6 cm/2-2½ inch patty tins. Set the oven at 200°C/400°F/gas 6. Sift the flour, baking powder and salt into a large bowl. Add the sugar and bran.

Dissolve the bicarbonate of soda in the milk. Melt the butter and syrup together. Add the milk, syrup and egg to the dry ingredients and mix with a wooden spoon until they are dampened and the mixture is lumpy. Do not over-mix. Spoon the mixture into the prepared patty tins, filling them only two-thirds full.

Bake for about 15-20 minutes or until brown and springy to the touch. Loosen from the tins with a palette knife. Cool on a wire rack. Serve while still just warm, or cold.

MAKES 20

VARIATIONS

APRICOT MUFFINS Add 100 g/4 oz soaked and roughly chopped dried apricots to the dough.

HONEY NUT MUFFINS Put 5 ml/1 tsp clear honey and 5 ml/1 tsp finely chopped nuts into each patty tin when half filled. Cover with the extra dough required. Serve nut side uppermost.

———————— ◆ ————————

PLAIN (AMERICAN) MUFFINS

Unlike English muffins, American muffins are quick breads. They are light, savoury or sweet buns made with a slightly more puffed, richer dough than scones. They are very popular breakfast breads.

butter for greasing
200 g/7 oz plain flour
15 ml/1 tbsp baking powder
2.5 ml/½ tsp salt
50 g/2 oz granulated sugar
50 g/2 oz butter
1 egg
200 ml/7 fl oz milk

Butter twelve 6 cm/2½ inch muffin tins or deep bun tins. Set the oven at 200°C/400°F/gas 6. Sift the flour, baking powder, salt and sugar into a bowl.

Melt the butter. Mix with the egg and milk in a separate bowl. Pour the liquid mixture over the dry ingredients. Stir only enough to dampen the flour; the mixture should be lumpy. Spoon the mixture into the prepared muffin tins, as lightly as possible, filling them only two-thirds full.

Bake for about 15 minutes, until well risen and browned. The cooked muffins should be cracked across the middle. Cool in the tins for 2-3 minutes, then turn out on to a wire rack to finish cooling.

MAKES 12

> **MRS BEETON'S TIP** American muffin tins should not be confused with ordinary patty tins. Muffin tins are slightly larger and far deeper than patty tins to allow room for the muffin batter to rise during cooking.

VARIATIONS

BRAMBLE MUFFINS Increase the sugar to 100 g/4 oz. Reserve 50 g/2 oz of the flour. Sprinkle it over 250 g/9 oz drained blackberries. Stir into the mixture last.

BLUEBERRY MUFFINS Reserve 50 g/2 oz of the flour. Sprinkle it over 225 g/8 oz firm blueberries. Stir into the mixture last.

JAM MUFFINS Before baking, top each muffin with 5 ml/1 tsp sharp-flavoured jam.

WALNUT MUFFINS Increase the sugar to 100 g/4 oz. Add 75 g/3 oz chopped walnuts before adding the liquids. After filling the muffin tins, sprinkle with a mixture of sugar, cinnamon, and extra finely chopped walnuts.

RAISIN MUFFINS Add 50 g/2 oz seedless raisins before adding the liquids.

ORANGE APRICOT MUFFINS Add 50 g/2 oz chopped ready-to-eat dried apricots and the grated rind of 1 orange before adding the liquids.

WHOLEMEAL MUFFINS Substitute 100 g/4 oz wholemeal flour for 100 g/4 oz of the plain flour. Do not sift the wholemeal flour, but add it after sifting the plain flour with the other ingredients.

AMERICAN COFFEE BREAD

This bread, made with walnuts, is served at coffee time.

fat for greasing
200 g/7 oz plain flour
100 g/4 oz light soft brown sugar
10 ml/2 tsp baking powder
5 ml/1 tsp salt
30 ml/2 tbsp butter
1 egg, beaten
200 ml/7 fl oz milk
75 g/3 oz walnuts, chopped

Grease a 23 × 13 × 7.5 cm/9 × 5 × 3 inch loaf tin. Set the oven at 180°C/350°F/gas 4.

Sift the dry ingredients into a large bowl. Melt the butter, add to the flour mixture with the egg, milk and walnuts. Beat thoroughly. Spread the mixture in the prepared loaf tin, then level the top.

Bake for about 1 hour, until risen, firm and browned. Cool on a wire rack.

MAKES ABOUT 12 SLICES

VARIATIONS

ORANGE NUT COFFEE BREAD Reduce the milk to 100 ml/3½ fl oz. Instead of sugar, use 250 g/9 oz orange marmalade.
BANANA NUT COFFEE BREAD Reduce the milk to 100 ml/3½ fl oz; add 3 ripe medium bananas, well mashed.

RICH GINGERBREAD

fat for greasing
225 g/8 oz plain flour
1.25 ml/¼ tsp salt
10 ml/2 tsp ground ginger
2.5-5 ml/½-1 tsp ground cinnamon or grated nutmeg
5 ml/1 tsp bicarbonate of soda
100 g/4 oz butter
100 g/4 oz soft light brown sugar
100 g/4 oz golden syrup
1 egg
45 ml/3 tbsp plain yogurt
30 ml/2 tbsp ginger preserve

Line and grease a 23 cm/9 inch square tin. Set the oven at 160°C/325°F/gas 3.

Sift the flour, salt, spices and bicarbonate of soda into a mixing bowl. Heat the butter, sugar and syrup in a saucepan until the butter has melted.

In a bowl, beat the egg and yogurt together. Add to the dry ingredients, with the melted mixture, to give a soft, dropping consistency. Stir in the preserve.

Spoon into the prepared tin and bake for 50-60 minutes until cooked through and firm to the touch. Cool on a wire rack.

MAKES ONE 23 CM/9 INCH CAKE

ALMOND BREAD

fat for greasing
75 g/3 oz almonds
250 g/9 oz plain flour
20 ml/4 tsp baking powder
pinch of salt
2 eggs
100 g/4 oz granulated sugar
90 ml/6 tbsp oil
few drops of almond or vanilla essence
flour
50 g/2 oz caster sugar

Grease and flour a baking sheet. Set the oven at 180°C/350°F/gas 4. Blanch and skin the almonds (page 22), then chop coarsely.

Sift the flour, baking powder and salt together. Beat the eggs and granulated sugar lightly together in a large bowl. Add the oil, flavouring, flour mixture and almonds, and mix to form a dough. With floured hands, form into a long roll about 7.5 ml/3 inches wide. Place on the prepared baking sheet.

Bake for about 30-40 minutes, until lightly browned. Reduce the oven temperature to 150°C/300°F/gas 2. Leave the bread on a wire rack until nearly cold, then cut slant-ways into slices about 1 cm/½ inch thick. Sprinkle lightly with caster sugar and place them on a baking sheet. Return to the oven for about 50-60 minutes until dry and lightly browned.

MAKES ABOUT 12 SLICES

———————— ◇ ————————

BANANA BREAD

Use ripe bananas in this popular recipe.

fat for greasing
300 g/11 oz plain flour
pinch of salt
5 ml/1 tsp bicarbonate of soda
75 g/3 oz margarine
100 g/4 oz granulated sugar
3 eggs, beaten
3 bananas
15 ml/1 tbsp lemon juice

Grease a 23 × 13 × 7.5 cm/9 × 5 × 3 inch loaf tin. Set the oven at 190°C/375°F/gas 5. Sift the flour, salt and bicarbonate of soda together.

Cream the margarine and sugar in a bowl. Beat in the eggs. Mash the bananas with the lemon juice. Add to the creamed mixture, then work in the dry ingredients. Put the mixture into the prepared loaf tin.

Bake for 50-60 minutes, until golden brown. Cool on a wire rack.

MAKES ABOUT 12 SLICES

BANANA AND WALNUT BREAD

fat for greasing
3 bananas
50 g/2 oz walnuts, chopped
200 g/7 oz self-raising flour
5 ml/1 tsp baking powder
1.25 ml/¼ tsp bicarbonate of soda
125 g/4½ oz caster sugar
75 g/3 oz soft margarine
grated rind of ½ lemon
2 eggs
50 g/2 oz seedless raisins

Grease a 23 × 13 × 7.5 cm/9 × 5 × 3 inch loaf tin. Set the oven at 180°C/350°F/ gas 4. Mash the bananas.

Mix all the ingredients in a large bowl. Beat for about 3 minutes by hand using a wooden spoon, or for 2 minutes in a mixer, until smooth. Put the mixture into the prepared loaf tin.

Bake for 1 hour 10 minutes, or until firm to the touch. Cool on a wire rack.

MAKES ABOUT 12 SLICES

APPLE LOAF

fat for greasing
200 g/7 oz plain flour
pinch of salt
5 ml/1 tsp baking powder
2.5 ml/½ tsp ground mixed spice
100 g/4 oz butter or margarine
150 g/5 oz caster sugar
50 g/2 oz currants
100 g/4 oz seedless raisins
200 g/7 oz cooking apples
5 ml/1 tsp lemon juice
2 eggs
about 25 ml/1 fl oz milk
50 g/2 oz icing sugar, sifted
1 tart red-skinned eating apple

Grease a 23 × 13 × 7.5 cm/9 × 5 × 3 inch loaf tin. Set the oven at 190°C/375°F/ gas 5. Sift the flour, salt, baking powder and mixed spice into a large bowl. Rub in the butter or margarine. Add the sugar and dried fruit.

Peel and core the cooking apples, slice thinly, then toss in the lemon juice. Add to the dry mixture. Stir in the eggs and enough milk to make a soft dropping consistency. Put the mixture into the prepared loaf tin.

Bake for about 50-60 minutes, until the loaf is golden brown and a skewer pushed into the centre comes out clean. Cool on a wire rack.

Add enough cold water to the icing sugar to make a brushing consistency. Core the eating apple, cut it into thin segments, and arrange these in a decorative pattern on the loaf. Immediately brush the apple with the icing sugar glaze to prevent discoloration. Leave the glaze to 'set' before serving.

MAKES ABOUT 12 SLICES

FATLESS FRUIT LOAF

fat for greasing
300 g/11 oz mixed dried fruit
150 g/5 oz dark Barbados sugar
200 ml/7 fl oz strong hot tea
1 egg, beaten
300 g/11 oz self-raising flour

Put the fruit and sugar in a large bowl. Pour the hot tea over them. Cover and leave overnight.

Next day, grease and line a 20 × 13 × 7.5 cm/8 × 5 × 3 inch loaf tin. Set the oven at 180°C/350°F/gas 4. Stir the egg into the tea mixture. Stir in the flour and mix well. Put the mixture into the prepared loaf tin.

Bake for 1½ hours. Cool on a wire rack. When cold, wrap in foil and store in a tin.

MAKES ABOUT 12 SLICES

> **MRS BEETON'S TIP** Vary the flavour of this fruit loaf by using different varieties of tea. As well as the lightly flavoured types, such as Earl Grey, try some of the stronger fruit teas and spiced teas.

DATE OR RAISIN BREAD

fat for greasing
200 g/7 oz plain flour
15 ml/1 tbsp baking powder
5 ml/1 tsp salt
large pinch of bicarbonate of soda
100 g/4 oz dates or seedless raisins
50 g/2 oz walnuts or almonds, whole or chopped
25 g/1 oz lard
50 g/2 oz black treacle
50 g/2 oz dark Barbados sugar
150 ml/¼ pint milk

Grease a 20 × 13 × 7.5 cm/8 × 5 × 3 inch loaf tin. Set the oven at 180°C/350°F/gas 4. Sift the flour, baking powder, salt and bicarbonate of soda into a large bowl. Chop the fruit and nuts finely if necessary, and add them to the dry ingredients.

Warm the lard, treacle, sugar and milk together in a saucepan. The sugar should dissolve, but do not overheat it. Add the liquid to the dry ingredients, then mix to a stiff batter. Pour into the prepared loaf tin.

Bake for 1½ hours. Cool on a wire rack. When cold, wrap in foil and store for 24 hours before cutting.

MAKES ABOUT 12 SLICES

MALT BREAD

fat for greasing
400 g/14 oz self-raising flour
10 ml/2 tsp bicarbonate of soda
100 g/4 oz sultanas or seedless raisins
250 ml/8 fl oz milk
60 ml/4 tbsp golden syrup
60 ml/4 tbsp malt extract
2 eggs

Grease a 23 × 13 × 7.5 cm/9 × 5 × 3 inch loaf tin. Set the oven at 190°C/375°F/gas 5. Sift the flour and bicarbonate of soda into a large bowl. Add the dried fruit. Warm the milk, syrup and malt extract in a saucepan. Beat in the eggs. Stir the mixture into the flour. Put into the prepared loaf tin.

Bake for 40-50 minutes, until a skewer pushed into the bread comes out clean. Cool on a wire rack.

MAKES 12 SLICES

☆ **FREEZER TIP**   Freeze teabreads and loaf cakes cut into slices. Seperate the slices with freezer film, then re-shape the loaf and pack it in a polythene bag. Individual slices may be removed as required.

COCONUT BREAD

fat for greasing
100 g/4 oz butter
150 g/5 oz granulated sugar
150 g/5 oz seedless raisins, chopped
50 g/2 oz chopped mixed peel
250 g/9 oz desiccated coconut
5 ml/1 tsp vanilla essence
1 egg
175 ml/6 fl oz milk
400 g/14 oz self-raising flour
pinch of salt
flour for kneading

Grease a 23 × 13 × 7.5 cm/9 × 5 × 3 inch loaf tin. Set the oven at 190°C/375°F/gas 5.

Cream the butter and sugar in a bowl. Add the raisins, then the rest of the ingredients. Mix well. Turn on to a floured surface and knead until smooth. Put the mixture into the prepared loaf tin.

Bake for 50-60 minutes, until golden brown. Cool on a wire rack.

MAKES ABOUT 12 SLICES

🥣 **MRS BEETON'S TIP**   This teabread is delicious served sliced and thinly topped with chocolate spread instead of butter.

SWEET DATE BREAD

Buy blocks of compressed, stoned dates sold specifically for cooking or look for packets of ready chopped dates, usually rolled in caster sugar.

fat for greasing
400 g/14 oz plain flour
pinch of salt
20 ml/4 tsp bicarbonate of soda
150 g/5 oz dark soft brown sugar
125 g/4½ oz sultanas or seedless raisins
75 g/3 oz walnuts, chopped
50 g/2 oz margarine
400 g/14 oz stoned dates, finely chopped
2 eggs
5 ml/1 tsp vanilla essence

Grease a 23 × 13 × 7.5 cm/9 × 5 × 3 inch loaf tin. Set the oven at 190°C/375°F/gas 5. Sift the flour, salt and bicarbonate of soda into a large bowl. Add the sugar and sultanas or raisins, then the walnuts.

Add the margarine to the dates and pour on 250 ml/8 fl oz boiling water. Add the date mixture, eggs and vanilla essence to the dry ingredients and mix thoroughly. Put the mixture into the prepared loaf tin.

Bake for 40-50 minutes, until the loaf is golden brown and a skewer pushed into the bread comes out clean. Cool on a wire rack.

MAKES ABOUT 12 SLICES

DATE AND CHEESE BREAD

Use a mild cheese such a Lancashire, Caerphilly, Wensleydale or mild Cheddar to enrich this bread rather than to give it a strong flavour.

fat for greasing
flour for dusting
200 g/7 oz stoned dates
1 egg
125 g/4½ oz mild cheese, grated
175 g/6 oz plain flour
5 ml/1 tsp bicarbonate of soda
1.25 ml/¼ tsp salt
50 g/2 oz granulated sugar
50 g/2 oz soft brown sugar

Grease and flour a 23 × 13 × 7.5 cm/9 × 5 × 3 inch loaf tin. Set the oven at 160°C/325°F/gas 3. Place the dates in a bowl and pour 125 ml/4 fl oz boiling water on to them. Allow to stand for 5 minutes.

Mix in the egg, then add the cheese. Sift the flour, bicarbonate of soda and salt into the date mixture. Add both sugars and mix thoroughly. Put the mixture into the prepared loaf tin.

Bake for about 50 minutes, until the loaf is springy to the touch and a skewer pushed into the centre comes out clean. Cool on a wire rack.

MAKES ABOUT 12 SLICES

HONEY BREAD

fat for greasing
100 g/4 oz margarine
100 g/4 oz caster sugar
2 eggs, beaten
90 ml/6 tbsp clear honey
250 g/9 oz self-raising flour or 250 g/9 oz
    plain flour and 15 ml/1 tbsp baking
    powder
5 ml/1 tsp salt
about 125 ml/4 fl oz milk

Grease a 20 × 13 × 7.5 cm/8 × 5 × 3 inch loaf tin. Set the oven at 180°C/350°F/ gas 4.

Cream the margarine and sugar in a bowl until pale and fluffy. Beat in the eggs and honey. Add the dry ingredients alternately with the milk until a soft dropping consistency is obtained. (Add the milk carefully as the full amount may not be needed.) Put the mixture into the prepared loaf tin.

Bake for 1¼ hours. Cool on wire rack. When cold, wrap in foil and keep for 24 hours before serving. Serve sliced and buttered.

MAKES ABOUT 12 SLICES

MRS BEETON'S TIP Warm the jar of honey by standing it in a dish of hot water for 5 minutes. This makes it more runny and easier to measure accurately.

ORANGE BREAD

This loaf is best left overnight before eating.

fat for greasing
50 g/2 oz lard
200 g/7 oz granulated sugar
2 eggs, beaten
400 g/14 oz plain flour
10 ml/2 tsp baking powder
10 ml/2 tsp bicarbonate of soda
pinch of salt
250 ml/8 fl oz orange juice
15 ml/1 tbsp grated orange rind
100 g/4 oz chopped mixed nuts

Grease a 23 × 13 × 7.5 cm/9 × 5 × 3 inch loaf tin. Set the oven at 190°C/375°F/ gas 5.

Melt the lard, then add to the sugar in a bowl. Beat in the eggs. Sift the flour, baking powder, bicarbonate of soda and salt. Add the flour alternately with the orange juice to the lard and sugar. Stir in the orange rind and nuts. Put the mixture into the prepared loaf tin.

Bake for 50-60 minutes, until the loaf is springy to the touch. Cool on a wire rack.

MAKES ABOUT 12 SLICES

MRS BEETON'S TIP Mixtures with bicarbonate of soda should be baked as soon as they are mixed. The bicarbonate of soda begins to work when it is moistened, then it becomes more vigorous as a raising agent when heated.

NORTH RIDING BREAD

This rich, dark fruit bread is better if kept in a tin for a week before use.

fat for greasing
400 g/14 oz plain flour
2.5 ml/½ tsp salt
15 ml/1 tbsp baking powder
2.5 ml/½ tsp grated nutmeg
100 g/4 oz lard
150 g/5 oz demerara sugar
150 g/5 oz currants
150 g/5 oz seedless raisins
75 g/3 oz chopped mixed peel
15 ml/1 tbsp treacle
2.5 ml/½ tsp almond essence
250 ml/8 fl oz milk

Grease a 23 × 13 × 7.5 cm/9 × 5 × 3 inch loaf tin. Set the oven at 190°C/375°F/ gas 5. Sift the flour, salt, baking powder and nutmeg into a large bowl. Rub in the lard. Add the sugar and dried fruit. Stir the treacle and almond essence into the milk and mix into the dry ingredients to give a soft dough. Put the mixture into the prepared loaf tin.

Bake for 45-50 minutes, until a skewer pushed into the bread comes out clean. Cool on a wire rack.

MAKES ABOUT 12 SLICES

CURLED WIGGS

Wiggs were made with milk and shaped into small or large cakes. Some 18th century cooks added yeast or the wiggs could be leavened with bicarbonate of soda, as here.

fat for greasing
400 g/14 oz golden syrup (in can)
75 g/3 oz unsalted butter
175 ml/6 fl oz soured milk
450 g/1 lb plain flour
5 ml/1 tsp bicarbonate of soda
pinch of salt
10 ml/2 tsp caraway seeds
10 ml/2 tsp ground ginger or mixed spice

Grease two 18 cm/7 inch sandwich tins or ovenproof soup plates, then place them on a sheet of foil on a baking sheet. Set the oven at 180°C/350°F/gas 4.

Warm the can of syrup in the oven, uncovered, to make measuring easier. Measure the syrup, put in a saucepan and add the butter. Heat together gently until the butter melts. Remove from the heat and add the milk. Sift the flour, bicarbonate of soda and salt into a large bowl. Add the seeds and spice. Stir in the syrup mixture. Divide the mixture between the prepared tins.

Bake for 25-30 minutes, or until the wiggs have risen and curled over the edges of the tins or bowls. Serve warm, cut in wedges, with butter.

MAKES 2 LARGE WIGGS

———————— ◆ ————————

TEA BRACK

'Brac' is a Celtic word for bread. The dried fruits in this tea bread are soaked overnight in tea to flavour and plump them up.

fat for greasing
500 g/18 oz sultanas
500 g/18 oz seedless raisins
500 g/18 oz soft light brown sugar
750 ml/1¼ pints black tea
3 eggs, beaten
500 g/17 oz plain flour
5 ml/1 tsp baking powder
15 ml/1 tbsp ground mixed spice
   (optional)
honey for glazing

Soak the dried fruit and sugar in the tea overnight.

Next day, grease three 20 × 10 × 7.5 cm/8 × 4 × 3 inch loaf tins. Set the oven at 150°C/300°F/gas 2.

Add the egg to the tea mixture, alternately with the flour in 3 equal parts. Stir in the baking powder and spice, if used. Turn the mixture into the prepared loaf tins.

Bake for 1½ hours, or until the loaves sound hollow when tapped underneath. Leave to cool. Melt the honey and brush it on the cooled loaves to glaze them.

MAKES 3 LOAVES

MOGGY

fat for greasing
350 g/12 oz flour
pinch of salt
7.5 ml/1½ tsp baking powder
75 g/3 oz margarine
75 g/3 oz lard
100 g/4 oz caster sugar
100 g/4 oz golden syrup
about 50 ml/2 fl oz milk

Grease a baking sheet. Set the oven at 180°C/350°F/gas 4. Sift the flour, salt and baking powder in a bowl. Rub in the margarine and lard, then mix in the sugar. Mix the syrup with the dry ingredients, adding enough milk to make the mixture into a stiff dough. Shape into a round or oval flat bun about 2.5 cm/1 inch thick. Place on the prepared baking sheet.

Bake for 25-35 minutes, until firm and light brown. Serve warm or cold, cut in wedges or slices, and thickly buttered.

MAKES ONE 675 G/1½ LB BUN

> **MRS BEETON'S TIP** To make the measuring of golden syrup easier, warm the syrup in the oven, uncovered, in its tin.

LINCOLNSHIRE PLUM BREAD

Prunes give a delightfully rich taste to this bread.

fat for greasing
100 g/4 oz prunes
100 g/4 oz butter
100 g/4 oz soft light brown sugar
2.5 ml/½ tsp ground mixed spice
2.5 ml/½ tsp ground cinnamon
2.5 ml/½ tsp gravy browning (optional)
2 eggs, lightly beaten
15 ml/1 tbsp brandy
100 g/4 oz sultanas
100 g/4 oz currants
175 g/6 oz self-raising flour
pinch of salt

Soak the prunes overnight in cold water. Next day, grease and line a 23 × 13 × 7.5 cm/9 × 5 × 3 inch loaf tin. Set the oven at 140°C/275°F/gas 1. Drain the prunes well and pat dry. Remove the stones and chop the prunes finely.

Cream the butter and sugar in a bowl until light and fluffy. Beat in the spices and gravy browning, if used. Mix the eggs with the brandy, then beat into the creamed mixture. Toss the chopped prunes and other dried fruit in a little of the flour. Mix the rest of the flour with the salt. Fold it into the creamed mixture, then fold in all the dried fruit. Turn the mixture into the prepared tin and level the top.

Bake for 3 hours. Cool in the tin. When cold, turn out and store in an airtight tin.

**MAKES ONE 23 × 13 ×7.5 CM/
9 × 5 × 3 INCH LOAF**

LAVENHAM BUNS

fat for greasing
325 g/11½ oz plain flour
100 g/4 oz ground rice
10 ml/2 tsp baking powder
100 g/4 oz butter
75 g/3 oz caster sugar
2 eggs, beaten
milk
75 g/3 oz currants or 35 g/1¼ oz caraway
    seeds
flour for rolling out

Grease a baking sheet. Set the oven at 180°C/350°F/gas 4. Sift the flour, ground rice and baking powder into a bowl. Rub in the butter and stir in the sugar. Add the egg to bind the dry ingredients to a firm dough. Stir in a very little milk, if required. Mix in the dried fruit or seeds.

On a lightly floured surface, pat or roll out the dough to 2.5 cm/1 inch thick. Cut out in 7.5 cm/3 inch rounds. Place on the prepared baking sheet.

Bake for 20-30 minutes, until firm and lightly browned. Serve hot with butter for tea or supper.

MAKES 12-16

SCONES

From basic scones and their many variations to deliciously different Pumpkin Scones: a few pages of ideas for some of the easiest and quickest of traditional baked goods.

PLAIN SCONES

fat for greasing
200 g/7 oz self-raising flour
2.5 ml/½ tsp salt
25-50 g/1-2 oz butter or margarine
125 ml/4 fl oz milk
flour for kneading
milk or beaten egg for glazing (optional)

Grease a baking sheet. Set the oven at 220°C/425°F/gas 7. Sift the flour and salt into a large bowl. Rub in the butter or margarine, then mix to a soft dough with the milk, using a round-bladed knife. Knead very lightly on a floured surface until smooth.

Roll out to about 1 cm/½ inch thickness and cut into rounds, using a 6 cm/2½ inch cutter. (Alternatively, divide into 2 equal portions and roll each piece into a round 1-2 cm/½-¾ inch thick. Mark each round into 6 wedges.) Re-roll the trimmings and re-cut.

Place the scones on the prepared baking sheet. Brush the tops with milk or beaten egg, if liked. Bake for 10-12 minutes. Cool on a wire rack.

MAKES 12

OTHER RAISING AGENTS

Scones can be made using plain flour with raising agents: For 200 g/7 oz plain flour, use 5 ml/1 tsp bicarbonate of soda and 10 ml/2 tsp cream of tartar. Or use 20 ml/4 tsp baking powder as the raising agent.

> **MRS BEETON'S TIP** Soured milk or buttermilk used instead of milk makes delicious scones. They are best made with the plain flour, 5 m/1 tsp bicarbonate of soda and 5 ml/1 tsp cream of tartar.

A VARIETY OF SCONE DOUGHS

CHEESE SCONES Add 75 g/3 oz grated cheese to the dry ingredients before mixing in the milk. Cut into finger shapes or squares.

SAVOURY HERB SCONES Add 50 g/2 oz diced cooked ham, 30 ml/2 tbsp grated Parmesan cheese and 5 ml/1 tsp dried mixed herbs to the dry ingredients before mixing in the milk.

CHEESE WHIRLS Add 75 g/3 oz grated cheese to the dry ingredients. Roll out the dough into a rectangle. Sprinkle with another 50 g/2 oz grated cheese, then roll up the dough like a Swiss roll. Cut into 1 cm/½ inch slices and lay them flat on greased baking sheets. Brush with milk or egg and bake as in the basic recipe.

FRUIT SCONES Add 50 g/2 oz caster sugar and 50 g/2 oz currants, sultanas or other dried fruit to the basic recipe.

GRIDDLE SCONES Add 50 g/2 oz sultanas to the basic dough. Roll out to 5 mm-1 cm/¼-½ inch thickness, then cut into 6 cm/2½ inch rounds. Cook on a moderately hot, lightly floured griddle or heavy frying pan for 3 minutes or until the scones are golden brown underneath and the edges are dry. Turn over and cook for about another 2 minutes until golden brown on both sides. Cool in a linen tea-towel or other similar cloth.

INVERARY MUFFINS Use only 75 ml/3 fl oz buttermilk or soured milk to make the dough, and add 25 g/1 oz caster sugar and 1 egg. Roll out 1 cm/½ inch thick, and cut into 7.5 cm/3 inch rounds. Cook on a griddle or heavy frying pan in the same way as Griddle Scones but for slightly longer.

NUT SCONES Add 50 g/2 oz chopped nuts to the basic recipe.

SCONES MADE WITH OIL Use 45 ml/3 tbsp olive oil or corn oil instead of the fat in the basic recipe. Reduce the milk to 75 ml/3 fl oz and add an egg.

POTATO SCONES Use 100 g/4 oz flour and 100 g/4 oz sieved cooked mashed potato. Reduce the milk to 60-65 ml/2½ fl oz.

RICH SCONES Add 25 g/1 oz sugar to the mixed dry ingredients for the basic recipe. Instead of mixing with milk alone, use 1 beaten egg with enough milk to make 125 ml/4 fl oz.

SYRUP OR TREACLE SCONES Add 20 ml/4 tsp light soft brown sugar, 2.5 ml/½ tsp ground cinnamon or ginger, 2.5 ml/½ tsp mixed spice and 15 ml/1 tbsp warmed golden syrup or black treacle to the basic recipe. Add the syrup or treacle with the milk.

WHEATMEAL SCONES Use half wholemeal flour and half plain white flour to make the dough.

MRS BEETON'S TIP Scones may be used to make cobblers, both savoury and sweet. For a savoury cobbler, overlap savoury scones on a meat sauce or vegetables in sauce, or on a casserole. For a sweet cobbler, overlap plain sweet scones on a poached or stewed fruit base.

SWEET WHEATMEAL SCONES

These scones are delicious filled with full-fat soft cheese or butter and spread with honey.

fat for greasing
200 g/7 oz wheatmeal flour
2.5 ml/½ tsp salt
15 ml/1 tbsp baking powder
50 g/2 oz margarine
50 g/2 oz light soft brown sugar
50 g/2 oz seedless raisins
1 egg plus milk to give 125 ml/4 fl oz
flour for rolling out

Grease a baking sheet. Set the oven at 220°C/425°F/gas 7. Mix the flour, salt and baking powder in a large bowl. Rub in the margarine, then stir in the sugar and dried fruit. Beat the egg and milk together. Reserve a little for brushing the tops of the scones and add the rest to the dry ingredients. Mix to a soft dough. Knead lightly.

Roll out the dough on a floured surface to just over 1 cm/½ inch thick. Cut into rounds, using a 6 cm/2½ inch cutter. Re-roll the trimmings and re-cut. Place the scones on the prepared baking sheet.

Bake for 10-15 minutes. Serve warm or cold, split and buttered.

MAKES 10 TO 12

VARIATION

BRAN SCONES Use 175 g/6 oz self-raising flour, 2.5 ml/½ tsp salt, 5 ml/1 tsp baking powder, 25 g/1 oz light soft brown sugar, 50 g/2 oz currants or sultanas, instead of the quantities given above. Add 25 g/1 oz bran when mixing the dry ingredients.

PUMPKIN SCONES

For these delicious scones, use leftover steamed or baked pumpkin cooked without liquid.

fat for greasing
300 g/11 oz well-drained cooked pumpkin
25 g/1 oz softened butter
15 ml/1 tbsp caster sugar
15 ml/1 tbsp golden syrup or honey
1 egg, beaten
250 g/9 oz self-raising flour
pinch of salt
2.5 ml/½ tsp ground cinnamon
1.25 ml/¼ tsp grated nutmeg
50-125 ml/2-4 fl oz milk

Grease a baking sheet. Set the oven at 230°C/450°F/gas 8. Mash the pumpkin.

Mix the butter with the sugar and syrup or honey in a bowl. Mix the egg with the pumpkin. Add to the butter and sugar, mixing thoroughly. Sift the flour, salt and spices into a bowl, then fold into the pumpkin mixture, alternately with 50 ml/2 fl oz milk. Add extra milk, if required, to make a soft but not sticky dough.

Knead the dough lightly and pat it out to 2 cm/¾ inch thick. Cut into rounds with a 5 cm/2 inch cutter. Put the scones on the prepared baking sheet. Bake for 12-15 minutes, until golden brown.

MAKES 12

PIZZA AND DOUGH BAKES

Pizza is now a familiar food but there are many versions which are far removed from this tasty snack of Italian origins. In this chapter there is a basic, traditional-style recipe as well as alternatives that are one step removed from authenticity.

ITALIAN-STYLE PIZZA

This should be thin and crisp with a slightly bubbly dough base and a moist topping.

fat for greasing
25 g/1 oz fresh yeast or 15 ml/1 tbsp dried yeast
5 ml/1 tsp sugar
450 g/1 lb strong white flour
5 ml/1 tsp salt
30 ml/2 tbsp olive oil
flour for rolling out

TOPPING
60 ml/4 tbsp olive oil
2 garlic cloves, crushed
1 large onion, chopped
15 ml/1 tbsp dried oregano or marjoram
1 (400 g/14 oz) can chopped tomatoes
30 ml/2 tbsp tomato purée
salt and pepper
375 g/12 oz mozzarella cheese, sliced

Grease 4 large baking sheets. Measure 300 ml/½ pint lukewarm water. Blend the fresh yeast with the sugar and a little lukewarm water. Set aside until frothy. For dried yeast, sprinkle the yeast over all the water, then leave until frothy.

Sift the flour and salt into a bowl, make a well in the middle and add the yeast liquid, remaining water and oil. Mix the flour into the liquid to make a firm dough.

Turn out the dough on to a lightly floured surface and knead thoroughly until smooth and elastic – about 10 minutes. Place the dough in a clean, lightly floured bowl. Cover with cling film and leave in a warm place until doubled in size. This will take about 2 hours.

To make the topping, heat the oil in a saucepan and cook the garlic and onion until soft but not browned – about 15 minutes. Stir in the oregano, tomatoes and tomato purée. Bring to the boil, reduce the heat and simmer for 15 minutes. Remove the pan from the heat and add salt and pepper to taste.

Set the oven at 240°C/475°F/gas 9. Knead the dough again, then divide it into four. Roll out each portion into a 25-30 cm/10-12 inch circle. Place a piece of dough on each prepared baking sheet. Top with the tomato mixture and mozzarella, then leave in a warm place for about 5 minutes, or until the dough bases begin to rise slightly.

Bake for about 15 minutes, or until the topping is well browned and the dough is crisp and bubbly. Serve freshly baked.

MAKES 4

CALZONE

Illustrated on page 159

A type of pizza pasty, calzone is a pizza which is folded in half to enclose its filling. Often filled with a meat sauce (bolognaise) and mozzarella, the filling may be varied according to taste.

fat for greasing
25 g/1 oz fresh yeast or 15 ml/1 tbsp dried
    yeast
5 ml/1 tsp sugar
450 g/1 lb strong white flour
5 ml/1 tsp salt
30 ml/2 tbsp olive oil
flour for rolling out

FILLING
225 g/8 oz minced beef
2.5 ml/½ tsp chilli powder
salt and pepper
1 quantity tomato pizza topping (opposite)
50 g/2 oz mushrooms, sliced
225 g/8 oz mozzarella cheese, sliced

Grease 2 baking sheets. Make the dough following the recipe for Italian-style Pizza (page 182) and leave it to rise.

Meanwhile, dry-fry the mince in a heavy-bottomed saucepan over medium heat until well browned. If the meat is very lean you may have to add a little olive oil. Add salt, pepper and the chilli powder. Stir in the tomato topping and bring to the boil. Cover, reduce the heat and simmer the mixture very gently for about 30 minutes. Set aside to cool. Stir in the mushrooms when the meat has cooled, just before it is to be used.

Set the oven at 220°C/425°F/gas 7. Knead the dough again, then divide it into quarters. Roll out one portion into a 23 cm/9 inch circle. Place it on a prepared baking sheet. Top one side with about a quarter of the meat mixture and a quarter of the mozzarella. Fold over the other half of the dough and pinch the edges together firmly to seal in the filling.

Repeat with the remaining portions of dough and filling. Use the second baking sheet to fill the second calzone, then slide it on to the first sheet next to the first calzone. To shape the last calzone, sprinkle a little flour over the calzone on the baking sheet, then lift the final portion of dough on to the sheet, allowing one half to drape over the filled calzone while filling the opposite side. Otherwise the large calzone can be difficult to lift once filled.

Leave the filled dough to rise in a warm place for about 5 minutes. Bake for 30-40 minutes, or until the dough is golden, risen and cooked. Leave to stand on the baking sheets for a few minutes, then transfer to individual plates.

MAKES 4

SCONE PIZZA

fat for greasing
225 g/8 oz self-raising flour
10 ml/2 tsp baking powder
salt and pepper
50 g/2 oz margarine
5 ml/1 tsp dried marjoram
2.5 ml/½ tsp dried thyme
150 ml/¼ pint milk

TOPPING
  1 (200 g/7 oz) can tuna in oil
  1 garlic clove (optional)
  1 onion, chopped
  15 ml/1 tbsp roughly chopped capers
  30 ml/2 tbsp chopped parsley
  4 large tomatoes, peeled and sliced
  100 g/4 oz Cheddar cheese, grated

Grease a large baking sheet. Set the oven at 220°C/425°F/gas 7. Sift the flour, baking powder and salt into a bowl, then rub in the margarine. Stir in the herbs and milk to make a soft dough. Knead the dough lightly.

Roll out the dough on a lightly floured surface into a 30 cm/12 inch circle. Lift the dough on to the prepared baking sheet and turn the edge over, pinching it neatly.

Drain the oil from the tuna in a small saucepan and heat it gently. Add the onion and garlic (if used) and cook for about 10 minutes, until the onion is just beginning to soften. Off the heat, add the capers, parsley and flaked tuna. Spread this topping over the scone base, cover with tomato slices, then sprinkle with the cheese.

Bake for 20-25 minutes, until the topping is bubbling hot and golden and the base is risen, browned around the edges and cooked through. Serve cut into wedges.

SERVES 4 TO 6

DEEP-PAN PIZZA

This is a thick-based, American-style pizza. Pepperoni sausage is a spicy uncooked sausage, available from delicatessens and large supermarkets.

fat for greasing
15 g/½ oz fresh yeast or 10 ml/2 tsp dried yeast
5 ml/1 tsp sugar
225 g/8 oz strong white flour
2.5 ml/½ tsp salt
15 ml/1 tbsp olive oil
flour for rolling out

FILLING
  30 ml/2 tbsp olive oil
  1 large onion, chopped
  1 green pepper, seeded and chopped
  1 garlic clove, crushed
  salt and pepper
  30 ml/2 tbsp tomato purée
  100 g/4 oz mushrooms, sliced
  100 g/4 oz pepperoni sausage, cut into chunks
  100 g/4 oz sweetcorn kernels
  75 g/3 oz Cheddar cheese, grated

Grease a 25 cm/10 inch loose-bottomed flan tin or sandwich tin. Make the dough following the recipe for Italian-style Pizza (page 182) and leave it to rise.

Roll out the dough on a lightly floured surface large enough to line the prepared tin. Press it into the tin, pinching it around the upper edges to keep in place. Cover with cling film and set aside. Set the oven at 220°C/425°F/gas 7.

To make the filling, heat the oil in a small saucepan and cook the onion, pepper and garlic until beginning to soften – about 10 minutes. Stir in salt, pepper and the tomato purée, then remove the pan from the heat and mix in the mushrooms. Spread this mixture over the dough. Top with the pepperoni sausage and sweetcorn, then sprinkle with the cheese.

Bake for about 40 minutes, until the dough and topping is golden brown and bubbling. Serve cut into wedges.

SERVES 4

PIZZA TOPPERS

Any of the following topping ingredients may be used for an Italian-style Pizza, Deep-pan Pizza or Scone Pizza. They may also be varied according to taste.

SPICY PRAWN PIZZA   Seed and finely chop 1 green chilli, then cook it with 1 chopped onion in some olive oil. Add 4 diced peeled tomatoes and 225 g/8 oz peeled cooked prawns (thawed and drained if frozen). Spread over the pizza and top with plenty of sliced mozzarella cheese (more if making 4 Italian-style bases than on a single pizza).

QUICKIE SARDINE PIZZA   This one is best on a scone base: arrange canned sardines like the spokes of a wheel on a scone base. Sprinkle with plenty of chopped spring onion, then arrange chopped peeled tomato between the sardines. Sprinkle with plenty of salt, pepper and grated cheese.

ANCHOVY AND OLIVES   Chop 1 (50 g/2 oz) can anchovy fillets with their oil. Divide between 4 Italian-style bases, sprinkling them over the tomato topping. Add the mozzarella, then top with 50 g/2 oz stoned black olives, either left whole or halved, as preferred. Sprinkle with 30 ml/2 tbsp chopped capers before baking.

HAM AND EGG PIZZA (illustrated on page 158)   Make the 4 Italian-style Pizzas or the dough for 1 Deep-pan Pizza. Spread the tomato topping for Italian-style pizzas over the chosen bases. Top with 225 g/8 oz roughly chopped cooked ham and 225 g/8 oz sliced mozzarella cheese. Make a slight nest in the middle of each Italian pizza or four in the deep pan pizza and crack 4 eggs into the nests. Bake as in the main recipes.

SALAMI AND WHOLE FLAT MUSHROOM   Top the chosen base with tomato purée and cooked chopped onion. Add slices of salami. Remove the stalks from small to medium flat mushrooms, allowing 4 each for individual pizzas, 8-12 for a large pizza. Chop the stalks and sprinkle them over the bases, then arrange the mushrooms on top. Sprinkle the mushrooms with salt and pepper, then top each with a thin slice of mozzarella before baking.

SPICY SAUSAGE TOPPING   Place 450 g/1 lb good quality pork sausagemeat in a bowl. Add 1 small grated onion, 2 crushed garlic cloves, 1.25-5 ml/¼-1 tsp chilli powder, 15 ml/1 tbsp ground coriander and 15 ml/1 tbsp paprika. Mix the ingredients really well, with a spoon at first, then wash your hands and knead the sausage mixture. Dot small lumps of the mixture over the chosen pizza, between any mozzarella topping or over any grated cheese so that the meat cooks and browns.

COURGETTE PIZZA   Make the tomato topping for the Italian-style Pizza. Spread the tomato mixture over the chosen base, then add a good layer of sliced courgettes and sprinkle them with lots of fresh basil leaves. Drizzle a little olive oil over the top and dust the courgettes with grated Parmesan cheese. Dot with a few pieces of mozzarella but leave at least half the courgettes uncovered so they brown slightly during baking.

*E*MPANADAS

Illustrated on page 160

*These Latin-American equivalents to pasties may
be made with pastry instead of bread dough,
and the filling may be varied to include poultry
and vegetables.*

far for greasing
15 g/½ oz fresh yeast or 10 ml/2 tsp dried
  yeast
5 ml/1 tsp sugar
225 g/8 oz strong white flour
2.5 ml/½ tsp salt
15 ml/1 tbsp olive oil
flour for rolling out

FILLING
30 ml/2 tbsp oil
1 small onion, chopped
1 green chilli, seeded and chopped
1 garlic clove, crushed
225 g/8 oz minced beef
15 ml/1 tbsp ground cumin
25 g/1 oz raisins
2 tomatoes, peeled and chopped
salt and pepper

Grease a baking sheet. Make the dough
following the recipe for Italian-style Pizza
(page 182) and leave it to rise.

To make the filling, heat the oil in a frying pan and gently cook the onion, chilli
and garlic for about 15 minutes, until the
onion has softened. Remove the pan from
the heat, then add the mince, cumin,
raisins and tomatoes. Add salt and pepper
to taste and make sure all the ingredients
are thoroughly combined.

Set the oven at 200°C/400°F/gas 6.
Knead the dough again and divide it into
quarters. On a lightly floured surface, roll
out one portion into a 15-18 cm/6-7 inch
round. Mound a quarter of the meat mixture on one half, leaving a space around
the edge of the dough. Dampen the dough
edge, then fold the dough over the filling
to enclose it completely in a semi-circular
pasty. Pinch the edges of the dough together to seal in the filling, then place the
empanada on the prepared baking sheet.

Fill and shape the remaining dough to
make 4 empanadas. Cover with cling film
and leave for about 5 minutes, so that the
dough begins to rise.

Bake for 30-40 minutes, until deep
golden brown. Serve freshly baked or
transfer to a wire rack and allow to cool.

MAKES 4

ONION FLAN

*This German-style savoury tray bake is
delicious hot or cold.*

fat for greasing
25 g/1 oz fresh yeast or 15 ml/1 tbsp dried
  yeast
5 ml/1 tsp sugar
450 g/1 lb strong white flour
5 ml/1 tsp salt
30 ml/2 tbsp olive oil
flour for rolling out

TOPPING
25 g/1 oz butter
450 g/1 lb onions, thinly sliced
15 ml/1 tbsp caraway seeds
salt and pepper
225 g/8 oz quark or curd cheese

Grease a 23 × 33 cm/9 × 13 inch oblong
baking tin. Make the dough following the
recipe for Italian-style Pizza (page 182) and
leave it to rise.

To make the topping, melt the butter in a large frying pan and cook the onions and caraway seeds, stirring often, for about 10 minutes, until the onions have softened slightly. Add salt and pepper to taste, then set aside.

Set the oven at 220°C/425°F/gas 7. On a lightly floured surface, knead the dough again, then roll out to fit the tin. Press the dough into the tin, then spread the quark or curd cheese over it. Top with the onions, spreading them in an even layer and pressing down lightly. Leave the dough in a warm place for about 15 minutes, until beginning to rise.

Bake for about 30 minutes, until golden brown. Allow the flan to stand for 5-10 minutes before serving, cut into oblong portions. Alternatively, it may be left until just warm or served cold.

SERVES 8

*P*LUM SLICE

Illustrated on page 157

fat for greasing
450 g/1 lb strong white flour
5 ml/1 tsp salt
50 g/2 oz butter
50 g/2 oz sugar
25 g/1 oz fresh yeast or 15 ml/1 tbsp dried
    yeast
150 ml/¼ pint milk

TOPPING
900 g/2 lb plums, halved and stoned
Apricot Glaze (page 126)

Grease a 23 × 33 cm/9 × 13 inch baking tin or line a roasting tin with foil and grease

that. Sift the flour and salt into a bowl. Rub in the butter and stir in the sugar, reserving 5 ml/1 tsp if using fresh yeast. Measure 150 ml/¼ pint lukewarm water.

Blend the fresh yeast with the reserved sugar and a little lukewarm water, then stir in the remaining water and set aside until frothy. For dried yeast, sprinkle it over all the water, then set aside until frothy.

Heat the milk until just lukewarm. Make a well in the centre of the dry ingredients and pour in the milk with the yeast liquid. Gradually mix in the dry ingredients to make a firm dough.

Knead the dough on a lightly floured surface until smooth and elastic – about 10 minutes. Place the dough in a clean bowl, cover with cling film and leave in a warm place until doubled in volume. This will take up to 2 hours.

Set the oven at 220°C/425°F/gas 7. On a lightly floured surface, knead the dough again, then roll out and press it into the prepared tin. Press the dough up around the edge slightly.

Arrange the plum halves on top of the dough, placing them cut sides down and pressing them in slightly. Leave in the warm for 30 minutes, until risen.

Bake for about 30 minutes, or until the dough is browned around the edges and cooked. Allow to cool slightly, then brush apricot glaze all over the plums. Serve hot, warm or cold with soured cream.

SERVES 8 TO 10

CRUMBLE SLICE

This is another sweet tray dough of Eastern European origins.

fat for greasing
450 g/1 lb strong white flour
5 ml/1 tsp salt
50 g/2 oz butter
50 g/2 oz sugar
25 g/1 oz fresh yeast or 15 ml/1 tbsp dried
    yeast
150 ml/¼ pint milk

TOPPING
    450 g/1 lb cooking apples, peeled, cored
        and sliced
    50 g/2 oz caster sugar
    10 ml/2 tsp ground cinnamon
    100 g/4 oz plain flour
    75 g/3 oz butter

Grease a 23 × 33 cm/9 × 13 inch baking tin or line a roasting tin with foil and grease that. Sift the flour and salt into a bowl. Rub in the butter and stir in the sugar, reserving 5 ml/1 tsp if using fresh yeast. Measure 150 ml/¼ pint lukewarm water.

Blend the fresh yeast with the reserved sugar and a little lukewarm water, then stir in the remaining water and set aside until frothy. For dried yeast, sprinkle it over all the water, then set aside until frothy.

Heat the milk until just lukewarm. Make a well in the centre of the dry ingredients and pour in the milk with the yeast liquid. Gradually mix in the dry ingredients to make a firm dough.

Knead the dough on a lightly floured surface until smooth and elastic – about 10 minutes. Place the dough in a clean bowl, cover with cling film and leave in a warm place until doubled in size. This will take up to 2 hours.

Set the oven at 190°C/375°F/gas 5. On a lightly floured surface, knead the dough again, then roll out and press it into the prepared tin. Press the dough up around the edge slightly.

To make the topping, lay the apples slices on the dough and sprinkle with half the sugar and the cinnamon. Cover with cling film and set aside in a warm place for the dough to rise. Sift the flour into a bowl, then rub in the butter. Stir in the sugar and sprinkle this crumble mixture over the apples. Set aside again, until the dough has had about 30 minutes rising.

Bake for 40-45 minutes, until golden and cooked through. Leave to cool in the tin, then cut into slices or fingers when warm or cold.

SERVES 12

> 🥣 **MRS BEETON'S TIP** Other fruits may be used as well as the apples. For example, try sprinkling raisins, chopped mixed peel or chopped ready-to-eat dried apricots over the apples before adding the crumble topping.

INDEX

Almond
   and apple triangles, 84
   bread, 170
      sweet, 149
   castles, 98
   filling, 66
   macaroons, 112
   maids of honour, 71
   paste, 102, 149
   pastry, 66
   rings, piped, 122
   soufflé, 92
   tartlets, 66
Ambassadrice soufflé, 92
American coffee bread, 169
   muffins, 168
Anchovy and olive pizza, 185
Anna potatoes, 44-45
Apple(s)
   and almond triangles, 84
   baked, 95
   charlotte, 95
   crumble slice, 188
   Eve's pudding, 96
   flan, Mrs Beeton's, 63
   loaf, 171
   pie, traditional, 63
   Somerset puddings, 98
   soufflé, 93
   strudel, 85
Apricot
   and walnut quick loaf, 165
   glaze, 126
   muffins, 167
   soufflé, 93
   triangles, 84
Aranygaluska borsodoval, 100
Asparagus and cheese custard, 31
Austrian hazelnut layer, 129
Avocados, hot stuffed, 31

Bacon
   quiche Lorraine, 59
   Wiltshire pie, 61
Bagels, 143
Banana
   and brandy pavlova, 130
   bread, 170
      nut coffee, 169
      walnut, 171
Bara brith, 150-1

Battenburg cake, 107
Béchamel sauce, 58
Beef
   Cornish pasties, 62
   see also minced meat
Biscuits, 112-4
Black Forest gâteau, 128
Bramble muffins, 168
Bran
   baking powder muffins, 167
   scones, 181
Brandy snaps, 123
Breads
   pizzas, 182-5
   scones, 179-81
   sweet yeast, 146-63
   teabreads, 169-78
   yeasted, 131-45
   yeastless, 164-6
Bridge rolls, 136
Brioches, 144
Brown bread, malted, 138
   Scottish, 138-9
Bun loaf, 148-9
Buns
   bagels, 143
   Bath, 162-3
   Chelsea, 152
   cream, 81
   hot cross, 161
   Lavenham, 178
   raspberry, 112
   revel, 162
   Sally Lunn, 144-5
Buttercream, 192
   coffee, 128-9
Butterfly cakes, 111
Butters, sweet, 94

Cabbage leaves, stuffed, 42
Cakes
   gâteaux, 70, 125-30
   large, 83, 102-10
   small, 66, 68-69, 71-72, 81,
      110-24
   see also tartlets
Calzone, 183
Cannelloni
   stuffed baked, 46-47
   with mushroom stuffing, 47

Caramel, 83
Caraway bread, 136
Castle puddings, 98
Challah, 142-3
Cheese
   and asparagus custard, 31
   and chicken scallops, 41
   and date bread, 174
   bread plait, 136
   éclairs, 82
   gratin dauphinois, 43
   pastry, 57
   phyllo and feta triangles, 84
   pudding, 49
   ramekins, 91
   sauce, 43, 46-47, 60
   scones, 180
   soufflé, 89
   stuffed baked cannelloni, 46-47
   whirls, 180
Chelsea buns, 152
Cherry bread, 150
Chicken
   and cheese scallops, 41
   and ham scallops, 41
   mayonnaise pastry horn, 69
   pie, 67
   scallops, browned, 41
   soufflé, 89
   triangles, 84
   Wiltshire pie, 61
Chocolate
   buttercream, 102
   custard, 126
   dream, 93
   gâteau, 127
   icing, 127
      glacé, 81
   loaf, plain, 108
   meringue tartlets, 65
   roll, 105
   sauce, 94
   sponge pudding, 97
Choux pastry, 54, 57, 81, 82
Christmas stollen, 163
Cobs, rye, 140
Cockscombs, 147
Coconut
   bread, 173
   sponge pudding, 97
Cod-stuffed avocado, 31

Coffee
    bread, American, 169
    buttercream, 102, 128-9
    gâteau, 128-9
    soufflé, 92
College puddings, 99
Confectioners' custard, 126
Corn pudding, 49
Cornbread, Texas, 166
Cornflour, 16
Cornish pasties, 62
    splits, 148
Cottage loaf, 134
    pudding, 98-99
Courgette pizza, 185
Crackers, crisp, 124
Cream, 94
    buns, 81
    éclairs, 81
    slices, 71
Crème frangipane, 126
    St Honoré, 126
Croissants, 145
Croquembouche, 83
Crumble
    nutty plum, 96
    slice, 188
Curled wiggs, 176
Custard
    cheese and asparagus, 31
    chocolate, 126
    confectioners', 126
    crème frangipane, 126
    crème St Honoré, 126
    tartlets, 72
    vanilla, 94

Danish pastries, 147
Date
    and walnut cake, 108
    bread, 172
        cheese and, 174
        sweet, 174
Deep-pan pizza, 184-5
Dough making, 132
    shaping 134
Duchesse potatoes, 44
Dumplings
    Hungarian golden, 100
    semolina, 48
Dundee cake, 106
Durham rabbit pie, 60

Eccles cakes, 72
Eclairs
    cheese, 82

cream, 81
Egg(s), 20-21
    and ham pizza, 185
    in cocotte, 32
    moulded, 32
    oeufs mollets en soufflé, 89
Empanadas, 186
English madeleines, 110
Enriched bread, 136
Eve's pudding, 96
Exeter pudding, 99

Fairy cakes, 111
Fats, 17-19, 24-25
Fatless fruit loaf, 172
Fish and potato soufflé, 90
Flaky pastry, 56, 57
Flan
    apple, 63
    onion, 186-7
    vegetable, 60
Flapjacks, 112
Flavourings, 23
Florentines, 123
Flour, 15-16
Forcemeat see stuffing
Frangipane cream, 126
French bread, 133
Fromage frais, 94
Fruit
    and liqueur pavlova, 130
    crumble, 96
    Eve's pudding, 96
    horns, 69
    soufflé, 93
Fruit, dried, 21-22
    bara brith, 150-1
    Bath buns, 162-3
    bun loaf, 148-9
    Chelsea buns, 152
    Christmas stollen, 163
    coconut bread, 173
    college puddings, 99
    cottage pudding, 98-99
    crumble slice, 188
    Dundee cake, 106
    Eccles cakes, 72
    fatless loaf, 172
    fruit bread, 136
    fruit snails, 147
    Lavenham buns, 178
    Lincolnshire plum bread, 178
    malt bread, 173
    North Riding bread, 176
    revel buns, 162

rich fruit cake, 100
    scones, 180, 181
    sweet date bread, 174
    tea brack, 177
Fruit, glacé: soufflé, 92

Gâteaux, 70, 125-30
Genoese sponge, 104
Ginger soufflé, 92
Gingerbread, 169
Glacé icing, 103
    chocolate, 81
Glaze, apricot, 126
Gnocchi, semolina, 48
Granary bread, 139
Grand Marnier soufflé, 92
Grant loaf, 139
Gratin dauphinois, 43
Griddle scones, 180

Haddock-stuffed avocado, 31
Ham
    and chicken scallops, 41
    and egg pizza, 185
    and tomato horns, 69
    stuffing for mushrooms, 41
    triangles, 84
Hazelnut layer, Austrian, 129
Herb
    forcemeat, 67
    pastry, 57
Honesty pudding, 97
Honey
    bread, 175
    nut muffins, 167
Hot cross buns, 161
Hot water crust pastry, 55, 86

Icing
    chocolate, 127
    glacé, 103
        chocolate, 81
    orange, 66
Inverary muffins, 180
Irish soda bread, 166
Italian-style pizza, 182

Jam
    and cream pastry horns, 69
    buns, 112
    cream slices, 71
    custard tartlets, 72
    glaze, 126
    mille-feuille gâteau, 70
    muffins, 168
    sauce, 94

Somerset puddings, 98
sponge pudding, 97

Kulich, 141

Lamb
Wiltshire pie, 61
see also minced meat
Lardy cake, 161
Lasagne verdi, 46
Lavenham buns, 178
Leek
tart, 58-59
turnovers, 62
Lemon
buttercream, 102
meringue pie, 64
soufflé, 92
sponge pudding, 97
tartlets, 64
Lincolnshire plum bread, 178
Liqueur soufflé, 92
Loaf see breads

Macaroons, almond, 112
Madeira cake, 106
Madeleines, English, 110
Maids of honour, 71
Malt bread, 173
brown, 138
Meringues, 121
lemon pie, 64
pavlova, 130
Mille-feuille gâteau, 70
Mince pies, 65
Minced meat
calzone, 183
empanadas, 186
moussaka, 45
pasticcio di lasagne verde, 46
stuffed cabbage leaves, 42
marrow, 43
peppers, 42
Mixed peel florentines, 123
Moggy, 177
Moulded eggs, 32
Moussaka, 45
Mrs Beeton's apple flan, 63
chicken pie, 67
custard tartlets, 72
Muffins, 167-8, 180
Mushroom(s)
and salami pizza, 185
stuffed, 41
stuffing, 47

Naan, 141
North Riding bread, 176
Nut(s), 22-23
bread, 136
coffee, 169
quick, 165
honey muffins, 167
scones, 180
Nutty plum crumble, 96

Oatcakes, 124
Oeufs mollets en soufflé, 89
Onion
and cheese soufflé, 89
flan, 186-7
Orange
boats, 66
bread, 175
nut coffee, 169
buttercream, 102
icing, 66
soufflé, 92
sponge pudding, 97

Parisian tartlets, 66
Parsnip soufflé, 91
Pasta see cannelloni; lasagne
Pasticcio di lasagne verde, 46
Pasties, Cornish, 62
Pastries, Danish, 147
see also cakes, small;
tartlets
Pastry
horns, 68-69
making, 50-57
recipes, 55-87
Pavlova, 130
Peach pavlova, 130
Pepperoni sausage pizza, 184
Peppers, baked stuffed, 42
Phyllo pastry, 54
and feta triangles, 84
Pies, 52
apple, 63
chicken, 67
Durham rabbit, 60
lemon meringue, 64
mince, 65
moulded raised, 86
pork, 87
veal, 87
Wiltshire, 61
Pineapple soufflé, 93
Piping, 125-6
Pizzas, 182-5
Plaits, bread, 134, 136

Plum
bread, Lincolnshire, 178
crumble, nutty, 96
slice, 187
Polenta
with cheese, 49
with smoked sausage, 48
Poppy seed bread, 136
Pork
pickled: Wiltshire pie, 61
pies, raised, 87
Potato(es)
Anna, 44-45
duchesse, 44
gratin dauphinois, 43
pastry, 61
scones, 180
soufflé, 90
Prawn
pizza, spicy, 185
quiche, 58
Princess rolls, 142
Prunes: wholemeal fruit bread,
151
Puddings
savoury, 49
sweet, 94-101
Puff pastry, 55, 57, 70
Pumpkin scones, 181

Queen of puddings, 101
Quiche
Lorraine, 59
prawn, 58
Quick bread, basic, 165

Rabbit pie, 60
Raisin
bread, 172
muffins, 168
see also fruit, dried
Raising agents, 16-17
Raspberry
buns, 112
soufflé, 93
Revel buns, 162
Rice
pudding, 101
stuffed peppers, 42
Rich pastry, 57
Rolls, 135
bridge, 136
dinner, 135
princess, 142
Rothschild soufflé, 92
Rough puff pastry, 56, 57

Rye
  bread, sour dough, 164
  cobs, 140

Sacher torte, 127
Saffron bread, 140-1
Salami and mushroom pizza, 185
Sally Lunn, 144-5
Sardine
  pizza, quickie, 185
  triangles, 84
Sauce
  béchamel, 58
  cheese, 43, 46-47, 60
  chocolate, 94
  jam, 94
  tomato, 42, 48
  white, 41
  white wine, 100
Sausage
  pizza, 184, 185
  smoked, polenta with, 48
Sausagemeat-stuffed marrow, 43
Savoury bakes, 30-49
  soufflés, 89-91
  strudel, 85
Scone pizza, 184
Scones, 179-81
Scottish brown bread, 138-9
Semolina gnocchi, 48
Short crust pastry, 57, 58
Shortbread, 122
Simnel cake, 109
Soda bread, Irish, 166
Somerset puddings, 98
Soufflés, savoury, 89-91
  sweet, 92-93
Sour dough rye bread, 164
Soured milk quick bread, 165
Spicy sponge pudding, 97
Spinach
  and cheese triangles, 84
  soufflé, 90

strudel, 85
stuffed cannelloni, 46-47
Sponge
  cake, 104
  chocolate roll, 105
  Genoese, 104
  pudding, baked, 97
  Swiss roll, 105
Stollen, Christmas, 163
Strawberry soufflé, 93
Strudel pastry, 85
Stuffed avocados, hot, 31
  baked cannelloni, 46-47
  cabbage leaves, 42
  marrow, baked, 43
  mushrooms, 41
  peppers, baked, 42
Stuffings
  herb forcemeat, 67
  mushroom, 47
Suet crust pastry, 53
Sugars, 19-20
Sweet pastry, 57
Sweetcorn see corn
Swiss roll, 105
Syrup scones, 180

Tart, leek, 58-59
Tartlets
  chocolate meringue, 65
  custard, 72
  lemon, 64
  Parisian, 66
Tea brack, 177
Teabreads, 169-78
Texas cornbread, 166
Tomato sauce, 42, 48
Treacle scones, 180
Tuna pizza, 184
Turkey breasts in pastry, 68
Turnovers, 52
  leek, 62

Vanilla
  buttercream, 102
  custard, 94
  slices, 71
  soufflé, 92
Veal
  pie, raised, 87
  Wiltshire pie, 61
Vegetable
  flan, 60
  pasties, 62
  strudel, 85
Victoria sandwich cake, 103
  one-stage, 103
Vol-au-vent cases, 69

Walnut
  and apricot quick loaf, 165
  and banana bread, 171
  and date cake, 108
  buttercream, 102
  muffins, 168
Watercress and cheese soufflé, 89
Wheatmeal
  bread, 137
  scones, 180
  sweet, 181
White
  bread, 132-3
    short-time, 137
  sauce, 41
  wine sauce, 100
Wholemeal
  fruit bread, 151
  muffins, 168
  quick bread, 165
  short crust pastry, 57, 60
Wiltshire pie, 61
Windmills, 147

Yeast, 131
Yogurt, 94